Multicultural America

Volume I

The Hispanic Americans

Multicultural America

Volume I

The Hispanic Americans

Rodney P. Carlisle
GENERAL EDITOR

Facts On File
An imprint of Infobase Publishing

Multicultural America: Volume I: The Hispanic Americans
Copyright © 2011 by Infobase Publishing

Facts On File, Inc.
An Imprint of Infobase Publishing
132 West 31st Street
New York, NY 10001

Library of Congress Cataloging-in-Publication Data
Multicultural America / Rodney P. Carlisle, general editor.
   v. cm.
   Includes bibliographical references and index.
   Contents: v. 1. The Hispanic Americans — v. 2. The Arab Americans —
v. 3. The African Americans — v. 4. The Asian Americans — v. 5. The
Jewish Americans — v. 6. The European Americans — v. 7. The Native
Americans.
   ISBN 978-0-8160-7811-0 (v. 1 : hardcover : alk. paper) — ISBN
978-0-8160-7812-7 (v. 2 : hardcover : alk. paper) — ISBN
978-0-8160-7813-4 (v. 3 : hardcover : alk. paper) — ISBN
978-0-8160-7814-1 (v. 4 : hardcover : alk. paper) — ISBN
978-0-8160-7815-8 (v. 5 : hardcover : alk. paper) — ISBN
978-0-8160-7816-5 (v. 6 : hardcover : alk. paper) — ISBN
978-0-8160-7817-2 (v. 7 : hardcover : alk. paper) 1.
Minorities—United States—History—Juvenile literature. 2.
Ethnology—United States—History—Juvenile literature. 3. Cultural
pluralism—United States—History—Juvenile literature. 4. United
States—Ethnic relations—Juvenile literature. I. Carlisle, Rodney P.
   E184.A1M814 2011
   305.800973—dc22   2010012694

Text design and composition by Golson Media
Cover printed by Art Print, Taylor, PA
Book printed and bound by Maple Press, York, PA
Date Printed: March 2011
Printed in the United States of America

11 10 9 8 7 6 5 4 3 2 1

CONTENTS

Volume I

The Hispanic Americans

AMERICANS HAVE HAD a sense that they were a unique people, even before the American Revolution. In the 18th century, the settlers in the thirteen colonies that became the United States of America began to call themselves Americans, recognizing that they were not simply British colonists living in North America. In addition to the English, other cultures and peoples had already begun to contribute to the rich tapestry that would become the American people.

Swedes and Finns in the Delaware River valley, Dutch in New York, Scots-Irish, and Welsh had all brought their different ways of life, dress, diet, housing, and religions, adding them to the mix of Puritan and Anglican Englishmen. Lower Rhine German groups of dissenting Amish and Mennonites, attracted by the religious toleration of Pennsylvania, settled in Germantown, Pennsylvania, as early as 1685. Located on the western edge of Philadelphia, the settlers and later German immigrants moved to the counties just further west in what would become Pennsylvania Dutch country.

The policies of the various other colonies tended to favor and encourage such group settlement to varying extents. In some cases, as in New Jersey, the fact that each community could decide what church would be supported by local taxes tended to attract coreligionists to specific communities. Thus in the colonial period, the counties of southern New Jersey (known in colonial times as West Jersey) tended to be dominated by Quakers, while townships in New Jersey closer to New York City were dominated by Lutheran, Dutch Reformed, and Anglican churches and settlers.

Ethnicity and religion divided the peoples of America, yet the official tolerance of religious diversity spawned a degree of mutual acceptance by one ethnic group of another. While crossreligious marriages were frowned upon, they were not prohibited, with individual families deciding which parents' church should be attended, if any. Modern descendants tracing their ancestry are sometimes astounded at the various strands of culture and religion that they find woven together.

To the south, Florida already had a rich Hispanic heritage, some of it filtered through Cuba. Smaller groups of immigrants from France and other countries in Europe were supplemented during the American Revolution by enthusiastic supporters of the idea of a republican experiment in the New World.

All of the thirteen colonies had the institution of African slavery, and people of African ancestry, both slave and free, constituted as much as 40 percent of the population of colonies like Georgia and South Carolina. In a wave of acts of emancipation, slaves living in the New England colonies were freed in the years right after the Revolution, soon joined by those in Pennsylvania, New York, and New Jersey. Although some African Americans in the south were free by birth or manumission, emancipation for 90 percent of those living south of Pennsylvania would have to wait until the years of the Civil War, 1861–65. Forcibly captured and transported under terrible conditions overland and across the ocean, Africans came from dozens of different linguistic stocks. Despite the disruptions of the middle passage, African Americans retained elements of their separate cultures, including some language and language patterns, and aspects of diet, religion, family, and music.

Native Americans, like African Americans, found themselves excluded from most of the rights of citizenship in the new Republic. In the Ohio and Mississippi Valley, many Native Americans resisted the advance of the European-descended settlers. In Florida, Creeks and Seminoles provided haven to escaped slaves, and together, they fought the encroachment of settlers. Some of the African Americans living with the Seminoles and other tribes moved west with them on the Trail of Tears to Indian Territory in what later became the state of Oklahoma. Other groups, like the Lumbees of North Carolina, stayed put, gradually adjusting to the new society around them. Throughout scattered rural communities, clusters of biracial and triracial descendents could trace their roots to Native-American and African ancestors, as well as to the English and Scotch-Irish.

The Louisiana Purchase brought the vast Mississippi Valley into the United States, along with the cosmopolitan city of New Orleans, where French exiles from Canada had already established a strong "Creole" culture. With the annexation of Texas, and following the Mexican-American War (1846–48), the United States incorporated as citizens hundreds of thousands of people of Hispanic ancestry. Individuals and communities in Texas and

New Mexico preserve not only their religion, but also their language, cuisine, customs, and architecture.

As the United States expanded to the west, with vast opportunities for settlement, waves of European immigrants contributed to the growth of the country, with liberal naturalization laws allowing immigrants to establish themselves as citizens. Following the revolutions of 1848 in Europe, and famines in Ireland, new floods of immigrants from Central Europe, Ireland, and Scandinavia all settled in pockets.

By the late 19th century, America had become a refuge for political and economic refugees, as well as enterprising families and individuals from many countries. More geographic-ethnic centers emerged, as new immigrants sought out friends and families who had already arrived, and settled near them. Neighborhoods and whole states took on some aspects of the ethnic cultures that the immigrants brought with them, with Italians settling in New York City, San Francisco, and New Jersey; Azoreans and continental Portuguese in Rhode Island and southern Massachusetts; Scandinavians in Wisconsin and Minnesota; Germans in Missouri; and Chinese and Japanese in a number of West Coast cities and towns. San Francisco and Boston became known for their Irish settlers, and Italians joined Franco-Hispanic Catholics of New Orleans. In some other scattered communities, such as the fishing port of Monterey, California, later Portuguese and Italian arrivals were also absorbed into the local Hispanic community, partly through the natural affinity of the shared Catholic faith.

As waves of immigrants continued to flow into the United States from the 1880s to World War I, the issue of immigration became even more politicized. On the one hand, older well-established ethnic communities sometimes resented the growing influence and political power of the new immigrants. Political machines in the larger cities made it a practice to incorporate the new settlers, providing them with some access to the politics and employment of city hall and at the same time expecting their votes and loyalty during election. The intricate interplay of ethnicity and politics through the late 19th century has been a rich field of historical research.

In the 1890s the United States suddenly acquired overseas territories, including Hawaii, and then Puerto Rico and Guam. Peoples from the new territories became American citizens, and although the great majority of them did not leave their islands, those who came to the continental United States became part of the increasingly diverse population. The tapestry of American culture and ancestry acquired new threads of Polynesian, Asian, Hispanic, and African-Hispanic people.

During the Progressive Era, American-born citizens of a liberal or progressive political inclination often had mixed feelings about immigrants. Some, with a more elitist set of values, believed that crime, alcoholism, and a variety of vices running from drug abuse through prostitution, gambling, and underground sports such as cockfighting, all could be traced to the new immigrants. The solution, they believed, would be "immigration reform": setting quotas that would restrict immigrants from all but Great Britain and northern Europe.

Other reformers took the position that the problems faced by new immigrants could be best dealt with through education, assistance, and social work. Still others approached the questions of poverty and adjustment of immigrants as part of the labor struggle, and believed that organizing through labor unions could bring pressure for better wages and working conditions. Meanwhile, immigrants continued to work through their churches, community organizations, and the complexities of American politics for recognition and rights.

Ultimately, two approaches emerged regarding how different ethnic groups would be viewed and how they would view themselves in America. For some, the idea of a "melting pot" had always held attraction. Under this way of thinking, all Americans would merge, with ethnic distinctions diminishing and the various cultures blending together to create a new American culture. Such a process of assimilation or integration appealed to many, both among American-born and immigrant groups. Others argued strongly that ethnic or racial identity should be preserved, with a sense of pride in heritage, so that America would continue to reflect its diversity, and so that particular groups would not forget their origins, traditions, and culture.

In 1882 the Chinese Exclusion Act prohibited further immigration of Chinese, and it was extended and made more restrictive in several amendments through 1902. Under the law, Chinese were prohibited from obtaining U.S. citizenship. In 1924 immigration legislation was enacted establishing quotas, based upon earlier census figures, so that the quotas favored those from Northern Europe. Under that law, Chinese were excluded, although between 1910 and 1940 more than 50,000 Chinese entered under claims they were returning or joining families already in the United States. The racial nature of the Chinese Exclusion and Immigration Acts tended to prevent the assimilation of Chinese into American society, with many cities, particularly in the west, developing defined Chinatowns or Chinese districts.

Whether an individual ethnic group should become homogenized, integrated, and assimilated into the total culture, or whether it should strive to maintain its own separate cultural identity, was often hotly debated. For some, like the Chinese, Native Americans, and African Americans, armed power of the state, law, and social discrimination tended to create and enforce separate communities and locales. For others, self-segregation and discrimination by other ethnic groups, and the natural process of settling near relatives and coreligionists led to definable ethnic regions and neighborhoods. Among such diverse groups as African Americans, Asians, Hispanics, Italians, Arab Americans, and Native Americans, leaders and spokesmen have debated the degree to which cultural identity should be sacrificed in the name of assimilation. In the 21st century, the debates have continued, sometimes with great controversy, at other times, the dialogues went on almost unnoticed by the rest of the country.

Armed conflict, race-wars, reservation policy, segregation, exclusion, and detention camps in time of war have shown the harsh and ugly side of enforced separation. Even though the multiethnic and multicultural heritage of the United States has been fraught with crisis and controversy, it has also been a source of strength. With roots in so many cultures and with the many struggles to establish and maintain social justice, America has also represented some of the best aspirations of humanity to live in peace with one another. The search for social equity has been difficult, but the fact that the effort has continued for more than two centuries is in itself an achievement.

In this series on Multicultural America, each volume is dedicated to the history of one ethnocultural group, tracing through time the struggles against discrimination and for fair play, as well as the effort to preserve and cherish an independent cultural heritage.

THE HISPANIC AMERICANS

This volume presents the story of people of Spanish ancestry in America. Perhaps more than any other ethnocultural group in the United States, the Latino or Hispanic group has a complex history. Different communities of Spanish settlers were incorporated into the United States during its 19th-century expansion. Under the Adams-Onís Treaty of 1821, Florida became part of the United States, where Spanish settlers had established forts, cities, and farms as early as the 16th century, well before the Pilgrims landed at Plymouth Rock. Texas seceded from Mexico in 1836. When Texas was admitted as a state to the United States in 1845, the Spanish settlers there became U.S. citizens. Locally, a distinction was made between the *tejanos* of Hispanic ancestry, and the Texians, who had come in from the other states of the United States.

The war with Mexico that ended in 1848 brought a vast sweep of territory into the country, with large communities of Hispanic ancestry, especially in what became New Mexico territory and later a state. Today, many New Mexicans of Hispanic ancestry still speak Spanish, noted for local retention of phrases and words more current in the 17th and 18th centuries in Spain. Smaller communities of Hispanics, such as the *californios*, also became U.S. citizens. Over the century and a half since California became a state, little remained of the original California Hispanic heritage except the unique mission architecture, place names, and the documentation of genealogists.

The Hispanic community in the United States was later expanded by separate waves of immigrants and migrants, particularly from Mexico, Central America, Cuba, Puerto Rico, and the Dominican Republic. Some of these waves of migration affected particular regions and cities more than others.

Central Americans and Mexicans flowed into the United States in great numbers from the 1930s onward. Not limited by a quota under the Immigration Act of 1924, many officially immigrated and took out citizenship in the United States, while others simply walked across the border in search of work. The waves of undocumented workers reached vast proportions late in the 20th century, creating legal, social, and political issues discussed in this volume in detail. Discrimination and hostility to Mexican Americans in the Los Angeles area in the 1940s led to so-called Zoot-suit riots.

Large communities of Cuban Americans settled in Florida, especially following the establishment of a communist government in Cuba under Fidel Castro following the 1959 revolution. Residents of Puerto Rico were declared citizens by an act of Congress in March 1917, and thus when they moved to the continental United States they were not immigrants, but simply U.S. citizens moving from one part of the country to another. Many sought work and settled in large east coast cities, particularly New York and Philadelphia. Many of these immigrants, including a number who were of African-Hispanic ancestry, frequently encountered racial discrimination.

Adding to the complexity of the various waves of Hispanic territorial incorporation, migration, and immigration, was the fact that smaller numbers of immigrants entered the United States from the countries of South America and Spain itself. Within the Latino or Hispanic communities in the United States, some have struggled to identify and maintain a distinct heritage based on the specific country or territory of origin. Others have sought to bridge the divisions within the community in hopes of gaining greater political leverage in the struggle for equal rights. This volume traces, in chronological sequence, the complexities of this many-sided story.

RODNEY CARLISLE
GENERAL EDITOR

CHAPTER 1

The Colonial Era: Beginnings to 1776

THE COLONIAL SPANISH settlements located in the present-day United States were on the borderlands of Spain's New World empire. The central settlements, wealth, and power of New Spain were located in the Caribbean, Central America, Mexico, and Peru. Its capital was Mexico City. Colonial Hispanic Americans lived in sparsely populated, multicultural frontier settlements in the present-day southeastern and southwestern United States, such as Florida, Texas, Arizona, New Mexico, and California. The Spanish sought to recreate Hispanic culture in the New World, but faced challenges from the new environment, particularly along the Spanish borderlands. Because of the vastness of the Spanish New World empire, its resources were strained and its borderlands were often neglected and economically underdeveloped. These borderland colonies primarily consisted of a presidio (fort), mission, and civilian settlement.

PRESIDIOS, MISSIONS, AND SETTLEMENTS

The colonies of New Spain came under the control of the Royal and Supreme Council of the Indies, created in 1524, as well as the Roman Catholic Church and a developing colonial bureaucracy. The near constant threat of attack made the presidios necessary, and gave the Spanish border settlements a military character, which they retained throughout the colonial period.

The dominance of the Roman Catholic Church in Spanish politics and culture and the establishment of missions to convert Native Americans to Christianity and Spanish culture also gave these settlements a religious character. The settlements usually began with a mission and a presidio; then civilian settlements, mines, or cattle ranches would develop nearby. Secular and spiritual power frequently went hand in hand, although they occasionally came into conflict. A common Hispanic background and frontier character created many similarities between the Spanish settlements in the American southeast and southwest, while regional differences gave each settlement distinct characteristics.

THE HIGH CONQUEST PERIOD

The earliest period of Spanish exploration in the New World is known as the high conquest period. Early explorers, known as conquistadors, represented the king of Spain, but were responsible for funding and preparing their expeditions. Renowned Spanish explorers in the high conquest period included Don Juan Ponce de León, Hernando de Soto, and Francisco Vázquez de Coronado. The early conquistadors had hopes of finding great wealth in gold and silver, as had been found in Mexico and Peru. Native-American accounts of wealthy, populous villages inspired dreams of possible riches. Catholic priests accompanied the early explorers to reinforce the religious conversion of Native Americans.

The illustration shows Spanish explorer Hernando de Soto with some of his company surveying Tampa, Florida, in 1539. Spanish conquistadors often wore up to 80 pounds of armor, like this reproduction 16th-century suit displayed at the De Soto National Memorial in Bradenton, Florida.

Spain was also interested in the southwest and southeast for defensive purposes, to protect the mining regions of Mexico and the treasure-laden fleets that sailed off the coast of Florida on their return to Spain. Florida was the first area of the present-day United States to be explored and settled by Hispanic Americans.

EARLY EXPEDITIONS IN LA FLORIDA

Although earlier Spanish slaving expeditions may have visited the southeastern U.S. coastline, historians credit Ponce de León with discovering and naming the southeastern Spanish colony of La Florida, which originally included all Spanish-controlled territory in the present-day southeastern United States. In 1513 Ponce de León, who had previous New World experience as a voyager with Christopher Columbus and as governor of Puerto Rico, sailed northward from that island. In his search for treasure or possibly the legendary fountain of eternal youth, he landed along the southeastern coast of present-day Florida. Ponce de León returned to Florida in 1521, accompanied by settlers, Catholic priests and friars, animals, and agricultural seeds and cuttings. Native Americans attacked Ponce de León's group, causing them to flee to the Spanish settlement of Cuba. Ponce de León suffered an arrow wound in the attack that eventually proved fatal.

Other early explorers who failed to find great wealth or establish colonies included Lucas Vázquez de Ayllón in 1526, Pánfilo de Narváez in 1527, Hernando de Soto in 1538, and Father Luis Cancer de Barbastro in 1549. Alvar Núñez Cabeza de Vaca, one of only four survivors of the Narváez expedition, left behind a rich account of the conquistadors' daily experiences. Cabeza de Vaca and others told of enduring harsh weather, from extreme temperatures and humidity, to storms and hurricanes; mosquitoes; swampy conditions; supply shortages; and disease, hunger, thirst, and exhaustion. Mutiny and the constant danger of Native-American attacks from tribes such as the Timucua, Calusa, Apalache, and Yamasee and intercultural misunderstandings also plagued these early expeditions and made settlement difficult. To further their disappointment, no fabulous cities or great mineral wealth were discovered. The hardships and failures of these expeditions led the Spanish king, Philip II, to abandon his attempts to settle La Florida until the Frenchman René de Laudonnière founded Fort Caroline near present-day Jacksonville in 1562.

ST. AUGUSTINE

Shortly after learning of the news of the French settlement, King Philip II sent one of his leading admirals, Don Pedro Menéndez de Avilés, to Florida to capture Fort Caroline and found a Spanish settlement. On September 8, 1565, Menéndez founded San Augustin (St. Augustine) on the northeast coast of present-day Florida. St. Augustine is the oldest continuously occupied town in the present-day United States. The city's founding marked

The Journeys of
Alvar Núñez Cabeza de Vaca

Alvar Núñez Cabeza de Vaca journeyed to the New World as second in command of the ill-fated expedition to conquer La Florida in 1528, led by the conquistador Pánfilo de Narváez. Narváez and his men experienced difficulties even before their arrival in La Florida, when two of his five ships and a number of men were lost in a hurricane off the coast of Cuba. Desertion and the return of some of the ships to Spain further reduced his forces to around 300 men when the expedition landed near present-day Tampa Bay on Florida's western coast.

Against Cabeza de Vaca's advice, the expedition then journeyed overland to the north in search of wealth, losing contact with the remaining ships. The overland expedition endured hunger, illness, and attacks led by hostile Native Americans. As Cabeza de Vaca described his account of their daily tribulations, "I cease here to relate more of this, because any one may suppose what would occur in a country so remote and malign, so destitute of all resource, whereby either to live in it or go out of it...." Narváez decided to build boats from any local resources they could find and take to the sea. Due to storms and the men's exhaustion and hunger, the boats became separated.

On November 6, 1528, Cabeza de Vaca's boat landed on an island off the coast of present-day Texas. As he described it, "The survivors escaped naked as they were born, with the loss of all they had; and although the whole was of little value, at that time it was worth much, as we were then in November, the cold was severe, and our bodies were so emaciated the bones might be counted with little difficulty, having become the perfect figures of death." He and his fellow survivors would then embark on a journey among the Native Americans of the region in search of Christian settlements that would last until their celebrated arrival in Mexico in 1536.

Cabeza de Vaca described his experiences as a healer and slave among the Native Americans, their customs, and the lands they inhabited. He described mosquitoes so thick that the men built fires to smoke them away, and of living off native plants such as prickly pear cacti. His accounts also continually remark on the daily guiding influence of his Roman Catholic faith and the necessity of converting the Native Americans. He also hinted at the wealth that could be found, fueling speculation and inspiring later expeditions such as that of Francisco Vázquez de Coronado. In one instance he noted, "Throughout this region, wheresoever the mountains extend, we saw clear traces of gold and lead, iron, copper, and other metals." Cabeza de Vaca's account of his travels was first published in 1542, and has since undergone numerous translations and reprintings.

the beginning of the First Spanish Period of Florida's colonial history, which would last until 1763.

Menéndez was accompanied by a group of families from the north of Spain linked by kinship and marriage. In 1573–74, King Philip II issued three sets of laws: the Ordinances of Pacification, Patronage, and Laying Out of Towns, which gave the Crown more direct control over La Florida. The now royal colony of La Florida would be protected by regular troops and presidios rather than mercenary soldiers, and would receive royal support for its residents and missions. The Spanish also maintained a settlement in Santa Elena to the north of present-day Florida, but abandoned it in 1587 to consolidate its southeastern base at St. Augustine, where most southeastern Hispanic settlers would remain.

A portrait of the Spanish admiral Don Pedro Menéndez de Avilés, who founded the Spanish outpost of St. Augustine in 1565.

St. Augustine was a garrison town in a military outpost, and its residents faced daily concerns for their survival. La Florida governors generally came from military backgrounds, and soldiering was the most common occupation. After several pirate raids and the establishment of British colonies to the north, Spain authorized the building of the massive Castillo de San Marcos, begun in the early 1670s. La Florida also received subsidies and supplies from Mexico City, Cuba, and wealthier parts of the Spanish empire on a regular basis under a system of revenue transfer known as the *situado*, to ensure its defense and survival. The situado was vital because of La Florida's unprofitable economy and daily hardships, such as supply shortages, hunger, unpredictable weather, illnesses such as malaria and yellow fever, and the hostility of some Native Americans as well as nearby British and French colonies and pirates.

EARLY MISSIONS IN LA FLORIDA

The Roman Catholic Church dominated the culture and governance of La Florida. Father Francisco López de Mendoza Grajales celebrated the first Catholic mass on St. Augustine's founding day, and its mission, Nombre de Dios (Name of God), was founded shortly thereafter. Jesuits first accompanied

Construction began on the Castillo de San Marcos in 1672, a century into the long Spanish occupation of St. Augustine. Its star shape was intended to make it more defensible and a harder target during cannon assaults; it survived to become the last 17th-century fort left in North America.

Menéndez to Florida, but it was the Franciscans who founded La Florida's system of missions. As elsewhere in the Spanish New World empire, La Florida's Native-American inhabitants were viewed as natural inferiors and wards of the Crown who needed instruction in Spanish religion and culture. Although the Spanish mission system in La Florida shared the same primary goal of the conversion of the Native Americans as missions in other parts of New Spain, its day-to-day operations differed. Native Americans were expected to aid in daily tasks in agriculture and construction under the Repartimiento de Labor (compulsory work) system, but there was no widespread enslavement due to the lack of mining or other labor-intensive work.

Another key difference was the location of the missions. In other parts of New Spain, missionaries built towns to relocate Native Americans. In La Florida, missions known as *doctrinas* were built in the larger, pre-existing Native-American towns and serviced by missionaries known as *doctrineros*. Smaller Native-American villages received visiting missionaries known as *visitas*. The La Florida mission system gradually expanded until British Colonel James Moore of South Carolina led a series of devastating raids from 1702 until 1704, causing the Spanish to abandon the more distant, vulnerable missions and concentrate once again around St. Augustine. A system of colonial La Florida laws developed to regulate the interaction between the converted Native Americans, termed the Republic of Indians, and the Hispanic settlers, known as the Republic of Spaniards.

OCCUPATIONS AND STATUS IN LA FLORIDA

The Spanish who came to La Florida included missionaries, farmers, soldiers, and various craftsmen, with the military as the principal source of employment. Other industries employing La Florida's Spanish residents included agriculture and citrus orchards, cattle ranching, timber and related industries, carpentry, blacksmithing, shoemaking, the deerskin fur trade, and fishing. A vibrant citrus industry developed after the Spanish introduction of orange and other trees to La Florida. There were also failed attempts to start silk and sugar industries. Many residents and even missionaries traded with wealthy seaports such as Havana, Cuba, and nearby British and French colonies, often evading royal taxes and regulations.

Hispanic Americans in colonial La Florida sought to transplant their Spanish culture in the New World, creating a bond of shared customs and beliefs. However, the mix of nationalities common in La Florida created a cosmopolitan environment of new customs and lifestyles for the area's predominant Hispanic culture. Spanish colonial culture remained hierarchical and male-dominated. Spanish-born *peninsulares* ranked above those Spaniards born in La Florida, known as *floridanos*. Next came the mestizos, those of mixed European and Native American heritage, the result of intercultural unions that were common in the colony's early years when there were few Spanish women.

As floridanos came to outnumber peninsulares over time and sex ratios evened out, intermarriage became less common, and segregation became more prevalent. Those of an inferior social status were expected to show deference to their superiors, but they also embraced the possibility of upward mobility, which was easier to achieve in the New World. At the bottom of the social ladder were Native Americans, mulattoes (those of mixed European and African blood), free blacks, and slaves. The Spanish later granted freedom to those slaves who escaped the British plantations to the north, and even established the runaway slaves in their own town, commonly known as Fort Mose. Many of the escaped slaves served in the weakened Spanish militia.

Residential housing and material possessions reflected social status. Many Spanish colonial-style houses and public buildings, including the Castillo de San Marcos, were constructed of coquina, a native shell rock

Coquina construction at the 1740 Fort Matanzas, which defended St. Augustine's southern approaches against British attacks.

formed when bits of shells are cemented by limestone. St. Augustine remains one of the best-preserved examples of Spanish colonial architecture in the present-day United States.

Colonists ate wheat, cassava, corn, onions, squash, vegetables introduced from Spain, beef, and pork. They also consumed other animals, grains, and vegetables found through foraging, agriculture, hunting, fishing, and trading with the Native Americans. The poor soils of the coastal areas they were confined to for defensive reasons often resulted in food shortages and periodic bouts of hunger.

RELINQUISHING LA FLORIDA

By the late 1600s La Florida remained an isolated, impoverished, neglected, and sparsely populated part of New Spain. St. Augustine was the only large town; even the promising port city of Pensacola remained a small, shabby settlement protected only by a diminutive wooden fort. As European wars and colonial revolts in other parts of New Spain turned the king's attention elsewhere, royal support became even less reliable. La Florida's inhabitants also became entangled in the Spanish rivalries with Britain and France as the three powers battled for control in both Europe and the New World. A series of European wars brought sieges and suffering to La Florida. In 1740 St. Augustine residents were forced to take refuge in the Castillo de San Marcos as British General James Oglethorpe of Georgia lay siege to the town. After siding with the French against the victorious British in the French and Indian War (Seven Years' War), Spain traded La Florida to the British in exchange for Havana, Cuba, in the 1763 peace treaty. Spain would later reclaim the separate colonies of East and West La Florida in 1783 and remain there until transferring possession to the United States in 1821 under the terms of the Adams-Onís Treaty.

EARLY EXPLORATION AND SETTLEMENT OF THE SOUTHWEST

Spanish exploration of the present-day southwestern United States began in 1539–40, as the Viceroy of New Spain sent expeditions north from Mexico in search of possible gold and silver. There was rampant speculation on the wealth to be found in the unexplored areas of North America, fueled by the stories of men such as Alvar Núñez Cabeza de Vaca, who told of Native American accounts of wealthy towns such as the legendary Seven Cities of Cibola. In 1539 Franciscan Friar Marcos de Niza led an unsuccessful expedition in search of wealth. Although some of his men were killed, Marcos returned to Mexico with stories of Cibola, fueling the Viceroy's desire to keep searching. The Viceroy next sent Francisco Vázquez de Coronado northward with a large number of soldiers, a few Franciscans, and a large support staff. The Native Americans Coronado encountered further fueled the rumors of great wealth. In particular, an Indian slave known as the Turk told of a wealthy kingdom named Quivira located to the north in the Great Plains area. Coronado trav-

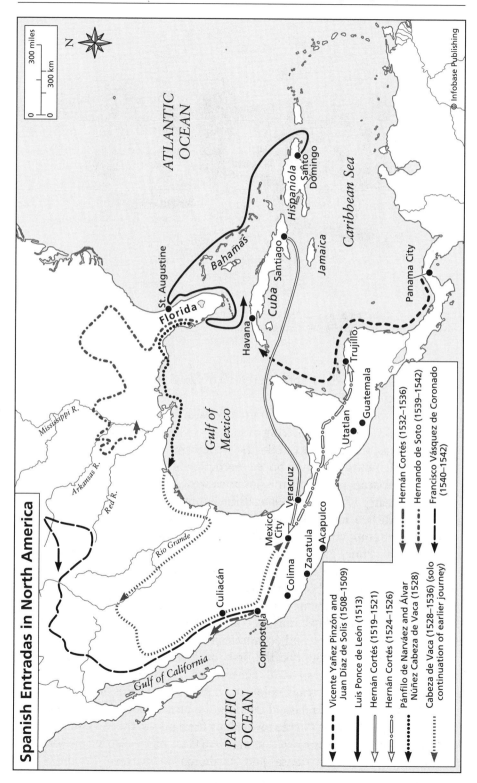

Spanish Entradas in North America

300 miles
300 km

N

ATLANTIC OCEAN

Caribbean Sea

Hispaniola
Santo Domingo

Bahamas

St. Augustine

Florida

Cuba
Santiago

Jamaica

Panama City

Havana

Trujillo

Guatemala

Utatlan

Gulf of Mexico

Mississippi R.

Arkansas R.

Red R.

Rio Grande

Veracruz

Mexico City
Zacatula
Acapulco

Culiacán

Colima

Zacatula

Compostela

Gulf of California

PACIFIC OCEAN

Vicente Yañez Pinzón and
Juan Díaz de Solís (1508–1509)

Luis Ponce de León (1513)

Hernán Cortés (1519–1521)

Hernán Cortés (1524–1526)

Pánfilo de Narváez and Álvar
Núñez Cabeza de Vaca (1528)

Cabeza de Vaca (1528–1536) (solo
continuation of earlier journey)

Hernán Cortés (1532–1536)

Hernando de Soto (1539–1542)

Francisco Vásquez de Coronado
(1540–1542)

© Infobase Publishing

A 19th-century depiction of part of Francisco Vásquez de Coronado's expedition marching through Colorado accompanied by Franciscan friars.

eled as far as present-day Kansas in search of Quivira, but returned to Mexico empty handed in 1542.

Although the Spanish found no great wealth in the American southwest, they eventually established a string of settlements in present-day New Mexico, Arizona, Texas, and California. Like the settlements of La Florida, these southwestern settlements remained on the borderlands of the Spanish New World empire. Franciscan and Jesuit missionaries would also found a series of missions in the early 17th through late 18th centuries in present-day Texas, Arizona, New Mexico, and California, just as they had earlier in La Florida. Here they would attempt conversion of the Native Americans who became known as the Pueblo, Pima, Papago, and Chumash, among others. Spanish settlers and missionaries would also be forced to confront those Native Americans who periodically resisted conversion and revolted, as well as those who raided the small Spanish settlements, such as the Navajo and Apache. Due to the military dangers and hardships, most of the southwestern settlements would also remain sparsely populated and economically underdeveloped.

Don Juan de Oñate founded the first southwestern Spanish settlement in present-day New Mexico in 1598. He traveled northward from Mexico with approximately 500 soldiers and colonists, settling in the lands of Native Americans whom the Spaniards named Pueblos. Oñate established a capital named San Juan in a pre-existing Pueblo town along the banks of the Rio Grande River, later moving it to a nearby town renamed San Gabriel. He also led explorations northward to present-day Kansas and Oklahoma, and westward to the Gulf of

California. The Franciscan friars who accompanied Oñate worked among the Pueblo Indians, converting thousands to Christianity and seeking to eradicate their native religion. Missions were founded along the Rio Grande River. Oñate also established the *encomienda*, a Spanish labor system granting land and the right to Native-American tribute to loyal Spaniards in the form of crops and labor, and occasionally personal service. The land grantee would then be responsible for the conversion and protection of those Native-American subjects, although that responsibility was not always fulfilled. The encomienda system was an important method of attracting colonists to New Mexico.

SOUTHWESTERN MISSIONS

The Spanish were disappointed not to find mineral wealth in New Mexico, but still felt New Mexico was important as a center of Native-American conversion, and as a buffer zone of defense for the wealthy mining areas to the south. Oñate would resign his post in 1608, when the Spanish king decided to make New Mexico a royal colony. Pedro de Peralta was appointed the new governor and founded the settlement of Santa Fe, which became the new provincial capital, in 1610. In that same year, the Spanish colonial-style Palace of the Governors was built in Santa Fe. Other settlements continued to develop, including Taos, which was founded in 1615. Missionaries continued to work with the Pueblos in both conversion and the raising of livestock, but harsh treatment of the Pueblos led to a buildup of resentment and ill will toward the Spanish, which would result in the Great Pueblo Revolt of 1680. Spanish colonial settlers were expelled from New Mexico until governor Diego de Vargas Zapata y Luján Ponce de León led a combined peacemaking and military campaign to subdue the Pueblo in 1692. By the early 1700s, the Spanish and Pueblo had resumed trading, and less religious pressure had improved relations.

The 1797 mission church of San Xavier del Bac near Tucson, Arizona, which was built using the labor of Papago Indians.

The Great Pueblo Revolt of 1680

The Great Pueblo Revolt of 1680, directed by a Native-American leader known as Popé, unified the majority of the New Mexican Pueblos in an organized attempt to rid the area of Spanish missions and settlements. There had been sporadic Pueblo resistance to religious conversion and the Franciscan attempts to extinguish their native religion, but the planning and execution of this revolt marked the first unified attempt at rebellion. The initial date of revolt was set for August 11, but the plan was executed on the 10th after the New Mexico governor at the time, Antonio de Otermin, learned of the plan. The Pueblos killed over 20 missionaries and more than 400 settlers, capturing all settlements north of El Paso, including the capital at Santa Fe. Targets included mission buildings, religious objects, and Spanish men. Survivors, many of whom were female, escaped to El Paso, not to return until 1692. The Great Pueblo Revolt purged the area of all Spanish colonists, making it one of the most effective revolts among colonial Native Americans.

Captured Pueblo Indian Pedro Naranjo, a member of the Queres from the Pueblo of San Felipe, gave his account of the 1680 revolt to government secretary Francisco Xavier, which was reproduced in historian Charles Wilson Hackett's *Revolt of the Pueblo Indians of New Mexico and Otermin's Attempted Reconquest, 1680–1682*. Xavier captures the religious focus of the attacks in his account of Naranjo's testimony:

Asked for what reason they so blindly burned the images, temples, crosses, and other things of divine worship, he stated that the said Indian, Popé, came down in person, and with him El Saca and El Chato from the Pueblo of Los Taos, and other captains and leaders and many people who were in his train, and he ordered in all the Pueblos through which he passed that they instantly break up and burn the images of the holy Christ, the Virgin Mary and the other saints, the crosses, and everything pertaining to Christianity, and that they burn the temples, break up the bells, and separate from the wives whom God had given them in marriage and take those whom they desired. In order to take away their baptismal names, the water, and the holy oils, they were to plunge into the rivers and wash themselves with amole, which is a root native to the country, washing even their clothing, with the understanding that there would thus be taken from them the character of the holy sacraments.

In 1692 the new governor Diego de Vargas arrived and suppressed the revolt. By 1700 the decreased missionary presence and increased trade in the area led to more peaceful interactions between the Spanish settlers and the Pueblos.

The Italian Jesuit Eusebio Francisco Kino founded a series of missions across southern Arizona in the late 1690s and early 1700s to convert the area's Pima and Papago Indians. The mission church of San Xavier del Bac near present-day Tucson, known as the White Dove of the Desert, exemplified the Spanish Renaissance architectural style common to the Spanish colonial settlements. Kino also introduced the care of animals such as cattle, sheep, goats, and horses, as well as the cultivation of wheat and other grains into the area. Hispanic Americans in Arizona also faced the periodic threat of Native American uprisings, which added an element of fear and caution to their everyday lives. Major Pima uprisings in 1695 and 1751 resulted in the death of missionaries and the destruction of mission buildings. A number of missions were also founded in present-day Texas, including the renowned mission and presidio known as the Alamo at San Antonio.

Hispanic Americans in the southwest had to adjust to daily life in a dry, sometimes mountainous land with few trees or water sources. Farmers and ranchers made a meager living, while merchants, soldiers, and government officials fared better economically. Wealthier residents could even afford servants to carry out their daily household chores. The Spanish settlements faced increasing raids from Navajo and Apache bands from the west and Kiowa and Comanche bands from the east, as well as the encroaching presence of French and British North American settlements. These continued military threats isolated the Hispanic settlers in the sparsely populated area, but trade continued to grow and link the settlers to outside communities. By the late 1730s, French traders had established a trade route from New France to Santa Fe along the Missouri–Santa Fe highway.

CALIFORNIA MISSIONS

Franciscan Friar Junípero Serra founded the Spanish missions of present-day California, called Alta California, beginning in 1769 in San Diego. California had a large Native-American population, and the missionary calling that prevailed in colonial Spanish settlements quickly took root. By the end of the Spanish control of California, a series of 21 missions stretched from San Diego northward to Sonoma, mostly along the Pacific coast. Well-known missions included San Diego, San Luis Obispo, and San Francisco. These mission complexes featured a central church surrounded by outbuildings and were the principal source of food, shelter, and protection for the missionaries, settlers, and Native Americans who lived within their walls. They featured Spanish colonial-style buildings of abode brick common throughout the American southwest. The missions sought to segregate Native-American converts, referred to as Mission Indians, from resistant Native Americans as they were immersed in teachings on Christianity, Spanish culture, and Hispanic lifestyle. Intermarriage between the Spanish and the Native Americans was rare.

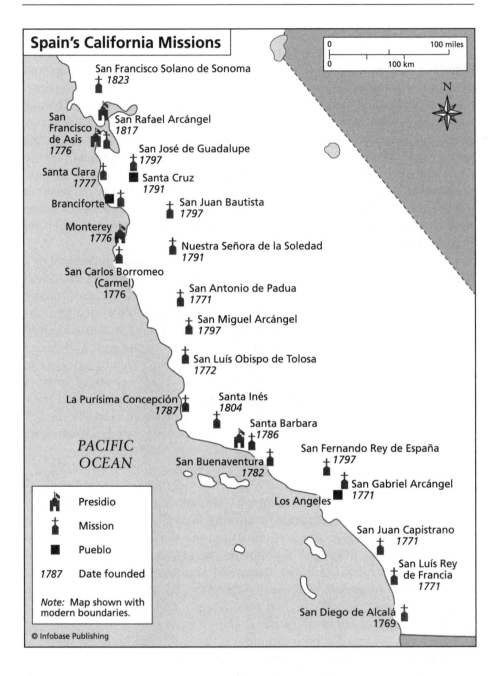

Spain's California Missions

0 _____ 100 miles
0 _____ 100 km

San Francisco Solano de Sonoma
+ 1823

San Francisco de Asis
1776

San Rafael Arcángel
1817

San José de Guadalupe
+ 1797

Santa Clara
1777

Santa Cruz
1791

Branciforte

San Juan Bautista
1797

Monterey
1776

Nuestra Señora de la Soledad
1791

San Carlos Borromeo
(Carmel)
1776

San Antonio de Padua
+ 1771

San Miguel Arcángel
+ 1797

San Luís Obispo de Tolosa
1772

La Purísima Concepción
1787

Santa Inés
1804

Santa Barbara
+1786

PACIFIC
OCEAN

San Fernando Rey de España
+ 1797

San Buenaventura
1782

San Gabriel Arcángel
1771

Los Angeles

San Juan Capistrano
+ 1771

San Luís Rey
de Francia
1771

San Diego de Alcalá
1769

Presidio

Mission

Pueblo

1787   Date founded

Note: Map shown with modern boundaries.

© Infobase Publishing

The missionaries also embarked on commercial and agricultural programs to help maintain their religious operations, including vineyards and wine cellars, olive presses, leather making, cattle ranching, and agriculture. Presidios and their troops supported the California missions as elsewhere and were accompanied by a few civilian settlements as well. Towns would usually de-

The Mission San Carlos Borroméo de Carmelo (or Carmel Mission) near Monterey, founded in 1770, was the second mission in California and became Father Junípero Serra's headquarters. This c.1790s view of the compound shows it as it looked prior to the construction of its sandstone church.

velop near the missions. Those involved in cattle raising lived in rural *haciendas*. Trade also became a key component of the colonial California economy, and the royal road El Camino Real allowed settlers and goods to travel more easily between Mexico and California. Some of the California missions became quite wealthy, unlike those of La Florida and elsewhere on the Spanish borderlands. Beginning in 1763, the Spanish crown placed its southwestern settlements under the jurisdiction of a new administrative agency known as the Provincias Internas, giving them a more secular orientation as Native American affairs came under the control of presidio commanders as opposed to missionaries.

CONCLUSION

The colonial period established the deep roots of Hispanic culture in the United States, roots that have sometimes been obscured by Anglo-American domination in later years. Nevertheless, the Spanish cultural heritage of the colonial period played a key role in shaping the culture of the former Spanish borderlands, including in the present-day states of Florida, Texas, Arizona, New Mexico, and California. This influence is apparent in many areas, from agriculture and the citrus fruits brought to Florida, to architecture that draws on the Spanish missions in the southwest and California. The experience of the Spanish in the southwest also foreshadowed the destructive relationships other European colonizers would have with Native-American tribes and America's long, traumatic struggle with issues of race and ethnicity.

MARCELLA BUSH TREVINO
BARRY UNIVERSITY

Further Reading

Altman, Ida. *Emigrants and Society: Extremadura and America in the Six-teenth Century*. Berkeley, CA: University of California Press, 1989.

Bolton, Herbert Eugene. *Bolton and the Spanish Borderlands*. Norman, OK: University of Oklahoma Press, 1964.

Cabeza de Vaca, Alvar Núñez. "The Narrative of Alvar Núñez Cabeza de Vaca" in *Spanish Explorers in the Southern United States 1528–1543*, Frederick W. Hodge, ed. Austin, TX: The Texas State Historical Association, 1990.

De la Teja, Jesus F. and Ross Frank. *Choice, Persuasion, and Coercion: Social Control on Spain's North American Frontiers*. Albuquerque, NM: University of New Mexico Press, 2005.

Elliott, John Huxtable. *Empires of the Atlantic World: Britain and Spain in America, 1492–1830*. New Haven, CT: Yale University Press, 2006.

Fuentes, Carlos. *The Buried Mirror: Reflections on Spain and the New World*. Boston, MA: Houghton Mifflin, 1992.

Gannon, Michael V. *The Cross in the Sand: The Early Catholic Church in Florida 1513–1870*. Gainesville, FL: University of Florida Press, 1965.

———, ed. *The New History of Florida*. Gainesville, FL: University Press of Florida, 1996.

Hackett, Charles Wilson. *Revolt of the Pueblo Indians of New Mexico and Otermin's Attempted Reconquest, 1680–1682*. Vol. 2. Albuquerque, NM: University of New Mexico, 1942.

Hoffman, Paul E. "Nature and Sequence of the Spanish Borderlands," in *Native, European, and African Cultures in Mississippi, 1500–1800*, Patricia K. Galloway, ed. Jackson, MS: Department of Archives and History, 1991.

———. *A New Andalucia and a Way to the Orient: The American Southeast during the Sixteenth Century*. Baton Rouge, LA: Louisiana State University Press, 1990.

Kessell, John L. *Spain in the Southwest: A Narrative History of Colonial New Mexico, Arizona, Texas, and California*. Norman, OK: University of Oklahoma Press, 2002.

Lake, Alison. *Colonial Rosary: The Spanish and Indian Missions of California*. Athens, OH: Swallow Press, Ohio University Press, 2006.

Lockhart, James and Stuart B. Schwartz. *Early Latin America: A History of Colonial Spanish America and Brazil*. New York: Cambridge University Press, 1983.

Lyon, Eugene. *Richer Than We Thought: The Material Culture of Sixteenth-Century St. Augustine*. St. Augustine, FL: St. Augustine Historical Society, 1992.

McAlister, Lyle N. *Spain and Portugal in the New World, 1492–1700*. Minneapolis, MN: University of Minnesota Press, 1984.

Milanich, Jerald T. and Susan Milbrath, eds. *First Encounters: Spanish Explorations in the Caribbean and the United States, 1492–1570*. Gainesville, FL: University of Florida Press, 1989.

Simmons, Marc. *The Last Conquistador: Juan de Oñate and the Settling of the Far Southwest*. Norman, OK: University of Oklahoma Press, 1991.

Thomas, Hugh. *Rivers of Gold: The Rise of the Spanish Empire, from Columbus to Magellan*. New York: Random House, 2003.

Truett, Samuel and Elliott Young, eds. *Continental Crossroads: Remapping U.S.-Mexico Borderlands History*. Durham, NC: Duke University Press, 2004.

Waterbury, Jean Parker, ed. *The Oldest City: St. Augustine: Saga of Survival*. St. Augustine, FL: St. Augustine Historical Society, 1983.

Weber, David J. *The Spanish Frontier in North America*. New Haven, CT: Yale University Press, 1992.

———, ed. *What Caused the Pueblo Revolt of 1680?* New York: St. Martin's Press, 1999.

CHAPTER 2

The American Revolution: 1775 to 1783

WHEN THE GUNFIRE of Lexington and Concord turned peaceful protests into open revolt in April 1775, the rebellious colonies enjoyed few advantages. They had no trained, professional army with which to confront the established British military that only a dozen years before had defeated its chief European rival, France, virtually eliminating any French presence in North America. They had no fleet to oppose the Royal Navy, arguably the most powerful seagoing force in the world. They had no significant industrial base to produce weapons and supplies necessary to engage in a major war since they had relied, by virtue of the English mercantilist laws, on the importation of manufactured goods from Britain. Because they had no established central government or treasury, they had little ability to secure loans to purchase what they needed for their own defense. They had no authoritative central government to manage economic or military affairs; rather, they had thirteen colonial governments that found it difficult to agree on the fundamental principles necessary to form an effective central government. Few would have wagered an English pound, a French *franc* or a Spanish *real* on the chances for colonial success against the world's most far-reaching empire.

To have any chance at all against the British Empire, the rebellious North American colonies would have to somehow raise enough money to purchase weapons and supplies overseas, solve the problem of transporting them to North America, and develop trained armed forces at least capable of defending their own territory. France would delight in seeing Britain's colonies rebel, as the British had expelled France from North America at the end of the Seven Years' War in 1763. In 1775, in addition to the 13 rebelling colonies, Great Britain's possessions in the Western Hemisphere included Canada, Bermuda, the Bahamas, Jamaica, and a string of outposts east of the Mississippi River stretching as far south as the area around today's Natchez, Mississippi. In addition Britain held Florida and West Florida, the latter including the southern portions of today's states of Alabama and Mississippi, both taken from Spain as a result of the Seven Years' War. New Spain included Louisiana; the North American continent west of the Mississippi River; Mexico; Central America; most of South America; and portions of the Caribbean region including Cuba, Hispaniola, and Puerto Rico. As England's primary rival for control of the Western Hemisphere, Spain would also be pleased to see dissension in the British Empire. But what nation would risk exposure to war with Britain in order to aid this improbable revolution? Sympathy was one issue, but open support of the rebels at the risk of being drawn into another worldwide war between the European empires was quite another matter.

CLANDESTINE SUPPORT FOR THE REVOLUTION

Although France and Spain were unwilling to provide overt aid, they nevertheless delighted at the inconvenience the revolution caused their longtime imperial opponent. When the British failed to quickly stifle the insurgents, both France and Spain sensed an opportunity to prolong their rival's discomfort through clandestine aid to the upstart colonists. To cloak their assistance, they agreed to funnel it through a bogus Spanish trading company they established for that purpose—Rodríguez, Hortalez y Compañía. Operations, which began six weeks before the Declaration of Independence, would be directed from St. Eustatius in the Lesser Antilles, with each of the two nations providing the equivalent of one million *livres* in initial funding. Shipments to the rebels would be made by water to Philadelphia, Charleston, or other Atlantic coast ports; or, if they were blockaded, through New Orleans, up the Mississippi and Ohio Rivers, then overland to the east.

Initial responsibility for Spanish policy was in the hands of the Marquis de Grimaldi, minister of state, who selected Pedro Pablo Abarca de Bolea, Conde (count) de Aranda, to direct operations in the Americas. Grimaldi's position was later assumed by José Moniño y Redondo, Conde de Floridablanca, but policy remained unchanged. Funded by the initial grants from France and Spain, the Conde de Aranda provided the American uprising with 216 brass cannons, 209 gun carriages, 27 mortars, 12,826 artillery shells, 51,134 musket balls, 300,000 pounds of gunpowder, 30,000 muskets with bayonets, 4,000 tents, and 30,000 uniforms.

French and Spanish assistance also helped bring in European military experts, who made significant contributions to eventual American independence—leaders such as the German Baron Friedrich Wilhelm Augustus von Steuben, and the Poles Tadeusz Kościuszko and Kazimierz Pułaski. During 1776 the government of King Carlos III also allowed American privateers the use of Spanish ports for provisioning and refitting.

In 1777 the Continental Congress sent Arthur Lee to Spain in search of additional aid. He met with Spanish officials in Burgos on March 1, with the wealthy Bilbao banker Diego María de Gardoqui serving as interpreter. Gardoqui would later establish his own company to channel aid to the colonies, and eventually become the first Spanish ambassador to the United States. As a result of these negotiations, Lee received 50,000 gold *pesos*, with larger sums forthcoming in April and June. From 1776 to 1778, Spain provided the Americans with 7,944,806 *reales* in financial assistance. Without this aid, it is difficult to imagine how the colonists would have been able to sustain themselves against the might of the British Empire.

SPAIN DECLARES WAR

By the fall of 1777 the American Revolution had been raging for two and a half years. The American victory over the British at the Battle of Saratoga in October marked the first time in history that an entire British army in the field had been forced to surrender. News of the patriot victory convinced many Europeans for the first time that the rebels had a real chance to win. France was the first to move, openly signing treaties with the Continental Congress recognizing the United States of America as a legitimate government, extending military aid and agreeing to commercial relations in 1778. Spain declared war on Great Britain on June 21, 1779. Spain saw in the American Revolution an opportunity to redeem colonial possessions lost to Britain during the Seven Years' War: Florida, West Florida, Jamaica, the Bahamas, Gibraltar, and Minorca. It was also a chance to eliminate all British outposts and settlements from Mexico, Honduras, and other areas claimed by Spain in the Americas.

Spain's declaration of war forced the British to spread their military and naval forces more thinly to protect their overseas possession from the combined French and Spanish fleets, and even begin to worry about threats to the British Isles themselves. The British fleet was forced to guard colonies from the Indian Ocean to the Caribbean, decreasing the effectiveness of their attempts to blockade the North American rebels or to hunt down American privateers preying on British merchant shipping. The British army was similarly required to deplete its strength by garrisoning overseas possessions, especially Gibraltar, which was besieged by Franco-Spanish forces. This limited the British forces that could be sent to North America and required the British, who were desperate for manpower, to rely heavily on mercenary troops hired from the kings and princes of the various German states.

Fort on the Bay

The Presidio La Bahia, meaning "fort on the bay," on the Gulf of Mexico coast in today's Texas had the distinction of being one of the only forts west of the Mississippi River to have participated in the American Revolution. It was built in 1721 along with the missionary chapel Our Lady of Loreto on the original site of explorer Rene-Robert de LaSalle's doomed Fort St. Louis on the western shore of Garcitas Creek, near present day Port Lavaca.

Because of conflicts with the Native American tribe Karankawa, in 1726 the fort was abandoned and moved 26 miles inland along the Guadalupe River near the location of Mission Valley, northwest of today's Victoria, in Victoria County. For the next 26 years La Bahia mission and presidio grew and prospered, supplying enough food for themselves and other nearby missions. In the autumn of 1749, the presidio and mission were relocated back to the original site by the Spanish government seeking a better tactical location to prevent further encroachment by the English and French.

During the American Revolution, Presidio La Bahia was responsible for the defense of the coast and eastern province of Texas after the abandonment of the Presidios at Los Adaes and Los Orcoquisac. Soldiers from Presidio La Bahia, along with the Spanish Army, fought the British along the Gulf Coast. Today, Presidio La Bahia is the oldest standing fort west of the Mississippi.

The Presidio La Bahia in Goliad, Texas, had a role in the American Revolution when it sent reinforcements to the Spanish Army fighting the British on the Gulf Coast.

In Europe, as well as the Caribbean, American privateers were welcomed in Spanish ports where they were able to refit, rearm, and resupply to continue their depredations on British shipping. American trade with Spanish possessions in the Caribbean and South America flourished, while supply routes continued through the Caribbean and Mexico with arms, equipment and other supplies sent directly from the French and Spanish governments to support American forces.

NEW ORLEANS SUPPLIES AMERICAN FORCES

In the spring of 1776 Captain George Gibson, along with 16 followers, arrived in New Orleans with a request from General Charles Lee, second in command of the American army after George Washington, to the Spanish governor Luis de Unzaga y Amézaga for weapons, gunpowder, blankets, and medical supplies. Gibson met with Oliver Pollock, an influential New Orleans businessman, who introduced him to the governor. Although Spain was officially neutral at that time, Unzaga was sympathetic to the Americans. Determined to assist them, he provided 1,000 pounds of gunpowder shipped to Philadelphia and another 9,000 pounds transported up the Mississippi and Ohio Rivers to Fort Pitt. This support was essential to saving the fort. Unzaga also sent a favorable report to the court of King Carlos III, who secretly ordered colonial officials in Havana, with businessman Eduardo Miguel acting as a front, to ship additional supplies to New Orleans. By July 1777 Spanish officials sent another 2,000 barrels of gunpowder, muskets, musket balls, blankets, shoes, and uniforms up the Mississippi, support that made its way to forces under George Rogers Clark and to Washington's Continental Army.

In 1776 Bernardo de Gálvez y Madrid received an appointment as colonel of the Spanish regiment stationed in New Orleans. On November 25, 1776, Carlos III ordered him to begin collecting information about British activities in the Floridas and elsewhere, inaugurating a successful espionage network that Gálvez ran for the rest of the war. Appointed governor of Louisiana effective January 1, 1777, Gálvez was introduced to Pollock by outgoing Governor Unzaga, and received secret orders from Madrid to offer covert assistance to the Americans. In response, he continued to provide secret aid, sending supplies of all kinds up the Mississippi under the protection of the Spanish flag. By the end of 1777, Gálvez had loaned Pollock some 74,087 Spanish dollars and provided cargo worth 25,000 gold *doubloons*, as well as over 100,000 Spanish dollars worth of weapons, provisions, and other supplies that were sent to Fort Pitt, Philadelphia, and other American destinations.

Yet Gálvez was not content with covert aid. In 1777 the Continental Congress sent Captain James Willing at the head of 30 men down the Mississippi to make contact with the Spanish governor. Along the way, Willing launched raids on British settlements and captured several British vessels plying the Mississippi. When he arrived in New Orleans, Gálvez provided the Americans with housing and provisions. He then took the extraordinary step of allowing them to sell their spoils to raise money for the purchase of military supplies for the American army. The governor also opened New Orleans to free American trade, allowed American privateers to use the port, and even launched actions that resulted in the capture of 11 British ships he deemed guilty of smuggling. After ordering all British subjects to leave Louisiana within two weeks, he further assisted Willing, who returned to Philadelphia aboard the ship *Rebeca* with a cargo of munitions, provisions, muskets, blankets, and medicine. Further Spanish supplies, provided through Gálvez's good offices, supported the American capture of Vincennes and other military operations in the Mississippi Valley area.

OUSTING THE BRITISH FROM THE MISSISSIPPI VALLEY
News of the Spanish declaration of war against Great Britain arrived in New Orleans in early August 1779. By the end of the month Governor Gálvez organized a force of over 600 men comprised of 170 professional soldiers from several Spanish regiments; 330 new recruits from Mexico and the Canary Islands for El Regimiento Fijo de Infantería de la Luisiana (the Fixed Infantry Regiment of Louisiana); 20 *carabineros*; 60 local white militia; 80 free blacks; seven Americans; and an assortment of volunteers from Cuba, Santo Domingo and Puerto Rico. Oliver Pollock acted as Gálvez's aide-de-camp. With this diverse collection he began a 90-mile march along the Mississippi River to Fort Bute at Manchac. Along the way Gálvez passed through German and Acadian settlements, where he added an additional 600 volunteers and 160 Native Americans. By the time he reached Manchac, his force numbered 1,427 men. Arriving on September 6, he took the small British fort by storm the following day, taking 20 prisoners from its 27-man garrison without losing a man.

With the fall of Fort Bute, Gálvez pushed on to Baton Rouge, which was defended by a sizeable force of 146 British regulars, 201 Waldeck mercenaries, 11 British artillerists, and 150 armed settlers and blacks. A sturdy fort mounting 13 cannons protected the garrison. By the time the Spanish force arrived on September 12, disease, fever, and the long marches—which most of Gálvez's troops had not previously experienced—had whittled the governor's troops down to an estimated 384 infantry from the Spanish and Louisiana regiments; 14 artillerymen; and some 400 militia, Native Americans, and blacks. Fearing his forces were not strong enough to overcome the fort by storm, Gálvez proved to be a solid military tactician by moving, under cover of night, a battery of artillery close enough to the British fort to open a destructive fire that began to shatter the fort's wooden walls. Unable to withstand the bombardment, with their walls collapsing, the British surrendered on September 21. Included in the terms of the surrender were 80 Waldeck infantry occupying Fort Panmure at Natchez.

Bernardo de Gálvez y Madrid

Born on July 23, 1746, in the village of Macharaviava near Málaga, Spain, Bernardo was the son of Matías de Gálvez y Gallardo; the nephew of José de Gálvez, president of the Consejo de Indias (Council of the Indies); captain general of Guatemala; and viceroy of New Spain. He entered the military as a lieutenant at age 16, rising to the rank of captain during the war with Portugal. In 1769 he accompanied his uncle when the latter was appointed Viceroy of New Spain. There he was wounded in skirmishes with the Apache Indians before returning to Spain in 1772. Once back in Europe, he was assigned to a Spanish regiment in France, where his French language education would later prove very useful in Louisiana.

The Spanish-born Bernardo de Gálvez founded Galveston, Texas, and achieved important victories over the British during the American Revolution.

In 1776 he arrived in New Orleans as colonel of the Fixed Infantry Regiment of Louisiana and assumed the role of governor of Louisiana on January 1, 1777. That same year, he married Doña Marie Felice de Saint-Maxent Estrehan. He founded Gálvez Town (later Galveston) in 1778 and encouraged the settlement of Nueva Iberia.

Following the capture of Pensacola in 1781, Gálvez led a Spanish force that captured the important British naval base at New Providence in the Bahamas on May 6, 1782, along with 12 privateers and 65 merchant ships. He left for Spain in 1783 to fight in the Netherlands, but returned to Nueva España in the following year as governor and captain general of Cuba. When his father died in 1785, Gálvez succeeded him as viceroy of New Spain. Taking his post in Mexico, he became very popular among the people for a number of reforms, including installing street lights in Mexico City, completing various highway projects, promoting scientific study, reducing abuses of Indian labor, and dedicating 16 percent of lottery income to charity. Unfortunately he became ill soon after taking office and died prematurely in Tacubaya, Mexico City, on November 30, 1786.

In addition to modern Galveston, Texas, St. Bernard Parish in Louisiana is named in Gálvez's honor, and in 1985 the United States issued a postage stamp in his honor. Few foreigners could claim to have contributed more to the American cause than Bernardo de Gálvez y Madrid.

In less than one month of energetic campaigning, Gálvez's patchwork force had swept the British from the Lower Mississippi Valley, capturing some 550 British and German regulars, 500 armed settlers and blacks, and three forts. He accomplished this with only one of his own men killed and two wounded. To this, Gálvez added the capture of eight British ships, and the British outposts at Thompson's Creek and Amite were taken by his subordinate officers. His success eliminated any threat to the Americans from British forces in the Lower Mississippi Valley, preserved the vital supply lines running through New Orleans, and forced the British to divert resources to protect their possessions in Florida, West Florida, and the Upper Mississippi Valley. Spanish success in the Lower Mississippi also provided support for American activities in the Upper Mississippi Valley.

SUPPORT FROM NUEVA ESPAÑA (NEW SPAIN)

Long before the American Revolution, Spanish explorers and settlers, though relatively small in number, had moved gradually north into what would become California, Texas, and the lands in between. One of their creations was the famed California mission system, many of which were founded by Father Junípero Serra and his fellow Franciscans. When word of Spanish participation in the Revolution arrived, Father Serra sent a letter to each of the missions asking people to pray for the success of Spain and the Americans. In Texas, about 2,800 Spanish settlers were located in the general vicinity of San Antonio de Bexar, La Bahia (Goliad), and El Fuerte del Cibolo, and scattered in the various missions.

Even at this early date an important economic occupation in Texas was cattle ranching. Most of the larger cattle *ranchos* were located in an area between San Antonio, Laredo, Brownsville, and Old Indianola, mostly in the lands bordering the San Antonio, Cibolo, and Guadalupe Rivers. The *rancheros* (ranchers) and local Spanish troops were reported to be sympathetic to the American Revolution. When Governor Gálvez began shipping provisions to the Americans, the rancheros drove herds of cattle to Nacogdoches, Texas. Under the protection of Lieutenant Governor Antonio Gil Ybarbo of the province of Texas, who also contributed his own cattle, the herds were then moved through Nachitoches and Opelousas, Louisiana, to New Orleans. Some of these cattle were sent on to supply the Americans, while the rest were used to support Gálvez's own campaigns against the British. Between 1779 and 1782, an estimated 9,000–15,000 head of cattle were sent to New Orleans, along with several hundred horses and a number of bulls. Some riders who accompanied the herds stayed on in Louisiana to join Gálvez's military campaigns.

On August 17, 1780, King Carlos III issued an order requiring all male Spanish residents in Nueva España to contribute two pesos and all male Indians to donate one peso, in cash or goods, to support the American Revolu-

Jorge Farragut

Born in Ciudadela, Minorca on September 29, 1755, Jorge Farragut went to sea at the age of 10, serving in the Russian navy in combat against the Turks. Some records suggest that he also worked in the shipbuilding yards before returning home. He left Minorca for good on April 2, 1772, traveling to Havana, Cuba, where he found employment on merchant ships.

By age 20 he captained a small schooner trading between Havana, Veracruz, and New Orleans. He likely learned about the American Revolution during a stop in Louisiana and became determined to join the rebels in their fight against the British.

Sailing his ship to Havana, he took on a cargo of weapons, munitions, and naval stores before set-

A portrait of Jorge Farragut, a native of Minorca who helped fight the British in the Revolution. His son David later rose to prominence in the navy during the American Civil War.

ting sail for Charleston, S.C., where he arrived in 1776. Since the British had controlled his native Minorca, Farragut was already conversant in English. In Charleston he served for a while as a lieutenant on a privateer before being appointed first lieutenant, and later captain in the South Carolina naval forces. In this capacity he fought against the British at Savannah and later Charleston, where he was captured. Once released, he again fought as a privateer until a serious wound brought his seafaring career to an end.

Not content to remain inactive, he joined the partisan forces led by General Francis Marion. He fought with the American forces at Cowpens, Wilmington, and Beaufort Bridge, rising to the rank of major by the end of the war.

Following the war he moved to Tennessee, married, and was named major of militia by Governor William Blount. He settled in Knoxville in 1792, fought against the Cherokee, and later moved to New Orleans, where he helped construct gunboats to defend the city in 1803–07, and was named captain of one of the gunboats during the War of 1812.

Jorge Farragut left the armed forces in 1814, dying three years later. One of his offspring was David Glasgow Farragut, who gained fame as an American admiral during the Civil War.

Spanish Participation in the American Revolution, 1777–1781

Legend:
- Spanish lands
- Cattle regions
- Spanish advances
- Cattle drives
- • Spanish settlements
- ✳ British settlements captured by Spain, 1779–1781

0   200 miles
0   200 km

N

St. Joseph 1781

St. Louis

UNITED STATES

Mississippi R.

Nacogdoches
Bucareli
Natchez 1779
West Florida
Mobile 1780
Baton Rouge 1779
Manchac 1779
San Antonio de Béjar
New Orleans
Pensacola 1781
East Florida
ATLANTIC OCEAN

Río Grande

Gulf of Mexico

© Infobase Publishing

Havana • CUBA

tion. Although it is not known exactly how much was collected, contributions continued to be gathered until 1784, when word arrived of the peace treaty ending the war.

ST. LOUIS AND THE UPPER MISSISSIPPI VALLEY

When the American General George Rogers Clark arrived on the banks of the Mississippi River on July 4, 1778, his troops suffered from a serious lack of supplies including gunpowder, musket balls, and even funds for their purchase. Clark sent a bill of exchange to Governor Gálvez in New Orleans, hoping for support from the only source of supplies that might keep his small army in the field. Although Spain was then technically neutral, the governor accepted the bill and provided Clark with the equivalent of more than $74,000 to purchase gunpowder and other supplies. At the same time, Clark established contact with the Spanish lieutenant governor in St. Louis, Fernando de Leyba, who furnished weapons, clothing, funds, and other support. With this assistance, Clark was successful in defeating the British forces at Kaskaskia and Cahokia.

A year later in 1779, Clark planned to oust the British from Vincennes in what is today southern Indiana. In addition to the aid provided by Gálvez and de Leyba, Clark received assistance from Colonel Francis Vigo, a Spanish citizen of Italian birth who used his personal fortune to help the American rebels and also acted as a spy for Clark, journeying to Vincennes to perform a reconnaissance on behalf of the Americans. Captured by the British, he was eventually able to escape. Vincennes fell to Clark on February 24, 1779. When the state of Indiana was formed, one of its southern counties was named in honor of Vigo.

By 1780 the British determined to reverse their string of losses in the west and cut off the flow of supplies into the rebellious colonies and their Spanish allies. Assembling a force of 300 regulars and Canadians and supported by upward of 1,000 Native-American allies, the British planned to recover Vincennes and Cahokia, then invade Spanish territory southward toward New Orleans. Warned of the impending British offensive, Lieutenant Governor de Leyba constructed Fort San Carlos, named in honor of King Carlos III, to defend St. Louis. But de Leyba could muster only 29 regulars from the Louisiana Regiment, 281 local militia, and a handful of American volunteers to defend the fort. Despite the disparity in numbers, de Leyba's force successfully repelled the British attack on May 26, preventing them from moving further south.

Detail from a mural in the Missouri state capital building depicting the 1780 attack on Fort San Carlos at St. Louis, in which the British and their Native-American allies were repelled because of the defenses planned by the Spanish lieutenant governor.

With the British retreat, de Leyba cooperated with the American Colonel John Montgomery near Cahokia in Illinois to launch reprisal attacks on the Native-American settlements at Bear River and Prairie du Chien. The following year, a force under Eugenio Purré, consisting of 65 Spaniards and 60 allied Native Americans, defeated the British outpost at St. Joseph near modern Niles, Michigan. By mid-1871 the only British garrisons remaining in the northwest were in the far north at Detroit and Mackinac. Gálvez and de Leyba had cooperated with the Americans to push the British out of the Upper Mississippi Valley, defeat a British counteroffensive, prevent the British from capturing Fort Pitt in Pennsylvania and Fort Henry in Virginia, and preserve the lifelines up the Mississippi and Ohio Valley that brought supplies essential to the American cause.

THE CAPTURE OF MOBILE

Returning from his successful campaign against the British in Louisiana, Bernardo de Gálvez determined to move against the British garrison at Mobile in modern Alabama. After his initial expedition was thwarted by a storm in January 1780, reinforcements arrived from Havana, enabling him to mount a second expedition. This second force sailed from New Orleans with 754 strong, including 234 regulars, 14 artillerymen, 26 *carabineros*, 323 white militia, 107 free blacks, 24 slaves, and 26 Americans. They landed near Mobile on February 10, marching overland to lay siege to Fort Charlotte, where the British garrison numbered a little over 300 men including regulars, loyalists, local militia, and blacks.

Reinforced by 567 infantry of the Regimiento de Navarra (Regiment of Navarre) who arrived from Havana on February 20, Gálvez opened fire on the defenders on February 29 and began digging siege approaches on March 9. Cut off, with their walls breached by Spanish artillery and a relief expedition from Pensacola delayed by bad weather, the garrison capitulated on March 14. Throughout the following year, after Gálvez withdrew all but a small garrison for his next campaign, Choctaw and Creek Indians allied with the British and continually harassed Spanish foragers, work parties, and others who ventured beyond the fort's walls.

In January 1781 a strong British force including 160 regulars from the 60th Regiment of Foot and the Waldeck Regiment, as well as an estimated 300 loyalists and Native-American allies, attacked the garrison at Mobile. Although Colonel José de Ezpeleta had only 40 men from the Regimiento de España, another 40-man black militia company from New Orleans, and eight cannons with 60 artillerists, he was able to withstand the assault. Fearing for the safety of the post should British forces in Pensacola launch another attempt, Gálvez reinforced the fort with two ships and 500 troops.

Delighted with Gálvez's successes, King Carlos III promoted him to governor of Louisiana and Mobile, with command of all Spanish operations in America.

THE SIEGE OF PENSACOLA

Pensacola was no small frontier outpost. The capital of West Florida, it was the most important British base on the Gulf Coast. Defended by a force of about 2,500 British, Germans, and Native Americans under Gen. Archibald Campbell, the base was crucial to the defense of the two Floridas, and provided the Royal Navy with an excellent base from which to attack American and Spanish shipping operations in the Caribbean. If Pensacola were to be taken, Gálvez would have to mount a much larger operation than his previous efforts.

Armed with his new titles and authority, Gálvez organized a force at Havana, but his first attempt in October 1780 was dispersed by a hurricane. To assemble a new expedition, Gálvez drew troops from Cuba, New

Francisco de Miranda

Born in Caracas, Venezuela on March 28, 1750, Miranda served as a captain in the Spanish Army's Aragon Regiment and aide to the governor of Cuba, where he proved very successful in arranging for supplies to support the French fleet under Admiral de Grasse, as well as loans to support General Washington's army during the Yorktown campaign. He fought under Bernardo de Gálvez during the siege of Pensacola and the capture of the Bahamas, negotiating the surrender as the representative of the governor.

Following the American Revolution, Miranda was instrumental in the movement to win Venezuelan independence from Spain, but after a series of reversals he capitulated to Spanish forces in 1812. Deported to Cádiz, he was imprisoned in Spain until his death in 1816. Statues commemorating Miranda's contributions are located in Washington, D.C., and Philadelphia, and in a number of other cities around the world. A park in Pensacola, Florida, is named in his honor.

A statue of Francisco Miranda, who fought for independence for both Venezuela and the American colonies.

Orleans, Mobile, and other Spanish possessions throughout the Caribbean. By the end of February 1781, he had assembled a new force ready to move on West Florida. Supported by a fleet of 16 Spanish naval vessels and dozens of transports, he left Havana on February 28 with a force of over 7,000 troops, most of whom were veterans from professional Spanish or colonial regiments. Spain sent 3,800 men from some of its most famous regiments; 2,000 from Cuba, Mexico, Puerto Rico, Costa Rica, Venezuela, Haiti, and Santo Domingo; 1,400 from New Orleans; and Colonel José de Ezpeleta commanded 500 from Mobile. In April another 1,600 reinforcements from Cuba under Governor Juan Manuel de Cagigal arrived to bolster Gálvez's expedition.

Arriving off Pensacola on March 8, Gálvez put some of his force ashore on Santa Rosa Island at the entrance of the bay to establish a base of operations. After accumulating supplies and awaiting the arrival of all of his forces, including a reinforcement of four French frigates and 725 French troops, Gálvez moved to the mainland to begin siege operations. With the Spanish navy preventing any reinforcement, the surrounded British fought stubbornly for two months as Spanish troops gradually pushed siege trenches toward Fort George, erecting artillery batteries within a half-mile of its walls. Daily

Spanish attackers moving in on the British forces at Fort George at Pensacola, just as the fort's powder magazine explodes after a direct hit from a Spanish shell.

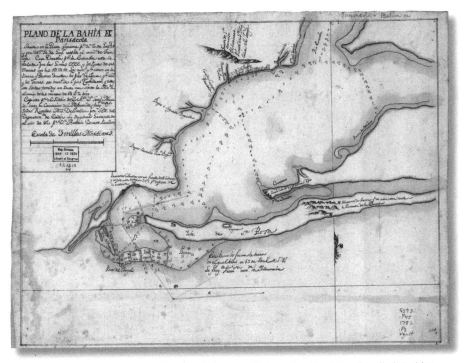

A 1782 Spanish-language map of Pensacola's strategic bay with directions for piloting ships through it; the map was made soon after the Spanish retook the outpost during the Revolution.

skirmishing and raids by the defenders determined to obstruct Spanish progress cost many casualties on both sides.

On May 8, a Spanish artillery shell penetrated one of the powder magazines in Fort George, resulting in an enormous explosion that killed nearly 100 defenders and destroyed a key fortification. Spanish infantry quickly moved forward to occupy the area. From their new position, Spanish artillery could sweep the exposed British positions inside Fort George. Recognizing that his position was now hopeless, General Campbell surrendered the fort with its 1,113 surviving defenders, as well as all of West Florida. Spanish losses were 74 killed and 198 wounded, including Gálvez.

The capture of Pensacola denied the British an important base of operations, while at the same time opening the bay for American and Spanish privateers to prey on British ships and providing another entry point for valuable supplies destined for the Continental Army. Following his victory, Gálvez provided his French allies with 500,000 pesos to refit and re-provision their ships for the forthcoming campaign at Yorktown. In appreciation for his services, King Carlos III promoted Gálvez to lieutenant general, named him governor and captain general of Louisiana and Florida, and awarded him a coat of arms with the title Conde of Gálvez, Viscount of Gálveztown.

Americans, British, and Hessians (German conscripts employed by the British) fighting at Yorktown. The American victory was made possible in part by emergency assistance from the Spanish.

THE SIEGE OF YORKTOWN

By the autumn of 1781 the Revolutionary War had been raging for six and a half long years. In an effort to at last subdue its rebellious colonies, Lord Charles Cornwallis led a British army north from the Carolinas into Virginia en route to a junction with British troops in New York. However, by the time he reached Virginia, his army was in need of resupply. To achieve this, he moved his troops out onto the York Peninsula, where they could be resupplied by the Royal Navy.

Learning of Cornwallis's position, General George Washington and his French allies under the Comte de Rochambeau and Admiral François Joseph Paul de Grasse determined to trap the British on the peninsula, surround them, and force them to surrender. To accomplish this, Washington and Rochambeau planned to move their troops to cut off Cornwallis's exit from the peninsula, while Admiral de Grasse's fleet blockaded Chesapeake Bay to prevent the arrival of the British fleet. De Grasse's fleet had been provisioned and supplied in the Spanish colonies of Santo Domingo and Puerto Rico at a cost to the Spanish of some 100,000 pesos. Further, de Grasse was able to move his fleet north because the Spanish fleet not only guarded French possessions in the Caribbean in de Grasse's absence, it also prevented the British from sending naval reinforcement against French forces off Virginia. In large part, de Grasse's victory over the British fleet at the Battle of the Virginia Capes,

Juan de Miralles y Trayllón

Born July 23, 1713, in Petrer, Spain, Juan de Miralles was a wealthy Spanish merchant in Havana, Cuba, when the Revolutionary War began. Well before Spanish entry into the conflict, José de Gálvez, head of Council of the Indies, appointed de Miralles the first envoy of King Carlos III to the North American rebels in 1778.

While en route to Philadelphia, de Miralles stopped in the southern colonies to arrange the transportation of clandestine Spanish aid through the ports at Charleston, South Carolina, and Baltimore, Maryland. He also made stops in North Carolina and Williamsburg, Virginia, to further establish communication and trade between the colonies and Spanish possessions in the Caribbean. Once in Philadelphia, he opened direct trade through that port, established a residence in the city, and met with members of Congress to further cooperation.

De Miralles became the primary organizer of trade between the American colonies and Havana. Becoming a close friend of George Washington, he spent time at the general's headquarters and sent him and his wife gifts of chocolate, wine, sugar, lemons, and other commodities. When De Miralles became seriously ill, he was treated by Washington's personal physician until his death on April 28, 1780. His remains were returned to Havana for burial.

which prevented relief from reaching Cornwallis, was made possible by this Spanish assistance.

The allies, however, had a serious problem—finances. The American treasury was empty; Continental paper money was so depreciated that merchants were reluctant to accept it. General Washington lacked the funds necessary for provisions, clothing, and other supplies. The situation was critical; without financial support, the allied siege of Yorktown might have to be abandoned.

To solve the problem, Admiral de Grasse dispatched three fast frigates to Havana, where Francisco de Saavedra de Sangronis, a Spanish envoy aboard one of the French ships, approached Governor Juan Manuel de Cagigal with a request for financial support. Cagigal, assisted by his aide Francisco de Miranda and Barbara Santa Cruz, Marquesa de Cárdenas, were able to raise in only six hours loans totaling some 4.52 million reales. Most historians agree that this financial assistance was crucial to the ultimate success of the Yorktown campaign. The surrender of Cornwallis's entire army was the last major military action of the war, sealing the future of American independence.

CONCLUSION

At the beginning of the American Revolution, Britain's rebellious colonies lacked the means of conducting a war against the vast power of the world's strongest empire. Not wanting to become involved in another worldwide war, the French and Spanish governments were reluctant to become involved, but at the same time relished the opportunity to discomfort the British, who had defeated them a dozen years prior in the Seven Years' War. Within a year of the outbreak of the Revolution, both nations were shuttling covert financial assistance through a bogus Spanish trading company, providing the weapons, gunpowder, uniforms, and other supplies Americans desperately needed to avoid subjugation. Much of this aid arrived through the port of New Orleans, where Spanish officials, sympathetic to the Revolution, provided not only weapons and supplies, but also sanctuary for American privateers and an espionage network that gained valuable intelligence.

Once Spain openly entered the war in 1779, Spanish forces threatened British positions in Europe and the Americas, pinning down British forces for the defense of its empire that could otherwise have been sent to subdue the American colonies. The Spanish fleet kept open valuable trade routes to supply the Americans, while at the same time raiding British shipping and threatening trade with their far-flung empire. Governor Gálvez's operations in the Mississippi Valley, Mobile, and West Florida were particularly important, for they eliminated the British presence in Louisiana and the Gulf coast and removed any threat to the Americans from the west. Spanish actions preserved the flow of supplies up the Mississippi and Ohio Rivers, providing essential supplies to American forces along the East Coast; saving Fort Pitt and Fort Henry, which guarded the western trade routes; and making possible the victories of George Rogers Clark against the British in Indiana and the Upper Mississippi Valley.

As early as November 1779, Thomas Jefferson wrote to Governor Bernardo de Gálvez to thank him for his assistance, and that of Spain, for the American cause. Following the Revolution, in his farewell meeting with his officers, General George Washington toasted Spain, and in 1784 Congress recognized both Spain and Gálvez for their contribution to American independence. Without Spanish and French assistance, it is indeed difficult to imagine how the Revolution could have succeeded.

JAMES S. PULA
PURDUE UNIVERSITY NORTH CENTRAL

Further Reading

Caughey, John Walton. *Bernardo de Gálvez in Louisiana 1776–1783.* Berkeley, CA: University of California Press, 1934.

Chávez, Thomas E. *Spain and the Independence of the United States: An Intrinsic Gift.* Albuquerque, NM: New Mexico Press, 2002.

Cockcroft, James D., *Latinos in the Making of the United States.* New York: Franklin Watts, 1995.

De Varona, Frank, ed. *Hispanic Presence in the United States: Historical Beginnings.* Miami, FL: Mnemosyne Publishing Company, 1993.

Fernández-Florez, Darío. *The Spanish Heritage in the United States.* Madrid: Publicaciones Españolas, 1965.

Fernández-Shaw, Carlos M. *The Hispanic Presence in North America.* New York: Facts on File, 1987.

Gann, L.H. and Peter J. Duignan, *The Hispanics in the United States: A History.* Boulder, CO: Westview Press, 1986.

Meier, Matt S. and Feliciano Ribera. *Mexican Americans—American Mexicans: From Conquistadors to Chicanos.* New York: Hill and Wang, 1993.

Thompson, Buchanan Parker. *Spain: Forgotten Ally of the American Revolution.* North Quincy, MA: Christopher Publishing House, 1976.

CHAPTER 3

The Early National Period and Expansion: 1783 to 1859

IN MANY RESPECTS, 1783 marked the beginning of the American nation. The Treaty of Paris formally recognized the United States as an independent country, ended the Revolutionary War, and established the new nation's boundaries from the Atlantic Ocean to the Mississippi River. In the same year Spain regained control of Florida, enlarging its land claims in North America to include roughly half of what would later become the modern continental United States. From Florida and its ambiguous border with Georgia in the east, Spanish territory stretched west through what it now Alabama and Mississippi to Louisiana. From there, Spain claimed all of the land west of the Mississippi River, its ships having already reached as far north along the Pacific Coast as Alaska.

Although the land holdings of each nation were vast, the populations were small. The U.S. census of 1790 recorded 3.9 million people, mostly spread out in the rural communities east of the Appalachian Mountains. Only five cities boasted populations of 10,000 or more, while the population west of the mountains consisted mostly of indigenous peoples interspersed with a few American trading posts and fledgling farming settlements. New Spain was even less populated. St. Augustine was the only sizeable settlement in Florida, with a population consisting mainly of Seminole and other Native American groups; while New Orleans, with its cosmopolitan Spanish, French, and mixed-blood population, was the only significant city.

West of the Mississippi, the series of Catholic missions reaching north into Alta California had resulted in small pockets of Spanish settlements at approximately 20 sites, including San Diego de Alcalá (1769), San Luis Obispo de Tolosa (1772), San Francisco de Asís (1776), San Juan Capistrano (1776), Santa Clara de Asís (1777), Santa Bárbara (1786), and San Fernando Rey (1797). By the end of the 1790s, the Santa Cruz Valley was home to some 1,000 Spanish settlers.

Likewise, a few settlements existed in Nuevo México and Texas, but the populations remained quite small. In Nuevo México, mission trading posts like those in Alta California served as small outposts of Spanish settlements, with most also raising crops and livestock. By the end of the 1790s, Texas boasted only six missions and a handful of sprawling ranchos raising large herds of cattle and sheep. The entire Spanish population of Texas numbered only about 3,500.

EARLY AMERICAN EXPANSION

The beginning of the French Revolution in 1789 inaugurated a quarter century of European wars that reached a peak during the reign of Napoleon Bonaparte as emperor (1804–14). As part of Napoleon's plan to reconstruct the former French overseas empire, France acquired the Louisiana Territory from Spain under the Treaty of Lunéville in 1801. Since use of the port of New Orleans was commercially important to America's western territories, President Thomas Jefferson offered to purchase the port from Napoleon. In the meantime, however, Napoleon's forces suffered a serious defeat at the hands of the Haitian revolutionaries. Because of this, and the increasing financial demands of the wars in Europe, Napoleon proffered the entire Louisiana Territory for the sum of $15 million in 1803. Acquisition of Louisiana virtually doubled the size of U.S. territory and, for the first time, brought significant numbers of Spanish-speaking people, along with their distinct culture, under American administration.

Westward expansion brought the United States into direct contact with the vast Spanish land holdings west of the Mississippi River. Moreover, since the boundaries of the Louisiana Purchase were open to interpretation, the claims of both nations overlapped in some areas, notably Texas and the Pacific Northwest. The latter had been claimed by Spain as early as 1493 by a papal bull (patent or charter issued by a pope), and through the voyage of exploration led by Vasco Núñez de Balboa in 1513. In fact, in the late 1700s the Spanish had solidified their claims by establishing a series of outposts along the Pacific Coast from California north into what today is British Columbia. With no clear agreement on the borders, Spain became increasingly concerned about further American expansion, especially when President Jefferson dis-

General Andrew Jackson fighting the British with a multi-ethnic force of U.S. soldiers, African Americans, and Spanish residents at the Battle of New Orleans on January 8, 1815.

patched an expedition under Meriwether Lewis and William Clark to explore the newly acquired lands as far west as the Pacific Ocean (1803–06).

The Barbary War (1801–05) and the escalating difficulties with England leading to the outbreak of the War of 1812, together with the need to pacify the area north of the Ohio River and east of the Mississippi, temporarily drew American attention away from the west. Spanish residents in New Orleans rallied to Andrew Jackson's call, including a battalion of men born in the Canary Islands, joining his motley army that dealt a major defeat to the British in the Battle of New Orleans. Yet at the same time, the Creek War (1813–14) brought American troops into areas between Georgia and Florida jointly claimed by both the United States and Spain, and stirred up animosity among many frontier Americans who felt that Spanish Florida was being used as a haven for hostile Native Americans.

A legacy of the War of 1812, Fort Apalachicola had been built by the British on Spanish land in East Florida. Following the British withdrawal, the location became a refuge for the Seminole and other Native Americans, as well as escaped slaves, all of whom were hostile to the United States. When an American force destroyed the fort in 1816, smoldering hostilities erupted into the First Seminole War. Sent south to pursue the Native Americans, Andrew Jackson led a full-scale invasion of Spanish Florida, capturing Spanish outposts and threatening to subjugate all of Florida. In what amounted to an ultimatum, the American minister in Spain accused the Spanish of provoking hostilities and demanded that they must either control Florida so that it posed no threat to Americans, or cede the territory to the United States. With little choice in the matter, Spain agreed to the Adams-Onís Treaty (1819).

Negotiated by Secretary of State John Quincy Adams and Spanish Foreign Minister Luis de Onís, the treaty settled the remaining border issues between the two nations. Under its provisions, Spain ceded East and West Florida in return for the United States assuming responsibility for the claims of American citizens against Spain for up to $5 million. Additionally, the United States agreed to give up its claims in Texas west of the Sabine River in return for

José Mariano Hernández

José Mariano Hernández of Florida, who was the first Hispanic American in the U.S. House of Representatives.

José Mariano Hernández was born in St. Augustine, Florida, in 1793, where his family owned the Mala Compra plantation, along with other holdings in Florida and Cuba. When Florida passed into American hands and the new Florida Territory was organized in 1822, Hernández accepted American citizenship and was elected as the first Hispanic delegate to the U.S. House of Representatives, serving until March 1823.

Following his service in Congress, Hernández enlisted in the U.S. army during the Second Seminole War (1835–42). During his service in 1837, he was responsible for constructing the Hernandez-Capron Trail, a road connecting St. Augustine with Fort Capron (near present Fort Pierce) on the St. Lucie River. In the same year he also commanded the expedition that captured the Seminole Chief Osceola. Hernández left the army in 1838, having gained the rank of brigadier general.

Elected to the territorial legislature, he became its presiding officer. As a member of the Whig Party, he ran for the U.S. Senate in 1845, but was defeated. Later he moved to Cuba, where he managed the family's sugar plantation in Coliseo, Matanzas Province, dying there in 1857.

Spanish recognition of a boundary line that went from the mouth of the Sabine west along the Red and Arkansas Rivers, and then due west along the 42nd parallel to the Pacific Ocean. Following the successful Mexican movement for independence, the Mexican government eventually ratified the same treaty in 1831.

The acquisition of Florida brought several thousand new residents into the United States, a mixture of Spanish settlers and Seminoles, along with smaller numbers of escaped slaves, English merchants, and Americans who had previously settled in the territory under Spanish rule. In 1822 José Mariano Hernández gained election as the first delegate from the Florida Territory to Congress, thus becoming the first Hispanic to serve in Congress. Two years later he was elected president of the Florida territorial legislature. Florida gained admission as a state in 1845.

TEXAS

When Mexico gained its independence from Spain in 1820, the northern portion of the new nation included the provinces of Alta California, Nuevo México, and Coahuila y Tejas (or Texas). In the same year the non-Native-American population of Texas numbered only about 4,000. With such a small population, the province was not very profitable, and could hardly be expected to defend itself. Led by Juan José María Erasmo Seguín, a representative from Texas in the Mexican legislature, laws were enacted to encourage migration into the province. In 1823 Stephen F. Austin received an *empresario* grant, which meant that he would receive a large tract of land free if he brought a specified number of settlers into Texas. In succeeding years, approximately 15 similar grants were made to U.S. citizens in an attempt to make the province profitable. The only conditions to the grants were that the immigrants become Mexican citizens and obey Mexican law.

Thousands of Americans, 80 percent of them from the south, moved into Texas in search of free or inexpensive land, increasing its non-Native-American population to 10,000 by 1827. Three years later Texas boasted a non-Native-American population of 18,000 Anglos; about 2,000 slaves brought from the United States, despite the fact that slavery was illegal in Mexico; and 4,000 Mexicans or tejanos. By 1835 Anglos would outnumber tejanos by about 30,000 to 5,000. The more prosperous of the Anglos followed the lead of the earlier Mexican upper class, establishing large ranchos on which they raised cattle or grew cotton. The large herds of cattle became the foundation for the subsequent cattle drives that became famous in Western legend, while also sparking a lively trade with Americans across the border.

NUEVO MÉXICO

Under Spanish rule, land in what would become Arizona and New Mexico was held under the *seignorial* system, a semifeudal arrangement whereby a

Santa Fe Trail

Following the Louisiana Purchase in 1803, American settlers began to push west from the Mississippi River, but trade with Mexico was prohibited by Spanish authorities. Nevertheless, a few individual traders crossed the largely desolate lands from the American territory to the Spanish provincial capital at Santa Fe, New Mexico, smuggling small amounts of trade goods on their horses and pack mules. When Mexico gained its independence from Spain in 1821, the trade restrictions of the Spanish colonial empire ended and a two-way commercial link opened.

What became known as the Santa Fe Trail stretched more than 1,200 miles through parched plains, barren desert, and rugged mountains, a trip taking at least eight grueling weeks. Two branches diverged once traders reached southwestern Kansas. One, known as the Mountain Route, followed the Arkansas River upstream into Colorado before turning south toward Santa Fe. The other, referred to as the Cimarron Cutoff, headed southwest across the arid desert to the Cimarron River and then on to Santa Fe. The former was more rugged, but offered water, game for food, and some shelter that was all but missing in the desert passage. Rattlesnake bites threatened sure death to any unwary traveler on either passage, while winds and storms could also threaten those caught in the open. Both routes also carried the danger of attacks by native Apaches, Comanches, or Osages. In 1825, the U.S. government authorized an official survey of the trail, negotiated a treaty with the Osage that provided for safe passage, and began to construct a series of forts for added protection. The Comanches often traded with those moving along the route west, or accepted payment in goods for safe passage, but raids on traders and settlers continued to be a threat into the 1870s. It has been estimated that despite its hardships the shorter desert route carried about 75 percent of the traffic since it saved an average of 10 days travel.

Between 1821 and the mid-1840s, about 80 wagons made the long trek each year. Once the territory passed into American hands following the war between the U.S. and Mexico, the trail became the main passageway for trade and settlers moving into the southwest, carrying some 5,000 wagons per year by the 1860s. It remained a major commercial and migration artery until completion of the Santa Fe Railroad in 1880 provided faster and cheaper shipment of goods, and more comfortable passenger travel.

large tract of land was granted to an individual, who then subdivided it for use by settlers who owed the landowner rents, and sometimes labor. In 1824 Nuevo México had a population of about 8,000 Native Americans (Navajo, Apache, and Ute) and 20,000 others, most of whom were *mestizos*, people of mixed Spanish and indigenous parentage. A few small mines produced copper, but the dominant economy was based on cattle and sheep ranching. At the top of the semifeudal society were a small group of *criollo* landowners, soldiers, and priests. In the Spanish class system, the criollo was a person of European parentage born in the New World.

In 1822 the 900-mile Santa Fe Trail linked the far northern regions of Nuevo México with Independence and St. Louis, Missouri. The new trail moved people and ideas in both directions. Commercial relations also developed, with a lively trade between the isolated settlements in northern Mexico and the United States. Since it was easier to move east than to go south to Mexico City, prosperous Mexican families often sent their children to St. Louis or other American cities to be educated. A small but steady stream of Americans began migrating into Nuevo México, many of them marrying into prominent Mexican families and settling down to ranching, but their loyalty remained suspect to Mexican officials.

ALTA CALIFORNIA

Spanish influence in Alta California had been spreading northward through the mission system after religious members of the Franciscan Order established a string of outposts northward through the region between 1769 and 1823. The missions had acquired huge grants of land from the Spanish government to support their activities. By 1815, for example, the San Diego Mission encompassed 50,000 acres with 1,250 horses, 10,000 cattle, and 20,000 sheep.

By 1830 cattle raising on the missions and private ranchos had become the largest industry in Alta California, sparking a prosperous trade in hides and tallow exported through the province's coastal ports along with wine, soap, cloth, and other products. It was through these missions that European livestock and agricultural products were introduced into what is today the southwestern United States.

The missions had become the centers of economic and social life, with the secular ranchos. By the end of Spanish rule in 1821, about 30 of these private grants had been awarded to rancheros who managed extensive land holdings. Following the Mexican Revolution, these were, for the most part, upheld by the new government. From 1822 to 1846, about 780 additional grants were made, many of them from former mission lands that had been secularized in 1833. About half of these new grants were awarded between 1840 and 1846. During this period, the few Americans who arrived in southern California, mostly by ships plying the commercial trading routes, generally settled among the local residents, became Mexican citizens, and often married into local californio families. Some even received land grants, such as William Hartnell at Rancho Patrocinio Alisal near Monterey, and William Dana at Rancho Nipomo in San Luis Obispo.

During the 1840s the opening of the Oregon Trail brought a steady stream of Anglo settlers into northern Alta California. Geographically separated from most of the californio settlements, the newcomers generally settled apart from the older residents. Unlike earlier Anglo arrivals, they also tended to arrive as families rather than individuals, with no intention of becoming Mexican citizens.

THE TEXAS REVOLUTION

Although Americans migrating into Texas were required to become Mexican citizens and abide by Mexican law, many simply ignored these and other requirements such as the Mexican law precluding slavery. Friction existed not so much between the Anglos (or Texians as they called themselves) and their tejano neighbors, but between the Texians and the Mexican government. In 1835 when President Antonio López de Santa Anna abolished the Mexican Constitution of 1824, unrest spread among the Texians as well as many tejanos, leading to a full-scale rebellion. After some initial revolutionary victories, General Santa Anna led a Mexican army into Texas to crush the rebellion.

One of the more famous incidents of the Texas revolt occurred when the Mexican army surrounded a group of rebels in the old Alamo mission outside San Antonio de Béxar. Although the defenders of the mission were mostly Texians, including such famous leaders as James Bowie and Davy Crockett, local tejanos were also numbered among the garrison. Among the latter was Juan Seguín, a prominent local tejano who managed to avoid the final massacre of the garrison when he was ordered to break through the encircling

The Alamo, originally called Mission San Antonio de Valero, was intended as a mission church for converting local Native Americans, but became a battle site and occasional military garrison.

The Paul Revere of Texas

Juan Nepomuceno Seguín was born in Mexico in 1806 to Erasmo Seguín, a postmaster and one-time *alcalde* (mayor) of Béxar who was instrumental in negotiating a Mexican land grant for Stephen F. Austin, inaugurating the large-scale movement of Anglos into Texas. Elected alcalde of San Antonio de Bexar at the age of 30, Juan Seguín lent his support to the Texas Revolution, raising a company of 25 tejanos to fight for independence. On the approach of General Santa Anna's Mexican army, Seguín took refuge with other revolutionaries in the nearby Alamo. During the siege that followed, Seguín was one of several defenders ordered by Colonel James Bowie, the makeshift fort's commander, to try to slip through the encircling Mexican army to deliver messages. Along with his orderly, he succeeded in breaking through; upon his return, he found that the Alamo had already fallen.

Locating General Sam Houston's Texas army, he was ordered to ride to the isolated frontier settlements to warn them of the approach of Santa Anna's army, earning him the nickname of the Paul Revere of Texas. Returning to Houston's army after the completion of his mission, he commanded a company that performed well at the Battle of San Jacinto, where Houston defeated and captured Santa Anna. In recognition of his services, the president of the Republic of Texas promoted him to lieutenant colonel.

Following the Texas Revolution, Seguín returned to San Antonio de Béxar. He was elected senator to the Second, Third, and Fourth Congresses of the Republic of Texas, where he supported the publication of legal documents in both Spanish and English. Elected mayor of San Antonio again in 1841, his outspoken support for tejano rights led to false accusations that he had secretly aided the Mexican army. Discouraged, he moved to Nuevo Laredo, Mexico, where his son resided. In later years he returned to the United States periodically, winning election as justice of the peace for Bexar County in 1852 and 1854, and county judge for Wilson County. He finally returned to Nuevo Laredo where his son was the alcalde, and died there on August 27, 1890.

Mexican lines with a message for the revolutionary leadership. Nevertheless, at least nine tejanos are known to have died defending the mission.

Tejanos, including Captain Seguín, also played a part in the final campaign of the war ending in the victory of General Sam Houston's army over Santa Anna's forces at the Battle of San Jacinto, where the Mexican president was captured and forced to sign a treaty granting Texas its independence. With Texan independence secured, Lorenzo de Zavala, one of the original signatories of the Texas Declaration of Independence, was elected vice president of the Republic of Texas. Although domestic political considerations prevented Texas from becoming an American state until 1845, the annexation of Texas eventually brought several thousand tejanos into the country, along with their distinctive culture.

THE MEXICAN WAR

By the 1840s American expansion westward had become embroiled in the growing sectional debates that eventually led to the Civil War. Although sentiment in the northern states was strong for annexing Oregon, those in the south opposed adding vast new territories that would potentially increase the dominance of northern representatives in Congress. Similarly, while those in the south favored annexing the Republic of Texas, those in the north opposed adding slave-holding territory to the country. In the presidential campaign of 1844, the Democrat candidate, James K. Polk, appealed to voters in both sections by promising to annex both areas. Following his electoral victory, an invitation was extended to Texas to become a state, an offer the Texas legislature accepted in 1845.

The annexation of Texas angered the Mexican government, which still harbored the hope of reasserting its claim to the lost land. As tensions escalated, President Polk answered calls for protection by ordering American troops to the border, while the Mexican government, concerned that its territory be protected, also ordered troops to the border. Unfortunately, each had a different concept of where the border lay. The Republic of Texas claimed the Rio Grande as its border, which Americans recognized when Texas became a state. However, the Mexican government claimed the Nueces River as the boundary. Since the Nueces was north of the Rio Grande, the area between the two nations wound up being claimed by both, thus ensuring a clash. When fighting erupted in the region, President Polk asked Congress for a declaration of war based on the argument that Mexican troops had invaded American territory.

Once hostilities began on April 25, 1846, the exiled General Santa Anna used the crisis to reclaim the presidency of Mexico on the promise to oppose any American invasion. In the United States, the war was unpopular in the north, where people believed it to be an attempt by southerners to extend slaveholding territory westward. Regardless, an American army of about 2,000 troops under General Zachary Taylor invaded northern Mexico and defeated troops under General Mariano Arista at the Battles of Palo Alto and Resaca de la Palma on May 8 and 9, 1846.

At the same time U.S. forces under Stephen W. Kearny advanced into northern Mexico from Ft. Leavenworth, and John C. Frémont led the Bear Flag Revolt in California, declaring the latter to be a republic. Supported by sailors and marines from a fleet led by Commodore Robert F. Stockton, these forces quickly compelled the Mexican garrisons to retreat further south into Mexico. In southern California, however, local californio citizens led by José María Flores forced the Americans to retreat, defeating them in several armed clashes. Eventually, when American reinforcements arrived, the californios were finally forced to surrender in January 1847.

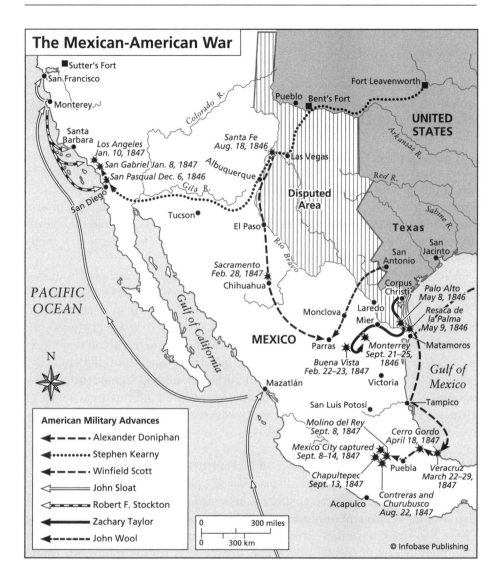

The Mexican-American War

Sutter's Fort
San Francisco
Monterey

Santa Barbara
Los Angeles
Jan. 10, 1847
San Gabriel Jan. 8, 1847
San Pasqual Dec. 6, 1846
San Diego

Tucson

Colorado R.

Pueblo   Bent's Fort

Fort Leavenworth

UNITED STATES

Arkansas R.

Santa Fe
Aug. 18, 1846

Albuquerque

Las Vegas

Gila R.

El Paso

Sacramento
Feb. 28, 1847
Chihuahua

Rio Bravo

Disputed Area

Red R.

Texas

Sabine R.

San Antonio

San Jacinto

PACIFIC OCEAN

Gulf of California

MEXICO

Parras

Monclova

Laredo
Mier

Monterrey
Sept. 21–25, 1846

Buena Vista
Feb. 22–23, 1847

Corpus Christi

Palo Alto
May 8, 1846

Resaca de la Palma
May 9, 1846

Matamoros

Gulf of Mexico

Mazatlán

Victoria

San Luis Potosí

Tampico

N

Molino del Rey
Sept. 8, 1847
Mexico City captured
Sept. 8–14, 1847
Chapultepec
Sept. 13, 1847

Acapulco

Cerro Gordo
April 18, 1847

Puebla   Veracruz
March 22–29, 1847

Contreras and
Churubusco
Aug. 22, 1847

American Military Advances

◄ ─ ─ ─ · Alexander Doniphan
◄ ·········· Stephen Kearny
◄ ─ ─ ─ · Winfield Scott
◄═══════ John Sloat
◄═ ═ ═ ═ Robert F. Stockton
◄─────── Zachary Taylor
◄ ─ ─ ─ ─ ─ John Wool

0   300 miles
0   300 km

© Infobase Publishing

While Taylor invaded Mexico from Texas and the struggle for California continued, General Winfield Scott led an army of 12,000 Americans in an amphibious landing at Veracruz, from where he began an overland campaign against Mexico City. Defeating General Santa Anna's army in a series of encounters, Scott's forces moved steadily on the Mexican capital, which fell on September 14, 1847, largely ending hostilities.

TREATY OF GUADALUPE HIDALGO

The Mexican War officially ended with the signing of the Treaty of Guadalupe Hidalgo on February 2, 1848. Under this agreement, Mexico recognized the southern border of Texas as the Rio Grande River, and was required to sell more than 500,000 square miles of land in Alta California and Nuevo México, about 55 percent of its entire national territory, to the United States for $15 million. The United States also agreed to assume $3.25 million in debts to American citizens owed by the Mexican government, but the total sum was still considerably less than the $25 million the United States had offered Mexico for essentially the same territory before the war. Additionally, the treaty contained provisions guaranteeing Mexican residents in the surrendered territory the right to become American citizens if they so chose, and the right to retain any property that they owned. These latter provisions, though struck from the final treaty, were reiterated in the informal Protocol of Querétaro. Nevertheless, over the succeeding years many Mexicans either sold their lands due to economic circumstances, or were forced off their land through various unscrupulous means.

Although it lost an enormous amount of land, Mexico lost only about one percent of its total population, since the northern regions had been so sparsely settled. Of the approximately 80,000 Mexican residents in what came to be known as the Mexican Cession, about 3,000 chose to move farther south into what remained of Mexico. This included approximately 1,000 from Texas, 1,500 from Nuevo México, and a few hundred from Alta California. The rest elected to remain under American authority, adding significantly to the nation's Hispanic population, and guaranteeing the continued existence of Hispanic cultural traditions in the southwest that eventually spread to other regions of the country.

THE GOLD RUSH AND CALIFORNIA STATEHOOD

In January 1848 James Marshall discovered gold at Sutter's Mill along the American River in northern California, inaugurating a rush to the gold fields that eventually brought an estimated 300,000 people flooding into the Pacific Coast. San Francisco, due west of the original discovery, grew into a boom town seemingly overnight, while towns and prospecting camps sprang up where only wilderness had previously existed. In 1849 alone, roughly 100,000 people arrived in California, including 87,000 Anglos along with about 8,000 Mexicans (mostly from Sonora), 4,000 Chileans and Peruvians, and a smaller number of Argentineans. The enormous influx of Anglos, although initially entering mostly northern California, rapidly spread south, overwhelming in number the approximately 13,000 californios. By 1850 only about 15 percent of the population spoke Spanish, which declined steadily to only 4 percent by 1870.

The rapid influx of people into California led to its application for statehood in 1849. Among the 48 delegates to the state constitutional convention were eight californios, including Mariano Vallejo, who was later elected to the California state senate. Largely because of his efforts, one of the first laws enacted was the requirement that all legal documents be printed in both Span-

In this 1851 photograph of Portsmouth Square in the boom town of San Francisco, at least one of the signs on the buildings is in Spanish, reflecting the continued influence of Hispanic culture, despite the fact that only about 15 percent of the population still spoke Spanish.

ish and English. California was admitted as the 31st state in 1850. In 1854 the permanent capital was located in Sacramento, an area that was then significantly Anglo in population.

Although a distinct minority of the population of California by 1850, californios remained a majority in the far southern region around what is today San Diego and Los Angeles, due in part to a small, but consistent migration of Mexicans from Sonora north into southern California. This stream of new migration kept the Spanish language and traditions alive in the region, and even managed to exert political influence, with the election of Juan Sepúlveda as mayor (alcalde) of Los Angeles, and Antonio Coronel as the city's first superintendent of schools. Although the relative economic prosperity of the region eased tensions between californios and Anglos, following that decade Anglos gradually increased in number, gaining prominence in social, economic, and political affairs.

CULTURAL HOSTILITIES

With the swift inflow and spread of Anglos, friction developed between them and the californios, as well as with the Native-American population and immigrants arriving from other countries. Disputes over "claims" and other issues increasingly led to violence, while many Anglos came to resent the recent Mexican and South American immigrants, many of whom proved quite successful because they had previous mining experience. This led vigilante groups to forcibly evict non-Anglos from claims, and led to the passage of the 1850 Foreign

Joaquín Murieta

An 1853 newspaper illustration purporting to depict the outlaw Joaquín Murieta.

Joaquín Murieta was a semi-mythical personality whose fame sprang from the 1854 novel *The Life and Adventures of Joaquín Murieta: The Celebrated California Bandit* by John Rollin Ridge. The character was a Robin Hood–type vigilante who attacked Anglo settlers in California in retaliation for racial discrimination at their hands.

Scholars disagree on whether he was born in Sonora, Mexico, or Quillota, Chile, but folk legend often describes him as a prominent criollo landowner. Others speculate that he arrived in California as part of the gold rush, seeking his fortune along with tens of thousands of prospectors. To avenge many wrongs committed against him, including the rape of his wife, he organized a gang called the Five Joaquíns after its members: Joaquín Botellier, Joaquín Carrillo, Joaquín Ocomorenia, Joaquín Valenzuela, and Murieta. Together with another compatriot, Manuel García, known popularly as Three-fingered Jack, the group embarked on a retaliatory wave of cattle rustling, robbery, and murder. Some sources believe they were responsible for stealing more than $100,000 in gold, rustling over 100 horses, and killing 19 people.

Legend has it that the gang was often supported by sympathetic californios. Largely due to the scare created by the growing legend of the Five Joaquíns, the California legislature created the California State Rangers to hunt down and eliminate members of the gang. When a shootout between the Rangers and a small group of Mexicans near Panoche Pass broke out in July 1853, leaving two Mexicans dead, claims were made that the two were Murieta and García. The Rangers beheaded the man they believed to be Murieta, placed the severed head in a jar of brandy to preserve it, and displayed it throughout California, charging the curious $1 to view it. Despite this, Murieta's sister claimed that the head did not bear a scar that would positively identity him, and sightings of Murieta continued to be reported after his supposed death.

Miners Tax of $20 per month for the right to mine, making it difficult for recent immigrants to comply with the law. Supposedly levied only on immigrants, it was often applied to californios as well. Although it was rescinded in about a year due to business protests and questionable constitutionality, it nevertheless increased resentment between the newcomers and California's traditional residents. This blatant discrimination led to reprisals, the most famous of which was led by the quasi-legendary Joaquín Murieta. With a popular image based largely on a novel published in the 1850s, Murieta was either a Mexican or Chilean who acted as a Robin Hood, leading a gang called the Five Joaquíns in attacks on Anglos in retaliation for racist discrimination he had encountered.

Further discriminatory laws in 1855 included a statute called the Anti-vagrancy Act, and other legislation that repudiated the previous law requiring the publication of all legal documents in both English and Spanish. The Anti-vagrancy Act outlawed bullfighting and cockfighting, and contained other provisions clearly aimed at eliminating Hispanics and their customs. Escalating passions over these and other actions, together with the increasing majority of Anglos, quickly destroyed the relative harmony that had existed between the communities before the Mexican War, leading to other moves by Anglos to further restrict californio influence in society.

LAND CLAIMS

With American acquisition of California, one of the most important issues to prominent californios was the status of their property rights. Among the approximately 13,000 residents, about 800 owned ranchos, about 50 of which were exceptionally large landholdings whose owners had wielded economic and political control over Alta California. The balance of the population was largely cholos, poor agricultural workers of mostly mestizo, mulatto, or other mixed-blood heritage. Native Americans ranked at the bottom of what was a clearly defined socioeconomic class system.

With the rapid influx of immigrants during the gold rush, property titles were called into question more frequently, leading to disputes over ownership. To sort out these issues, in 1851 the California legislature passed the Land Act, which created a Board of Land Commissioners to investigate and adjudicate land claims. However, instead of focusing on specific disputes, the Land Act provided that each claimant must prove ownership. For many californios, this proved difficult. In 1849 about 200 californio families held an estimated 14 million acres of land under grants from the Spanish or Mexican governments. When the Land Courts were established, only 813 claims were made, most based on the Spanish/Mexican tradition of "usage and custom," rather than documented titles. Mexican land claims often lacked specific boundaries other than markers such as trees, rocks, or streambeds, which could often change over time. Precise surveys were not required, and transfers of property could be made verbally without the actual change of ownership being registered. But the Land Courts demanded documentary evidence of land ownership, and for those who sought proof, the process could be lengthy and quite costly.

Of the 813 claims filed with the courts, 467 were from californios. Eventually, 614 of the claims were validated, covering about nine million acres of the original 14 million in question. Yet this did not end the issue. Some claimants sold their lands at discount prices rather than going through the uncertain process of verification and running the risk of losing everything. Others who persisted in their claims, and had them upheld, often ended up selling large portions of their lands to pay outstanding legal bills amassed during the process of verification.

Further financial burdens came from new and increased taxes. Under Mexican rule, taxes were based on productivity. Once California came under U.S. rule, property taxes replaced the earlier system in 1850, placing an even greater financial burden on families already struggling with the legal costs of proving ownership of their property. Between 1850 and 1856, property tax rates increased twice, but the northern mining areas were largely exempt, placing the burden of the new tax system more heavily on the owners of the extensive ranchos.

As a result of the land claims process, many californios lost their land through one circumstance or another, forcing many to take low-paying jobs as unskilled workers in the agricultural, cattle, or sheep businesses, or to migrate to the cities where they took lower-paying jobs in construction, on railroads, or in mining. As male income declined, women began to move increasingly into positions outside the home as domestics, seamstresses, or unskilled industrial workers. The net result was to seriously erode the socioeconomic position of the californios, and their corresponding political influence.

ARIZONA AND NEW MEXICO

When Colonel Stephen Kearny moved into Nuevo México with 1,500 men during the Mexican War, he met no serious resistance. Relations with the local population were generally friendly, probably because of the frequent contacts fostered by the Santa Fe Trail. In creating a new government, Kearny retained most of the Mexican officials in place, with important positions held by a mixture of Anglos and Mexicans. Charles Bent, who had married into a prominent Mexican family, became acting governor; Donaciano Vigil was appointed territorial secretary; and Antonio J. Otero served as one of three territorial justices.

The gold rush that populated California largely bypassed what was now the New Mexico Territory, except for a few miners in the northwestern areas of the region. Most people continued to live as they had before American rule, working in cattle ranching, sheepherding, mining, and agriculture within a community that was predominantly Spanish-speaking. In fact, the New Mexico legislature continued to conduct its meetings in Spanish until 1859.

Yet changes also began to occur in the mid-1850s. Americans, eager to increase commerce and trade between east and west, began to seriously press for the construction of a transcontinental railway. Southerners in particular, who sought the economic benefits of linking the south with California, began thinking in terms of a railroad route through the Mexican Cession, but the topography proved too mountainous. Largely under the influence of Secretary of War Jefferson Davis, a Mississippian, President Franklin Pierce began negotiations with Mexican President Santa Anna for the purchase of additional land along the southern border of modern Arizona and New Mexico. Although Pierce had designs on significant areas of northern Mexico, including all of Sonora and Baja California, the Treaty of La Mesilla (better known as the Gadsden Purchase) gave the United States a 29,670-square-mile area in return for $10 million. Many Mexicans were furious with President Santa Anna for agreeing to sell additional Mexican territory, an animosity that exists for many to this day.

The Gadsden Purchase brought an additional 2,000 Spanish-speaking people into the United States. The eventual construction of the southern transcontinental railway after the Civil War brought with it new jobs in construction, cattle ranching, and other businesses, as well as an increase in the Anglo population, although the majority of the population of the area remained Spanish-speaking until well after the Civil War. New Mexico eventually entered the Union as the 47th state, and Arizona as the 48th state, both in 1912.

THE CART WAR

By the time Texas became a state, the tejano population formed only a small minority. In 1836, for example, tejanos held all 15 of the land grants in what would become Nueces County, but by 1859 only one was in tejano hands. Loss of land led inevitably to loss of economic and political influence, and social standing. Gradually, tejanos were displaced, migrating to the cities and towns, or remaining on the land as low-paid, unskilled agricultural workers.

One of the occupations to which many tejanos and Mexican immigrants gravitated was hauling freight as a teamster along well-traveled routes from San Antonio to the coastal port of Indianola and settlements in between. Increasing attempts by Anglo teamsters to run the tejanos out of the business beginning in 1855, in violation of the terms of the Treaty of Guadalupe Hidalgo, erupted into violence in 1857 in the so-called Cart War. The absence of local authorities' attempts to curb increasing violence against tejano teamsters, including murder, led to a rebellion headed by Juan Nepomuceno Cortina against Anglos in southern Texas. Cortina defeated both the Brownsville militia and the Texas Rangers sent to subdue him, but was eventually forced to flee into Mexico when army reinforcements arrived.

News of the violence led to strong protests by Manuel Robles y Pezuela, the

Juan Nepomuceno Cortina, who became a Mexican folk hero for his resistance to Anglo domination.

Mexican minister to Washington, which prompted Secretary of State Lewis Cass to intercede with Texas governor Elisha M. Pease. In a message to the Texas legislature, Pease called upon them to approve additional expenditures for the state militia because "It is now very evident that there is no security for the lives of citizens of Mexican origin engaged in the business of transportation, along the road from San Antonio to the Gulf." With the approval of the measure, tejano teamsters were provided with armed escorts, and what had become an international incident gradually faded.

CONCLUSION

The three-quarters of a century between 1783 and 1859 was an especially important era for the future development of Hispanic history and culture in the United States. Beginning at a time when Hispanic participation in America was largely limited to a few individuals and the sometimes close relations between Spain and the United States through Spain's alliance with France, this period saw the United States grow from a cluster of isolated communities east of the Appalachian Mountains, to an expansive nation stretching from the Atlantic to the Pacific. In the process, it absorbed tens of thousands of Spanish-speaking people in Florida, Louisiana, Texas, Nuevo México, and Alta California, people who contributed their language, culture, and traditions to the growing mosaic of the United States.

In addition to the people who found themselves in the United States without immigrating, there were also those, though much smaller in number, who

Brownsville, Texas, depicted above in an 1850 illustration, was the center of Juan Cortina's attempted uprisings against the growing Anglo power in the region.

migrated north willingly during this period. Although census records reveal only an average of 44 immigrants from Central America arriving during the 1830s, the number increased gradually to more than 1,000 per year in the early 20th century. The same records show 10 times as many immigrants from South American nations during the 19th century as there were from Central America. By 1830 there were 20,000 Mexicans already living in Chicago, while Cuban and Puerto Rican migration was already well underway to New York City, where exiled Ramón Emeterio Betances organized one of the first movements to establish an independent Puerto Rican republic. The Cuban priest Félix Varela, exiled from his native island, built churches, schools, and orphanages in New York City, serving also as vicar general of the archdiocese. Cigar factories produced Cuban cigars in Florida, Louisiana, and New York, while many working-class Cubans sought jobs in the growing industries of New England and the Middle Atlantic states. It is estimated that by 1850, the population of 23 million Americans included over 100,000 Hispanics.

The V. Rev. Felix Varela, D. D.

A print of Father Félix Varela published in 1853, the year he died. Varela was honored on a U.S. postage stamp in 1997.

Despite the ongoing, if small, migrations from the Caribbean and Central and South America, the vast majority of Hispanics who found themselves in the United States—either through migration or American expansion—originated from the former Spanish-controlled areas in Florida, Louisiana, and Mexico. It was people from these areas, and in particular Mexico, who infused the American language with new words, imported celebrations such as Cinco de Mayo, enriched American culture with their music and literature, and otherwise contributed to the American mosaic.

JAMES S. PULA
PURDUE UNIVERSITY NORTH CENTRAL

Further Reading

Alonzo, Armando C. *Tejano Legacy: Rancheros and Settlers in South Texas, 1734–1900* Albuquerque, NM: University of New Mexico Press, 1998.

Cockcroft, James D. *Latinos in the Making of the United States.* New York: Franklin Watts, 1995.

De Varona, Frank, ed. *Hispanic Presence in the United States: Historical Beginnings.* Miami, FL: Mnemosyne Publishing Company, 1993.

Fernández-Florez, Darío. *The Spanish Heritage in the United States.* Madrid: Publicaciones Españolas, 1971.

Gann, L.H. and Peter J. Duignan. *The Hispanics in the United States: A History.* Boulder, CO: Westview Press, 1986.

Meier, Matt S. and Feliciano Ribera. *Mexican Americans—American Mexicans: From Conquistadors to Chicanos.* New York: Hill and Wang, 1993.

Nieto-Phillips, John. *The Language of Blood: The Making of Spanish American Identity in New Mexico, 1850–1940.* Albuquerque, NM: University of New Mexico Press, 2004.

Officer, James E. *Hispanic Arizona, 1536–1856.* Tucson, AZ: University of Arizona Press, 1987.

Pitt, Leonard. *Decline of the Californios: A Social History of the Spanish-Speaking Californias, 1846–1890.* Berkeley, CA: University of California Press, 1969.

Simmons, Marc. *Hispanic Albuquerque 1706–1846.* Albuquerque, NM: University of New Mexico Press, 2003.

CHAPTER 4

The Civil War to the Gilded Age: 1859 to 1900

THE YEAR 1860 was a momentous time in American history. Tensions ran high between factions in the North and South over economic, political, and social differences that had been growing for decades. The election of Abraham Lincoln as president convinced many in the South that their sectional interests were in jeopardy. In December South Carolina declared its exit from the Union, leading to the secession of 10 other Southern states, the formation of the Confederate States of America, and the beginning of the Civil War. The 1860 census counted 38,315 Hispanics living in the United States who were born outside of the country. The total number of Hispanics is unknown, since the census did not clearly differentiate between people born in the United States, except by race. One thing is certain, however; many were as deeply divided as other Americans. About 27,500 Hispanics in America were Mexican Americans who, as residents of the southern borderlands, were called upon early in the conflict to choose between the warring sides. In Texas in particular, the Civil War became in many respects a civil war pitting Spanish-speaking community members against one another, much as Americans were divided nationally.

HISPANICS IN GRAY

Research by John O'Donnel-Rosales suggests that as many as 13,000 Hispanics served the Confederacy in various capacities. Some held influential positions. The Cuban poet José Agustín Quintero served as the Confederate Commissioner to northern Mexico, a particularly important post because it entailed responsibility for the critical supply routes through Mexico that the Southerners used to circumvent the Northern naval blockade. His efforts were apparently so successful that at one point the governor of the Mexican provinces of Coahuila and Nueva León considered leading a movement to secede from Mexico and join the Confederacy. Another Cuban, Ambrosio José González, who is credited with designing the modern Cuban and Puerto Rican flags, served as chief of ordnance for General Pierre G.T. Beauregard in Charleston, South Carolina, at the outbreak of the war, and later chief of artillery for the Department of South Carolina, Georgia, and Florida. American-born David C. DeLeón received an appointment as surgeon general from President Jefferson Davis to organize the Confederate medical department.

Throughout the southeastern states, Hispanics generally served in integrated detachments. Among those that included fairly large numbers of Hispanics were Manigault's South Carolina Battalion, the Spanish Guards from Mobile (Alabama), the Cazadores Españoles (Louisiana), the 1st Florida Cavalry, the 55th Alabama Infantry, the 6th Missouri Infantry, the Chalmette Infantry (Louisiana), and the Louisiana Zouave Battalion.

While most Hispanics sided with their section in the conflict, loyalties were not so clear in Texas, where strong antislavery traditions and ethnic conflict led some tejanos to question allegiance to the state. Of those who initially volunteered in 1861, about 2,550 served in the Confederate forces and 950

This 1864 newspaper illustration depicts the thriving trade in Confederate cotton that continued at the Mexican border after other outlets closed to Southern growers.

served in Union units. Among the federal forces raised in the state were 12 Mexican-American companies that became the 1st Texas Cavalry. Of those who donned Confederate gray, units with numerous tejanos included the 2nd Mounted Rifles and the 10th Texas Cavalry.

The most important Confederate tejano was Santos Benavides. Born in Laredo in 1823, he gained election as mayor of his hometown in 1856. At the outbreak of the war he enlisted as a captain, rose quickly to the rank of colonel, and became the highest-ranking Mexican American in the Southern army. When Confederate forces withdrew from the lower Rio Grande Valley, Colonel Benavides led the only force remaining to defend the Laredo area. In March 1864 he received a request from Brigadier General Hamilton P. Lee asking him to march to the rescue of Brownsville, which was besieged by Union forces. At the head of his 33rd Texas Cavalry, Col. Benavides defeated the Federals, who included the 2nd Texas Cavalry formed from Brownsville tejanos, lifting the siege. The efforts of Benavides and other tejanos in gray preserved for the South its critically valuable trade routes from Mexico.

THE SÁNCHEZ SISTERS

The Sánchez family was one of many that settled in Florida from Cuba prior to the Civil War. Living along the east bank of the St. John's River opposite Palatka in 1861, the parents were in ill health and the son was away serving in the Confederate army, leaving three sisters—Eugenia, Lola, and Panchita—to run the household. With the occupation of Federal troops in St. Augustine, the sisters began providing intelligence information to the Confederates about the plans and activities of nearby Northern troops. Suspecting the family, Federal authorities arrested Lola's father, placed a guard on the house each evening, and occasionally searched the premises for any incriminating evidence. Despite the suspicions, Union officers often visited, no doubt drawn by the attractive sisters. Evenings frequently included light conversation between the women and the Yankee officers, with singing accompanied by the tunes of a guitar. Any information that the sisters gleaned from these social occasions was quickly sent to Confederate authorities.

One evening, when the women adjourned to their kitchen to prepare dinner for three visiting officers, Lola was able to eavesdrop on a conversation the men were having in the belief they were alone. She learned the Federals were planning two expeditions for the following day: a raid on a rebel camp upriver using a gunboat and troop transport, and a foraging expedition. The three sisters quickly determined that Panchita would entertain the Yankees while Eugenia cooked dinner, supposedly assisted by Lola. With the officers distracted and suspecting nothing, Lola would slip out of the house to convey the information to Captain J.J. Dickison of the 2nd Florida Cavalry on the other side of the St. John's River. The trip required a dangerous journey of some two miles during which she had to navigate woods, swamps, and

David Glasgow Farragut

Born on July 5, 1801 at Campbell Station near Knoxville, Tennessee, Farragut was the son of Jorge Farragut, the famous Minorcan who came to the colonies to fight for their independence during the American Revolution. At the age of nine, following the death of his mother, Farragut was taken in by a family friend, Commodore David Porter, and changed his given name of James to David in honor of Porter. Farragut went to sea as a midshipman at age nine, and at age 11 was wounded when his ship, the frigate U.S.S. *Essex*, was captured off the coast of Chile during the War of 1812. Fluent in Spanish, he accompanied Minister Joel Poinsett on his mission to Emperor Agustín de Iturbide in Mexico. He visited Spain aboard the frigate U.S.S. *Independence* in 1815 and again in 1819, made several trips to Mexico, and visited Uruguay and Argentina in 1842. From 1867–68 he visited Mahón on Minorca, where he viewed his father's baptismal records to acquaint himself more fully with his family history.

At the beginning of the Civil War he was given command of the West Gulf Blockading Squadron, charged with blockading the Confederate Gulf Coast. In one of the key events of the war, in April 1862 he successfully pushed his fleet past the Mississippi River defenses to capture New Orleans. New Orleans, the largest city in the Confederacy, denied its port to the Confederacy and provided Farragut with a base of operations from which to pursue his blockade. To reward him, the navy appointed him to the newly created rank of rear admiral.

In 1864 his fleet attacked Mobile Bay in an effort to capture the city and eliminate the last Confederate port on the Gulf Coast still open to blockade runners. The bay was defended by minefields, then called torpedoes, and one of the weapons sank the monitor U.S.S. *Tecumseh,* causing the other Federal ships to hesitate. When informed of the problem, Farragut yelled what became one of the most famous lines in U.S. naval history: "Damn the torpedoes! Full speed ahead!" Once again, Farragut led his ships into the bay, defeated Confederate naval forces arrayed to meet him, passed the forts designed to defend the city, and closed the port to Confederate use. In 1866 Congress created another new rank for him—admiral. Following the war Farragut commanded the European Squadron. He died in Portsmouth, New Hampshire, on August 14, 1870.

Admiral David G. Farragut, naval hero of the Civil War, had roots in Minorca.

the river. Her mission accomplished, she returned home in time to have dinner with the unsuspecting visitors.

Armed with the information the Sánchez sisters provided, the Confederates arranged an ambush that captured the gunboat and transport and defeated the foraging party, capturing many of the infantry as well. Following this episode, the sisters continued to provide a steady flow of information to Confederate forces, resulting in the capture of several woodcutting parties, foragers, and an occasional unsuspecting officer.

HISPANICS IN BLUE

Hispanics living in the North at the time of the war generally remained loyal to the Union, several making major contributions to the Northern war effort. Julio P. Garesché du Rocher, a native of Cuban and French descent and a graduate of the U.S. Military Academy, served under General Zachary Taylor during the Mexican War. Garesché later established the Society of St. Vincent de Paul in Washington, D.C., to assist distressed families. When the Civil War began, he designed fortifications defending Washington, D.C., until November 1862, when he was assigned as chief-of-staff to the Army of the Cumberland commanded by his friend Major General William S. Rosecrans. During the campaign that followed, Garesché's promising career was cut short when, during the Battle of Stones River, he was beheaded by a cannonball.

Federico Fernández Cavada, another native of Cuba, moved to the United States where he enlisted in the 23rd Pennsylvania Infantry on the outbreak of the Civil War. Adept at recruiting, he raised a company of which he was appointed captain. Assigned as an engineer during the Peninsula Campaign in 1862, he made several ascents in a balloon to observe Confederate lines. Later appointed lieutenant colonel of the 114th Pennsylvania, he was captured at the Battle of Gettysburg and confined in a Richmond prison until January 1864. In the same year he published *Libby Life*, a memoir of his confinement in Libby Prison that historians still use as an important source.

Luis Fenollosa Emilio was born in Salem, Massachusetts, in 1844, the son of immigrants from Spain. In May 1863 he enlisted as a captain in the 54th Massachusetts Infantry, a regiment whose officers were Caucasian while the enlisted men were African American. Accompanying the regiment south, he fought in South Carolina, including the disastrous assault on Fort Wagner that left him acting commander of the regiment when all of the senior officers were killed or wounded. Following the war, he penned his memoirs under the title *A Brave Black Regiment*, an important source for the filming of the 1989 movie *Glory*.

The most famous and influential Hispanic to serve in the Civil War was Admiral David G. Farragut. Born in Tennessee as the son of a Spanish immigrant and Revolutionary War hero, he spoke fluent Spanish and kept in touch with his Spanish heritage. He served in the Mediterranean, Caribbean, Atlantic, and Pacific, including the War of 1812 and the Mexican War. During the Civil War, he led the successful Union effort to capture New Orleans and open the Mississippi River. Promoted to the newly created rank of vice admiral, he led the successful Union assault on Mobile Bay in August 1864 where, when his ships were imperiled by Confederate naval mines, he uttered the famous words "Damn the torpedoes, full speed ahead!" He was further rewarded when he became the first person in American history to hold the rank of admiral.

THE NEW MEXICO CAMPAIGN

While Hispanics in the lower South tended to support their local, pro-South governments during the Civil War, most loyalties further west lay with the

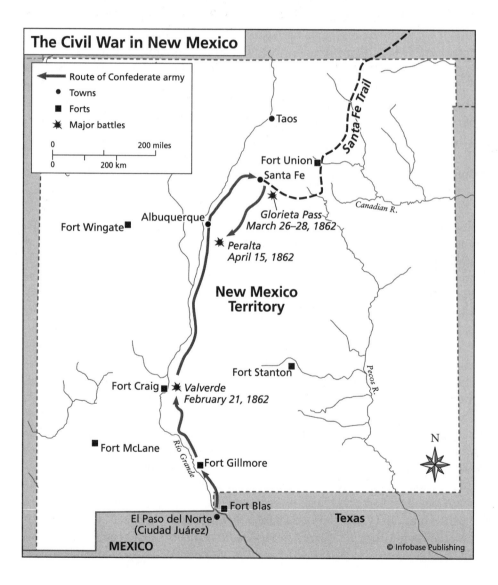

The Civil War in New Mexico

Union. In 1863 the Federals established four companies that were organized into the 1st Battalion of Native
Cavalry under Major Salvador Vallejo.
Numbering some 469 men of Mexican
and Spanish origin, they served in California and Arizona guarding supply
lines and fighting bands of Indians and
the occasional Confederate. In New
Mexico, most of the Hispanic population also remained loyal to the Union.
The territorial militia quickly enrolled
five regiments numbering some 4,000
troops in the Union effort, and added
six independent militia companies
commanded by Mexican Americans.

In early January 1862, Confederate Brigadier General Henry Hopkins
Sibley led an army of some 2,600 men
up the Rio Grande Valley, defeating a
Federal force at the Battle of Valverde.

*José Chaves, pictured above, was one of
a number of Hispanics who fought in the
Civil War with the 1st New Mexico Infantry
and other regiments in the southwest.*

From there he pushed west, determined to raise the Confederate flag over
New Mexico and Arizona. Among the Union troops that opposed him were
the 1st New Mexico Infantry under Colonel Rafael Chacón, a graduate of the
Mexican Military Academy in Chihuahua, and the 2nd New Mexico Infantry
under Colonel Miguel E. Pino. In March, at the Battle of Glorieta Pass near
Santa Fe, troops under Lieutenant Colonel Manuel Chávez of the New Mexico
militia outflanked the Confederate force and destroyed its supply base, forcing the rebels to retreat back into Texas and saving New Mexico and Arizona
for the Union.

Following the Confederate retreat, New Mexican forces continued skirmishing with occasional Confederate raiders and Native Americans. Their defense
of the New Mexico Territory denied the Confederates access to the gold and
silver mines in the southwest, and maintained an active front that forced the
Confederates to assign troops to guard their supply routes through Texas that
would otherwise be threatened by the Union troops on their western flank.

MEDAL OF HONOR

The Medal of Honor was established by Congress in July 1862 to recognize
individuals who distinguish themselves through conspicuous gallantry at the
risk of life above and beyond the call of duty while engaged combat operations. Between its origin and 1900, four Hispanics were recognized with their
nation's highest award. The first Hispanic to be so honored was Corporal

This photograph taken after the January 1865 battle at Fort Fisher, in which the Chilean-American sailor Philip Bazaar earned fame by surmounting the rebel fortifications, highlights the muzzle of a gun that had been broken by a bomb blast during the fierce fight.

Joseph H. de Castro of Company I, 19th Massachusetts Infantry. Born in Boston in 1844, he was not yet 19 years old when his regiment was deployed to oppose the famous Pickett's Charge at Gettysburg on July 3, 1863. During the height of the fighting, he held the very dangerous position of color bearer for his regiment, holding aloft the Massachusetts state colors. As Confederates charged into his regiment's ranks, de Castro thrust his own flagstaff at a Confederate color bearer, knocking him down and capturing the colors of the 19th Virginia Infantry.

Seaman John Ortega, a native of Spain, was assigned to duty aboard the sloop-of-war U.S.S. *Saratoga*. His ship formed part of the naval blockade designed to prevent the Confederacy from receiving critical imports of weapons, munitions, and other supplies from Europe. Stationed in the vicinity of Charleston, South Carolina, in the fall of 1864, he distinguished himself as a member of several landing parties that conducted successful raids on the Confederate coast, capturing prisoners and destroying considerable amounts of military equipment and supplies, bridges, and an important salt works. In addition to the Medal of Honor, his conspicuous conduct also brought promotion to acting master's mate.

Another sailor, Ordinary Seaman Philip Bazaar, was born in Chile. Serving aboard the sidewheel steamship U.S.S. *Santiago de Cuba*, in January 1865 he participated in the vital Union assault on Fort Fisher, the gateway to Wilmington, North Carolina. The capture of Fort Fisher was particularly important because in Union hands it would effectively close the last major port open to Confederates on the Atlantic Coast. Bazaar was detailed to accompany the assault forces that landed near the fort. In the successful attack that followed, he was one of six seamen to enter the rebel fortifications, and distinguished himself by carrying dispatches under heavy fire during the assault.

Following the Civil War, Private France Silva became the first Hispanic member of the U.S. Marine Corps to be awarded the Medal of Honor. Born in California of Mexican heritage, he was assigned to the U.S.S. *Newark*, the first modern cruiser in the U.S. fleet. Arriving in China following the Spanish-American War, Silva was detailed as a legation guard to protect the diplomatic missions in Beijing. During the Boxer Rebellion in June 1900, which broke out within days of his arrival, a serious bullet wound through his arm and elbow made it impossible for him to work his rifle. Refusing an order from his captain to go to sick bay for treatment, Silva traded his rifle to the captain for the officer's pistol, and continued to defend the walls from June 18 until the relief of the siege by allied forces on August 17, 1900. The citation for his medal noted that he had "distinguished himself by meritorious conduct."

THE WESTWARD MOVEMENT

Following the Civil War, the westward movement that had begun during the antebellum era was renewed with vigor. Union Army veterans, Southerners made destitute by the war, and ex-slaves lured by the prospect of abundant and inexpensive land swelled the great westward migration. Facilitating this was completion of the Southern Pacific Railroad to Los Angeles in 1876 that linked the vast southwest to the eastern states. This provided inexpensive, relatively speedy, and comfortable transportation to the southwest resulting not only in sizeable increases in population, but also important changes in the ethnic composition of the population of this area. The influx of Anglo settlers into Texas had reduced tejanos to less than 10 percent of the state's population long before the Civil War, and with this came a corresponding loss of political influence. With the completion of the railroads, Anglo settlers quickly surpassed the californio population on the West Coast. As early as 1863, when Arizona was granted territorial status, its first legislature included 22 Anglos and only three mexicanos. As Anglos arrived, they established their own schools, churches, and social institutions, quickly altering the traditional culture of the Spanish-speaking areas. Only in the New Mexico Territory did the Spanish-speaking residents constitute a majority of the population and maintain political influence well into the 1890s.

As settlers moved into the more arid regions of the southwest, water became an essential element in making the land productive. Irrigation techniques learned earlier by the Spanish settlers from the Pueblo Indians proved central to effective agriculture, as did knowledge of canal and aqueduct construction they brought with them from Spain. All of these skills were shared with the newly arriving Anglo settlers in the postwar era. With irrigation, the cultivation of sugar beets spread into California and Colorado in the 1890s, while citrus fruits and cotton grew steadily in the region from California eastward through Arizona and New Mexico into the lower Rio Grande Valley in Texas. The timber industry also grew in the upland areas and mountain foothills. The increasingly large landholdings necessary for commercial agriculture also required large amounts of labor, but only during certain seasons; a large, year-round labor force was too expensive to support. The result was the beginning of massive seasonal migrations of Mexican labor into southern California, Texas, and to a lesser extent, Arizona and New Mexico beginning in the 1880s.

RANCHING

In the antebellum years, cattle ranching was a typical occupation from Texas into the west, but most ranchers raised only enough to supply their own needs and sell excess meat and hides at local markets. This situation changed significantly when Philip Danforth Armour established a meat-packing business in Chicago. By 1866 the demand for meat in the east was increasing dramatically, raising the price of cattle, and making it profitable for Texas ranchers to raise and sell larger herds to Armour and others who entered the industry. By 1867 a railhead with cattle pens had been established in Abilene, Kansas, inaugurating the Chisholm Trail that brought over 36,000 head of cattle to Abilene each year. Demand increased so rapidly that just 10 years later, Dodge City, Kansas, shipped 500,000 head of cattle to the east. The rapid expansion of the cattle industry opened new job opportunities for Mexican vaqueros, with some historians arguing that as many as a quarter of all the cowboys working the herds in Texas were Mexicans.

Yet the rise of the cattle industry occurred at the same time that sheep herding began a period of unprecedented growth due to the new railroad connections that made shipment affordable, as well as the demand for wool. By the 1880s, most of the commercial cattle operations were owned by Anglos, while sheep herding was largely a *mexicano* activity. Cattle owners believed that sheep destroyed the ranges for cattle grazing, leading to frequent confrontations that quickly took on ethnic overtones. Further, with the invention of barbed wire, owners of larger landholdings began to fence their land, limiting the amount of open range, and gradually forcing out small- and medium-sized landowners. Because of this, many tejanos, unable to compete with the larger ranches, sold their land to Anglos and sought wage-earning jobs. Over time this led to further economic class divisions between upper-class Anglo landowners and business proprietors, and the mexicanos who were increasingly identified as landless wage-laborers in an era when land ownership equaled economic, political, and social status.

MINING

Aside from agricultural and livestock pursuits, another lure for immigrants was the thriving southwestern mining industry. The discovery of gold north of Taos, New Mexico in 1867, the reopening of silver mines in the southwest in the 1870s, new silver strikes in the 1870s and 1880s, and the reopening of the Santa Rita copper mines after the defeat of the Apaches all brought an influx of Anglos to those areas. Toward the end of the century, coal mining around Gallup, Santa Fe, and Raton in northern New Mexico brought additional employment opportunities. Historically, skilled miners from Mexico, Chile, and Peru had brought with them Spanish techniques that were used to work the mines prior to the American acquisition of the southwest. These skills were passed along to Anglo miners over a period of years. The new mineral strikes brought an influx of Mexican and other South and Central American miners into the southwest—especially after the exclusion of Asians in 1882—but they generally met with discrimination from Anglo owners, who paid them less than Anglo miners performing the same tasks. Additionally, the freighting industry, which was largely in mexicano hands before the advent of the railroads, went into serious decline as both mine owners and commercial agricultural operations found they could transport their produce faster and cheaper by rail than over the traditional freight trails.

In Santa Clara County, California, the New Almaden mercury mine's many Hispanic workers were segregated into an isolated area called "Spanishtown," shown above in an 1876 photograph, while Anglo workers lived in better conditions in "Englishtown."

Overall the widespread migration of settlers from the east had largely negative consequences for tejanos, mexicanos, and californios. Their population submerged beneath the rapid influx of Anglos, Hispanics found their environment forever transformed. In the process, many would lose their land, and most would lose their economic and political status as the economy changed from individual agricultural holdings to commercial agriculture, mining, and other industrial pursuits.

THE COWBOY

Few historical icons identify the United States more than the cowboy. One of the most popular topics of the new dime store novels that caught the imagination of Americans during the last quarter of the 19th century were stories with Western themes—Buffalo Bill, Wild Bill Hickok, and, of course, the cowboys who roamed the range. Buffalo Bill's Wild West Show played to sold-out audiences in the east, dramatic productions featured Western themes, and as the decades passed, movies and television shows about the Old West were popular both in the United States and abroad. Surely, nothing was more American than the cowboy.

But, of course, the origin of the cowboy was the Spanish vaquero. As far back as medieval Spain, owners of large land grants on the Iberian Peninsula allowed their herds to graze across the plains under the watchful eye of mounted vaqueros, who used their skills to manage the herds. During the 16th century, Spanish settlers brought horses, cattle, and the vaquero tradition to the Americas. As Spanish influence spread northwest into what is today the southwestern United States, large haciendas spread through the region with surplus cattle herded from Texas and Nuevo México south to Mexico City. With the annexation of the southwest by the United States, cattle continued to move south, but some also found their way east to American markets.

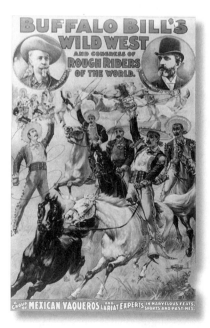

This advertisement for Buffalo Bill's Wild West Show specifically features "Mexican vaqueros" rather than "cowboys."

Following the Civil War, the explosion in demand in the eastern United States, coupled with the construction of western railroads, brought a boom in the cattle industry, and with it the need for large numbers of vaqueros; or, as the Anglos translated the term, "cowboys." Some vaqueros migrated north from Mexico.

Cinco de Mayo

Distinct among celebrations of national culture like the fourth of July or the French Bastille Day, *Cinco de Mayo* is more popular in the United States than in Mexico, its country of origin. European-Americans sometimes confuse *Cinco de Mayo* with Mexico's Independence Day, which is September 16 and is the country's most important patriotic holiday. The day actually celebrates the unexpected victory of outnumbered Mexican forces against the French army in the May 5, 1862 Battle of Puebla.

The Battle of Puebla was a key battle in the Franco-Mexican War, which had begun the previous year with the invasion of Mexico by the French army. Emperor Napoleon III of France attempted to take advantage of American distraction during the Civil War to enlarge its colonial possessions by asserting control over Mexico. Napoleon III had justified the invasion as a response to the bankrupt Mexican government's temporary suspension of interest payments to foreign countries. Thanks to a well-fortified Mexico City and the French general's underestimation of how hard the Mexicans would repel the attack, the battle was the first major Mexican victory in the war—and remained one of the few. On Independence Day of that year, then Mexican President Benito Juarez declared May 5—*Cinco de Mayo*—a national holiday in remembrance of the forces of Puebla, but the French invasion ultimately succeeded when their army took Mexico City in 1863 and installed Archduke Maximilian of Austria as a new emperor of Mexico. Not until 1867 was the Mexican Republic restored and Juarez returned to power.

In the meantime, the celebration of *Cinco de Mayo* had become popular in American regions with large Mexican-American populations. It has been celebrated in California every year from 1863 to the present. During the period of French occupation, such celebrations of the Puebla victory by Mexican-Americans in California took on a deeper meaning than simply a celebration of their heritage—it was an anticipation of the eventual freedom of their families and countrymen. Even when Mexican rule was restored in Mexico, such celebrations continued throughout Mexican-American communities, as a way to reconnect with and celebrate their heritage. Festive Mexican dishes (especially those involving a great deal of preparation or labor, such as *moles* or *tamales*) were prepared for the family or to share with friends, while dances (*baile folklorico*) and *mariachi* demonstrations would be held in parks, churches, or community centers. Later in the century, especially large Mexican-American communities held *Cinco de Mayo* street festivals and carnivals, sometimes lasting throughout the first week of May, though this became more common in the 20th century. In some cases, a reenactment of the Battle of Puebla was performed.

A minor holiday in Mexico, *Cinco de Mayo* has been transformed into a Mexican-American holiday across the border.

Newcomers from the east without cattle experience learned the new skills they would need from the experienced vaqueros. Since cowboys often moved about, it is quite difficult to estimate the proportions of the different groups that comprised the cowboys at any particular time. Census records suggest that by the 1880s, approximately 15 percent of cowboys were of Mexican descent, but this varied from region to region, with some researchers claiming that as many as one-third of the cowboys active on the great cattle drives north from Texas were of Mexican heritage. Regardless of their exact number, it was the vaqueros who were the prototype of the American cowboy, who passed along their skills at herding cattle, and who first introduced the rodeo to display their individual livestock handling skills. The ancestor of the famous Texas longhorn came from Spain, as did the origin of many of the terms associated with the cowboy—bronco, chaps, corral, lariat, lasso, ranch, poncho, rodeo, and buckaroo, to mention just a few.

NEW MEXICO

In New Mexico, the upper economic class of *nuevomexicanos*, often referred to as *los ricos* (the rich), had generally welcomed American control of the area. Unlike the other areas in the southwest, the New Mexico Territory remained largely nuevomexicano in population, and they dominated the legislature into the 1880s. Fearing that nuevomexicano children would be Americanized, and preferring that they be taught in Spanish in Catholic schools, the legislature opposed creating a public school system until 1891. In the previous year the legislature had voted against statehood for fear of endangering the parochial school system, and because leaders saw a financial advantage in territorial status where the federal government paid many of the expenses that nuevomexicano taxes would have otherwise had to pay as a state.

Between 1860 and 1900, there was a clear distinction between the majority of nuevomexicanos who were peones and the ruling oligarchy of los ricos who cooperated with Anglo businessmen in a clear economic-class alliance. Although legally eliminated by Congress in 1867, vestiges of the old seigniorial system with its strict class structure remained in New Mexico into the 1890s, causing some ethnic tensions with the gradually increasing Anglo population. Similarly, the failure to promptly rule on land claims from the era of Spanish and Mexican rule also created friction between nuevomexicanos and Anglos. Thirty years after the American annexation of the region, over 1,000 land claims had been filed, but less than 150 had been fully investigated, with only 71 settled.

Land use also resulted in other frictions. As the sheep and cattle industries both grew, hispano sheepherders moved eastward, colliding with Anglo cattlemen expanding westward from Texas. The rivalry for grazing land, combined with ethnic prejudices, led to instances of violence. Cattle ranchers, homesteaders, and the railroads that were beginning to cross the territory

A room in Mariano Guadalupe Vallejo's adobe ranch at Petaluma, California. The large ranch flourished after the original 1834 land grant, but fell into decline after the Bear Flag Revolt.

Mariano Guadalupe Vallejo

Born in Monterrey, California, July 4, 1807, Mariano Guadalupe Vallejo graduated from the military academy in Monterrey in 1823, then served as a cadet in the Mexican army. Later appointed commandant of the presidio in San Francisco, he fought Indians, explored northern California, and encouraged colonization. Elected to the legislature in 1830, he sided with it in a revolt against the governor in 1831–32. When a new governor granted an amnesty, Vallejo turned his efforts to colonization in the Sonoma Valley, founding Petaluma and Santa Rosa. When a new revolt against Mexican authority broke out in 1836 under Vallejo's nephew, Juan Bautista Alvarado, Vallejo acted as military commander. Vallejo was an early supporter of U.S. annexation, at least in part because Mexico appeared either unwilling or unable to protect northern California from Indian raids or the border claims of Britain and Russia.

Imprisoned by the Americans during the Bear Flag Revolt in 1846, Vallejo nevertheless appealed to californios to peacefully consent to American annexation. One of seven californios elected to the constitutional convention, he also journeyed to Washington, D.C. in 1863–65 in an attempt to settle outstanding land claims issues. Although he lost much of his land in the process, he continued to cultivate his land and vineyards. After attempting to author a history of early California, only to see his effort destroyed in a fire, he gave his large collection of original papers and documents to Hubert Howe Bancroft in 1873. Known as the Vallejo Documents, they formed the nucleus for an exceptional collection of early California manuscripts that was later donated to the University of California. He died at his home on January 18, 1890. His portrait was hung in the state capitol, and the city of Vallejo was named for him. His home at Rancho Petaluma Adobe is now the Petaluma Adobe State Historic Park and a national historic landmark.

each began fencing in land that sheepherders had used to graze their flocks. One result was the formation of various nuevomexicano vigilante groups such as the La Mano Negra (The Black Hand) and Las Gorras Blancas (The White Caps) that waged campaigns of sabotage by destroying barbed wire fences, cutting telegraph lines, breaking railroad ties, and occasionally burning ranches and homesteads. Some of these groups gradually turned to politics and legal challenges to protect their interests.

These range conflicts and land claims issues, coupled with an increasing number of Anglo settlers arriving on the completed southern transcontinental railroad, resulted in a rise in the transfer of land ownership from nuevomexicanos to los ricos and their Anglo allies. As the demand for land increased and land claims continued to go unresolved, a major upsurge in land disputes erupted. Anglos and los ricos allied with bankers and attorneys to force lands into foreclosure so they could be purchased and then resold to settlers at a profit, or retained to form large commercial agricultural businesses. The Santa Fe Ring, for example, was estimated to have gained over a million acres of land, while its attorney, Thomas B. Catron, was believed to have obtained ownership of two million acres and part ownership in another four million acres. The loss of land, together with a downturn in sheepherding, forced a major change in the economic condition of lower- and middle-class nuevomexicanos who moved in large numbers into employment with the railroads, mining, lumbering, and other wage-labor positions. This marked a major change in the nuevomexicano economic position from landholders and independent entrepreneurs to lower-paid, wage-labor positions.

HISPANIC-AMERICAN JOURNALISM

Between 1860 and 1900, as Hispanic Americans encountered discrimination and watched as Anglo culture spread into Hispanic areas, hundreds of Spanish-language newspapers and magazines appeared in the southwestern United States. Some were closely affiliated with revolutionary or vigilante movements. The influential californio newspaper *La Crónica* (The Chronicle) began publication in 1861 and circulated into Arizona and northern Mexico into the 1890s. Texas, New Mexico, and Arizona each supported scores of newspapers, many with specialized purposes such as *El Defensor del Pueblo* (The Defender of the Village), established by Juan José Herrera in Albuquerque as an official organ of the Knights of Labor; Néstor Montoya's *La Voz del Pueblo* (The Voice of the Village), affiliated with *Las Gorras Blancas* to speak on behalf of the poor against the corrupt land practices of los ricos and their Anglo allies; and Arizona's *El Fronterizo* (The Border), founded by Carlos Velasco, an influential artist and intellectual who also established the important mutual aid society Alianza Hispano-Americana, both of which fought discrimination against Hispanics. In addition to these Hispanic publications, there were several journals devoted to promoting revolution against Spanish control in Latin America. Chief among these were *Patria* (Motherland) and *La Revolución* (The Revolution), the latter edited by the Cuban Isaac Carrillo O'Farril. Both were early publications associated with José Martí and the Cuban independence movement.

HISPANIC-AMERICAN LITERATURE

Some of the early Spanish-language publications in America originated in New York, where Francisco Sellén published *Estudios Poéticos* (Poetic Studies) in 1863, and Antonio Sellén issued *Cuatro Poemas* (Four Poems) in 1877. Since the Hispanic population of New York at this time included a number of Cuban activists, they exerted a clear influence on the literature of the period. Anselmo Suárez y Romero's *Francisco*, published posthumously in 1880, presented a popular story of slaves who married despite their master's prohibition, providing pointed social commentary. Another Cuban, Cirilo Villaverde, authored *El Penitente* (The Penitent) in 1889, providing a glimpse into the folklore of manners common to Spanish literature in the Romantic period. Spanish-born George Santayana, the first Hispanic writer to earn a doctorate at Harvard University, began his prolific career in 1896 with the publication of his first book, a tract on aesthetics titled *Sense of Beauty*.

Generally considered to be the first Spanish-language novel published in the southwestern United States, Manuel M. Salazar's *La Historia de un Caminante, o Gervacio y Aurora* (The History of a Traveler on Foot, or Gervacio and Aurora) in 1881 was a romantic adventure set against a quaint picture of pastoral life in New Mexico. A popular topic of many novels was the "social bandit," a Robin Hood figure who robbed from the rich—especially the Anglos—to give to the poor. *Las aventuras de Joaquín Murieta* (The Adventures of Joaquín Murieta), serialized in the Santa Barbara newspaper *La Gaceta* in 1881, was followed by Eusebio Chacón's *El hijo de la tempestad* (Son of the Tempest) in 1892, which presents another version of the social bandit. Manuel C. Baca's *Historia de Vincente Silva, sus cuarenta bandidos, sus crímenes y retribuciones* (History of Vincente Silva, His Forty Bandits, His Crimes and Retributions) from 1896 introduces a twist on the topic when the protagonists appear as robbing Anglos and their own people to make money. Another variation in this genre of social commentary was Chacón's *Tras la tormenta la calma* (The Calm After the Storm), a romance featuring two suitors who contend for the hand of charming young lady, one of them from the working class and the other from the middle class, thus opening the way for commentary on the economic and social class system.

The first Hispanic known to have published a novel in English was María Amparo Ruiz de Burton, who authored in 1872 *Who Would Have Thought It?*, a satirical look at Anglo attitudes toward Mexicans, Native Americans, and African Americans. In a similar vein, Ruiz de Burton in 1881 published *The Squatter and the Don* from the viewpoint of the Mexican population

Loreta Janeta Velázquez

A portrait of Loreta Janeta Velázquez printed in her 1876 book.

Born in Havana, Cuba, on July 26, 1842, Loreta Janeta Velázquez moved to New Orleans to live with an aunt while receiving her education. Most of what is known about Velázquez comes from her memoir, *The Woman in Battle: A Narrative of the Exploits, Adventures, and Travels of Madame Loreta Janeta Velazquez, Otherwise Known as Lieutenant Harry T. Buford, Confederate States Army*, published in 1876. In this work she claimed to have enlisted in the Confederate army disguised as a man, and fought as Lt. Harry T. Buford at First Bull Run, Ball's Bluff, and Fort Donelson.

After her gender was finally discovered, she was discharged, but she maintained that she enlisted again in the 21st Louisiana Infantry and fought at Shiloh. When she was again discovered and discharged, she determined to continue aiding the Confederacy by becoming a spy. In her memoirs she claims to have pursued her career in espionage in Washington, D.C., where she met Secretary of War Edwin Stanton and President Abraham Lincoln. She also wrote that she visited Ohio and Indiana, where she took part in a plan to free Southern prisoners of war. Following the war she traveled to Europe, married, and lived for a time in Caracas, Venezuela, until her husband died. She then traveled west, meeting Brigham Young before she settled in Austin, Nevada. She is believed to have died in 1897.

When her memoirs were published, they were denounced as fraudulent by several Civil War veterans, including the prominent Confederate Gen. Jubal Early. Most historians consider her work largely fiction, pointing to the general improbability of her many adventures, vague or inaccurate descriptions, incorrect place names, and the lack of corroborating evidence for her many claims. In 2007 The History Channel broadcast *Full Metal Corset,* in which Velázquez's claims were presented as fact, but most historians continue to question their reliability.

of the southwest who struggled against the loss of their land to squatters, banks, and railroads.

INFLUENCE ON ANGLO-AMERICAN LITERATURE

During the second half of the 19th century, Hispanic themes also had an influence on Anglo-American literature. There were instances of negative characterizations such as those portrayed in Richard Henry Dana's *Two Years Before the Mast* or William Perkins's *Journal of a Forty-Niner in Sonora.* Yet reaction against this negative portrayal also appeared among Anglo authors, some of whom moved in the opposite direction by presenting a romanticized version of californios, nuevomexicanos, and tejanos. Works such as Helen Hunt Jackson's *Ramona* and Gertrude Atherton's *The Splendid Idle Forties* portrayed Spanish life in California as an extension of the old, romanticized aristocratic traditions of peninsular Spain.

Spanish culture can also be seen in the works of a number of other popular authors. Critics have commented on Spanish influence in the writing of Mark Twain, Herman Melville, and Edgar Allan Poe. Washington Irving, who once served as U.S. Minister to Spain, authored several works with Spanish themes such as *Christopher Columbus*, *Moors*, and *Alhambra*. Lew Wallace's *The Fair God* in 1873 chose as its theme the arrival of the Spanish in Mexico and the Night of Sadness. Much taken with Spanish culture, Bret Harte penned *The Legend of Monte del Diablo* and *The Lost Galleon*. His *A Knight-Errant of the Foot-Hills* owes an obvious debt to *Don Quixote*, while the unique history of the Spanish mission system formed the background for *The Miracle of Padre Junipero* and *The Mystery of the Hacienda*. James Russell Lowell, who was appointed U.S. minister to Spain, published *Yorick's Love* in 1878 as an adaptation of *Un Drama Nuevo* by Tamayo y Baus.

This 1885 Harper's Weekly featured "Maruja," one of Bret Harte's Mexican-themed stories.

By the last four decades of the 19th century, Hispanic writers were active in the United States, and Spanish culture formed a basis for themes adopted by Anglo writers.

FINE AND PERFORMING ARTS

Much as in literature, Spanish themes influenced the creations of some prominent artists in the United States. These included William Merritt Chase and John Singer Sargent, both of whom were greatly influenced by Diego Velázquez. Among the most prominent Hispanic artists was the Mexican landscape painter José María Velasco, who became the first Hispanic to win a major U.S. art award at the Centennial International Exhibition in Philadelphia in 1876. Also noted for his photography and lithography, Velasco won first prize at the Chicago World's Fair in 1893, and in 1889 exhibited his paintings at the Universal Exhibition in Paris, where he was made Chevalier de la Légion d'Honneur. Another important artist of this period was the sculptor Miguel Herrera, a noted *santero* sculptor. Santeros were images of the saints used to decorate churches, or displayed in homes for the special protection the saints might offer.

The California missions were a popular theme for artists and composers. Meredith Willson's symphony "The California Missions," Harl McDonald's two nocturnes "San Juan de Capistrano" and "Mission," and McDonald's symphony "Rumba" are examples of this genre. A unique musical form that developed in the southwest was the *corrido*, a form of folk music used to convey mexicano views on their cultural conflict with Anglos and to celebrate social bandits who opposed the Anglos. The first extant example of this was "El Corrido de Kiansis" (The Ballad of Kansas) dating from the 1860s. Another uniquely mexicano musical expression that arose along the Texas-Mexico border during the later 19th century was the *música norteña*, a local folk music that became very popular among the working class. The música norteña groups were centered on the accordion supported by the *tambora de rancho* (ranch drum) and the *bajo sexto* (12-string guitar). This became the standard folk music form during the last two decades of the 19th century.

Another popular activity in southwestern mexicano communities was the theater. During the 1860s several traveling theatrical companies began to settle in the southwest, notably Gerardo López del Castillo's Compañía Española de la Familia Estrella. Professional and amateur plays were staged in communities throughout the area. By the mid-1870s there were 14 theatrical companies active in California, with Los Angeles home to two of the more famous, Compañía Española de Angel Mollá and Compañía Dramática Española, directed by Pedro C. de Pellón. Both toured into Baja California and Arizona, with Pellón's company eventually settling in Tucson in 1878. As the railroads extended into the southwest, theatrical touring companies, including some from Mexico, began to make regular circuits from Laredo west through Los Angeles and north to the San Francisco area. The typical production provided an entire evening of entertainment beginning with a three- or four-act drama, followed by songs and dances, then concluding with a single-act comedic performance. Most of the dramas featured works by peninsular playwrights. Performances were family affairs attended by people of all classes.

THE SPANISH-AMERICAN WAR

As the 19th century came to a close, tensions rose between the United States and Spain, eventually leading the United States into war once again. Resentment of Spanish rule had existed in Cuba for several decades during the mid- and late-19th century. Support for this growing movement came from Cuban exiles in Florida, and especially in New York City, where they formed an active lobbying effort on behalf of Cuban independence. In 1892 José Martí established the Partido Revolucionario Cubano (Cuban Revolutionary Party) in New York City, which led to an increase in revolutionary activity such as the publication of newspapers and pamphlets. By 1895 a Cuban government-in-exile in New York led by Tomás Estrada Palma was providing arms, supplies, and volunteers directly to the revolutionary movement in Cuba. At the same time, Puerto Rican exiles led by Ramón Emeterio Betances and Santiago Iglesias Plantín (founder of the Socialist Party in Puerto Rico) pursued similar revolutionary

This lithograph of Cuban heroes was published for a Cuban-American Fair held at Madison Square Garden in New York City in May 1896.

activities, including publishing the newspaper *El Postillón* (The Coachman) in New York.

The explosion of the battleship U.S.S. *Maine* in Havana Harbor with the loss of 260 American sailors, an ill-advised letter from Spanish Minister Enrique Dupuy de Lôme in which he insulted President William McKinley, and the incendiary "yellow journalism" of competing New York newspapers combined to produce a state of war between the two nations in 1898. The outbreak of war divided opinions among Hispanics. Some, especially those with roots in Cuba, supported American entry into the war in the hope of gaining eventual freedom for Cuba. Others tended to favor Spain, most notably the Mexican miners in the southwestern United States.

Once war was declared, the most important military campaign of the war was the U.S. invasion of Cuba. The operation enjoyed the support of Cuban revolutionary forces under Gen. Calixto García, who cleared the area around the proposed American landings of any Spanish soldiers, allowing American troops to land unopposed. Gen. García's forces fought alongside the Americans, provided valuable intelligence throughout the campaign, and tied down Spanish reinforcement that otherwise could have been deployed against U.S. forces. Accompanying the invasion were scores of Hispanic soldiers in the regiments assembled for the invasion.

General Calixto García (center) meeting with American Brigadier General William Ludlow as the American army landed in Cuba.

Among the famous 1st U.S. Volunteer Cavalry, better known as the Rough Riders and led by Col. Leonard Wood and Lt. Col. Theodore Roosevelt, were Mexican-American troops from Texas, New Mexico, and Arizona. These included Capt. Maximiliano Luna and Sgt. Jorge W. Armijo. Descended from conquistadors who settled along the Rio Grande River around 1650, Luna attended Georgetown University and had been elected sheriff in Valencia County, New Mexico, before the war. Following the conflict, a military camp was named in his honor. Armijo survived the war to be elected to the U.S. Congress.

CONCLUSION

During and immediately after the Civil War, Hispanic participation on both sides meant a number of Hispanics rose to national prominence. At the same time, other national trends were affecting Hispanics in less positive ways, as Anglo settlers moved westward in large numbers after the war, and changed the economic environment of the areas where they settled. The ongoing dispossession of Hispanic landowners worsened, threatening the established cultures of Hispanic communities in Texas, California, and the southwest. Despite their deep roots in these regions and their often superior skills in irrigation, ranching, and mining, many Hispanics suffered a decline in status as traditional small farms and ranches could not compete with large-scale agriculture instituted by Anglo settlers. This change set in motion another trend that has since influenced the lives of innumerable Hispanics: the expansion of commercial agriculture, with its need for large numbers of seasonal migrant laborers rather than full-time workers. At the end of the century, the outcome of the Spanish-American war left another legacy that would impact Hispanic-American population patterns throughout the 20th century—U.S. control of the island of Puerto Rico, which would lead to American citizenship for Puerto Ricans in 1917.

JAMES S. PULA
PURDUE UNIVERSITY NORTH CENTRAL

Further Reading

Cockroft, James D. *Latinos in the Making of the United States: The Hispanic Experience in the Americas*. New York: Franklin Watts, 1995.

De Varona, Frank, ed. *Hispanic Presence in the United States: Historical Beginnings*. Miami, FL: Mnemosyne Publishing Company, 1993.

Fernández-Florez, Darío. *The Spanish Heritage in the United States*. Madrid: Publicaciones Españolas, 1965.

Fernández-Shaw, Carlos M. *The Hispanic Presence in North America*. New York: Facts on File, 1987.

Gann, L.H. and Peter J. Duignan. *The Hispanics in the United States: A History*. Boulder, CO: Westview Press, 1986.

Meier, Matt S. and Feliciano Ribera. *Mexican Americans—American Mexicans: From Conquistadors to Chicanos*. New York: Hill and Wang, 1993.

Military.com. "Adm. David Glasgow Farragut." Available online, URL: www .military.com/Content/MoreContent?file=ML_farragut_bkp. Accessed April 2009.

O'Donnell-Rosales, John. *Hispanic Confederates*. Baltimore, MD: Clearfield Co., 1997.

Rodríguez, Ricardo J. *Hispanics in the U.S. Civil War: A Compiled List of Men Who Fought for the Confederacy and the Union,* 2 vols. San Antonio, TX: Ricardo J. Rodríguez, 2008.

Thompson, Jerry D. *Vaqueros in Blue and Gray*. Austin, TX: State House Press, 2000.

Weber, David J. *Foreigners in Their Native Land*. Albuquerque, NM: University of New Mexico Press, 1973.

CHAPTER 5

The Progressive Era and World War I: 1900 to 1920

IN THE FIRST two decades of the 20th century, Hispanic Americans were largely concentrated in the southwestern states of Texas, New Mexico, Colorado, Arizona, and California. Sizeable Hispanic American populations also resided in Florida, New York, New Jersey, and Illinois. The term *Hispanic American* encompasses a wide variety of groups of diverse national, ethnic, and racial backgrounds. Some Hispanic Americans had long roots in the United States, dating back to the colonial times when California, Florida, and the southwest were on the borderlands of the Spanish empire. Californios, floridanos, tejanos, and hispanos had lived in these areas for generations and built cultures centered around family and religion.

The first decades of the 20th century were also a time of sizeable immigration from Mexico. Another large group of immigrants in the beginning of the 20th century consisted of Spanish, Cuban, and Puerto Rican political exiles. These new immigrants often encountered conflicts as they sought to maintain their cultural heritage and to adjust to life among older Hispanic communities and mainstream American society. The reform spirit of the Progressive Movement, and the national unity inspired by U.S. entry into World War I, would help the process of assimilation and the development of vibrant new communities and cultures among both established and recently arrived Hispanic Americans.

A family of Mexican peasant refugees waiting on the banks of the Rio Grande in Mexico in a photograph dated between 1908 and 1919. The majority of the estimated 250,000 refugees from the Mexican Revolution (1910–20) ended up in Texas.

HISPANIC IMMIGRATION IN THE EARLY 20TH CENTURY

Hispanics arrived as immigrants to United States in the early 20th century in small, but significant numbers, during a time when foreign suspicion and anti-immigrant sentiment were widespread. Many Americans feared that the flood of immigrants, which began in the late 19th century, was threatening traditional American life with new languages and customs. The largest groups of Hispanic immigrants to the United States at this time were from Mexico and Puerto Rico. Economic and political instability in various Latin American nations, increasingly restrictive immigration laws against Asians, and the growth of large-scale agribusinesses with their need for large labor forces fueled the growth of Hispanic immigration to the United States. For example, the Immigration Act of 1907, which increased the head tax on new immigrants and allowed the president to deny admission to immigrant groups believed to be negatively influencing labor conditions, was designed to halt Japanese immigration, which furthered the need for other sources of cheap immigrant labor. There were few restrictions on Mexican immigration before 1917.

The new Hispanic arrivals included both legal and illegal immigrants and refugees, temporary workers, and permanent residents. Beginning in the early 1900s, Mexican immigrants crossed the border into the United States in ever-increasing numbers for political and economic reasons. During this time an economic gap between Mexico and the United States had begun to develop, meaning that workers could earn more money for the same occupations in the United States. Agricultural, mining, and railroad companies desperate for workers even sent recruiters into Mexico, often employing deceptive tactics such as the promise of high wages and the imposition of a transportation fee that left the new arrival in debt. The political and economic instability of the Mexican Revolution (1910–20) drove approximately 250,000 upper-class, middle-class, and peasant Mexicans (approximately 10 percent of the Mexican population), to flee into the American southwest. Key points of arrival included Los Angeles, California, and El Paso and San Antonio, Texas, with Texas housing the bulk of the new arrivals. These refugees lived in what they termed *México de afuera,* meaning Mexico in exile. The Mexican Revolution would also have a military impact on the United States, especially along the border.

PANCHO VILLA AND THE *BANDIDO* STEREOTYPE

In 1916, when U.S. President Woodrow Wilson recognized the government of Mexican President Venustiano Carranza, he angered Carranza's rival, the revolutionary fighter Francisco "Pancho" Villa. In January of that year, Villa stopped a train in the northern Mexican town of Santa Ysabel, killing a group of American citizens on board. In March Villa entered U.S. territory when he launched a raid that resulted in the burning of the town of Columbus, New Mexico and the killing of 19 people. General John J. Pershing and his men had already been stationed in Texas in 1915 to guard the border due to a number of raids that had been conducted in Texas, New Mexico, and Arizona. After the public outcry over the destruction of Columbus, Wilson sent Pershing into Mexico to pursue Villa in what became known as the Punitive Expedition. The expedition was unsuccessful and would be recalled in 1917, but the actions along the border provided valuable experience as the country began mobilizing for its

This 1916 cartoon depicting a face-off between Villa and Pershing employs a bandit stereotype that became widespread in U.S. culture.

eventual entry into World War I. Villa would later surrender his forces to Mexican President Adolfo de la Huerta and live on a hacienda until his death in an ambush in 1923.

Villa captured the American imagination and helped fuel the stereotype of the villainous Mexican *bandido* (bandit) that became a staple of Hollywood movies for years to come. The incidents arising out of the Mexican Revolution would further strain U.S.-Mexican relations and heighten the discrimination Mexican Americans already felt.

PATTERNS OF MEXICAN DISCRIMINATION

The pattern of displacement of the landed tejano class that had begun in the second half of the 19th century would largely be complete by 1920. Thus the majority of Mexican Americans, both established citizens and new arrivals, now worked as migrant agricultural laborers. Migrant workers followed the harvests, often living in numerous places throughout the year. Some even returned to Mexico for several months each year as they waited for the next harvest season. Agricultural work was often monotonous, backbreaking, and a daily struggle with harsh conditions, including inclement weather and the necessity of constant stooping and carrying heavy loads. Many lived in migrant labor camps as they followed the harvests, resulting in poor access to health care and education for their children. Mexican Americans were the largest group of migrant workers, but not the only Hispanic Americans to suffer the daily hardships of migrant life. In 1919 nearly 100 Puerto Rican laborers died on an Arkansas farm due to malnutrition and harsh living conditions. Large numbers of Mexican Americans also still worked as vaqueros, an occupation with roots dating back to Spanish colonial times.

Those Hispanic Americans who worked in other industries and held such jobs as railroad workers, miners, and factory workers, also faced differential pay scales, harsh working conditions, and segregation at home, at school, and in the workplace. Hispanic Americans, like African Americans, faced daily battles with racism, discrimination, and the decline in the social acceptability of inter-racial marriages, once common along the Spanish colonial frontier. The often brutal attacks on Mexican Americans living in the southwest, including lynch-ings, led to a formal protest by the Mexican ambassador to the United States in 1912. Many Mexicans who worked in the United States hoped to eventually return permanently to Mexico, and few sought to become U.S. citizens. This made them even more vulnerable to exploitation and discrimination.

This upsurge in immigration increased demands for restrictive legislation. Many Mexicans were able to elude the new restrictions, however, due to their importance as a low-paid labor force. The Immigration Act of 1917 instituted a literacy test that excluded those immigrants who could not read or write in English or in their native language. The literacy test and higher head tax ex-cluded many Mexican laborers, which initially increased the number of illegal

This man photographed driving a donkey cart near Nuevo Laredo, Mexico, in 1912 was on his way to the United States a few years before the short-lived literacy test and head tax.

immigrants. Due to the demand for workers, however, the federal government soon waived the literacy test and head tax for Mexicans, instituting a Mexican worker program that allowed workers to stay up to six months. The special program remained in effect until 1921. There was no formal federal Border Patrol until 1924.

SPANISH, CUBAN, AND PUERTO RICAN IMMIGRATION
Spanish, Cuban, and Puerto Rican political exiles began arriving in the United States in the late-19th century as Cuba and Puerto Rico struggled to win their independence from Spain. After the Spanish-American War ended in 1898, the 1900 Foraker Act established a civilian government in Puerto Rico, with a parliament elected by the people and a governor appointed by the U.S. president. In 1901 Federico Degetegu became the first Puerto Rican to serve in the U.S. House of Representatives as resident commissioner of the island. The new immigrants mainly settled in areas they called *colonias* in New England and mid-Atlantic cities such as in New York, Philadelphia, New Orleans, Tampa, and Key West, as well as in Chicago. Hawaiian plantation workers also recruited a number of Puerto Rican workers. Puerto Ricans would become the most urban of the Hispanic American groups in the 20th century. New York City in particular saw the establishment of a large Puerto Rican population in neighborhoods such as El Barrio by the end of the first decade of the 20th century. In 1901 Luis Muñoz Rivera began publication of the bilingual newspaper the *Puerto Rican Herald*. The term *Nuyorican* was coined to describe those

Machismo and Marianismo

Some cultural historians use the terms *machismo* and *marianismo* to refer to the Latin American ideal cultural male and female roles, while others argue that they are mere stereotypes of the traditional Hispanic man and woman. Machismo is the older term, while marianismo is relatively newer. The ideas trace their heritage back to Spanish colonial days in Latin America, where a patriarchal society and the dominance of the Roman Catholic Church were in place.

The ideal cultural roles prescribed by machismo and marianismo were meant to shape the division of labor and guide the everyday lives of Hispanic men and women. Men would inhabit the public sphere of politics and business, while women would inhabit the private, domestic sphere of home and family.

According to machismo, the Hispanic male was the household protector, defender, and provider. Common male characteristics included aggressiveness, self-confidence, and dignity. According to marianismo, the Hispanic female was to pattern her actions after the Virgin Mary. Common female characteristics included gentleness, caring, self-sacrifice, virtuousness, sexual purity, humbleness, and emotional behavior. Both males and females were expected to place family needs over individual needs. Whether scholars accept machismo and marianismo as cultural ideals or stereotypes, the majority agrees that they were not necessarily attainable in everyday life, especially among the poor and working class where economic necessity brought women into the workplace. Urban life and the pressures for cultural assimilation also served to weaken ties to older cultural ideals.

of Puerto Rican descent who were born in New York. They maintained close social, political, and economic ties with their home country while adapting to life in the United States.

HISPANIC AMERICANS AND THE PROCESS OF ASSIMILATION

Hispanic Americans, both old and new arrivals, experienced the cultural tensions of assimilation during the first two decades of the 20th century. Most Americans expected immigrants to assimilate (or acculturate) into mainstream American society. Conflicts often arose between Hispanic and Anglo cultures, as well as between individual national and ethnic identities within the Hispanic-American population. The process of assimilation was made more difficult by the segregation, discrimination, poverty, and low educational levels most Hispanic Americans faced. Other sources of conflict and differences included rural versus urban lifestyles, class tensions, generational tensions between parents and their often more acculturated children, and between new arrivals and more settled populations. The stigma attached to new immigrants often led native Hispanic Americans to distance themselves from new arrivals; conversely, the new arrivals often looked down on the natives, who had abandoned many of their old customs. Recent Mexican-American immigrants even coined a term, *el pocho*, to describe a Mexican American who they felt had lost touch with their Mexican heritage. Despite the pressures to assimilate, most Hispanic Americans maintained many of their old customs, often blending them with new American ways of life. Rural, agricultural families tended to maintain more of the old lifestyles, while urban families tended to be the most acculturated.

The traditional Hispanic-American family tended to be large, with multiple generations and extended relations such as grandparents, aunts, uncles, and cousins sharing the same household. Hispanic culture placed a great emphasis on the family as the center of daily life, and *la familia* was valued above an individual's wants or needs. An individual was a representation of their family and was expected to act accordingly. Males and females within the family had traditional roles that were meant to guide their daily actions. These would come to be known by the terms *machismo* and *marianismo*. The patriarchal household was to be ruled by the working father, while the mother cared for

Mexican sugar beet workers, including a large family with small children, standing before their shack in Rocky Ford, Colorado, in July 1915.

A Cinco de Mayo celebration featuring fiddles, horns, and a clarinet winding through the mining town of Mogollon, New Mexico, in 1914, during the town's heyday. Mexican-American cultural celebrations like this one have persisted in the region, but Mogollon later became a ghost town.

home, children, and the family's spiritual wellbeing. Cultural historians debate whether these terms were meant to serve as cultural ideals or merely represent stereotypes.

Many Hispanic Americans also placed a great emphasis on the role of religion in guiding everyday life. While Hispanic Americans practiced a variety of religious faiths, a majority were Roman Catholics, a tradition dating back to colonial times when the Roman Catholic Church was the state-sponsored religion and a dominant guiding force in Spain and its American colonies. New immigrants also introduced Afro-Caribbean religions such as Santeria into the United States. Religious art and objects were often prominently displayed.

The result of the twin pressures of maintaining one's cultural heritage and assimilating into mainstream society often produced a rich, blended Hispanic-American culture, and helped introduced Hispanic customs into the broader American culture. The English and Spanish languages were often blended to various degrees to create a hybrid language that would come to be known as Spanglish. Prominent traditional holidays, such as the Mexican *Dia de los muertos*, were celebrated along with American holidays such as the Fourth of July. Renowned Mexican painters such as Diego Rivera traveled to the United States to paint murals in cities such as New York, Los Angeles, and Detroit. Prominent Hispanic baseball players such as José Méndez played in the U.S. Negro League, achieving recognition despite the insults and abuse often heaped on them by American audiences. The legendary Cuban player Adolfo Luque became the first Latino to appear in the World Series, helping set the stage for the future breaking of the color barrier in Major League Baseball.

Mexican Americans in the southwest in particular developed a new culture that blended customs and traditions. Tex-Mex food included the introduction of such Mexican dietary staples as the taco, quesadilla, and tamale to the American diet. Popular daily music forms included the development of tejano music and the *corrido*. Tejano music blended Mexican folk songs with Texas music, as well as European influences, including the polka and the waltz. Corridos had their roots in Mexican folk ballads, and consisted of rhyming stanzas, a chorus that told the story of a legendary hero or event, and the accompaniment of a guitar or other

These corrido *lyrics from 1909 tell the story of Jesús Negrete, who was a notorious Mexican bandit at the turn of the century.*

stringed instrument. One popular early 20th-century example is the "Ballad of Gregorio Cortez," which tells the story of a Mexican American who killed a Texas sheriff and led the Texas Rangers on one of the largest manhunts in the state's history.

Mexican Americans also continued to establish small printing presses and Spanish-language newspapers to educate their communities and tell their stories. Mexican-American literature developed further, centered on humorous stories of daily life, collections of Mexican tales and legends, and romantic works set in pre-Revolutionary Mexico. Well-known authors included Maria Cristina Mena (Chambers), Vicente Bernal, and Luis Pérez. Ignacio Lozano founded the newspaper *La Prensa* in 1913 in San Antonio, Texas.

ASSIMILATION DURING WORLD WAR I

The process of assimilation into American society would be greatly aided by U.S. participation in World War I, which the United States entered in 1917 after declaring war on Germany. The Selective Service Act of 1917 instituted a draft by lot; males between the ages of 21 and 30, later expanded to those between 18 and 45, were eligible. Hispanic Americans would be mobilized

The Ballad of Gregorio Cortez

Gregorio Cortez was born June 22, 1875 near Matamoros, Mexico, and moved with his family to the small town of Manor, Texas in 1887. His parents were migrant workers, and his two brothers, Tomás and Romaldo, were charged with horse theft on various occasions. Cortez married several times and fathered several children while working as a farmhand and vaquero in Texas. In 1901 Cortez and his brother Romaldo were tenant farmers on the W.A. Thulemeyer ranch when county sheriff W.T. "Brack" Morris showed up to investigate a horse theft, after learning that Gregorio had recently acquired a mare. After misunderstandings arose as a result of faulty language translations during the interview with the Cortez brothers, the sheriff shot and wounded Romaldo, and his brother Gregorio in turn shot and killed the sheriff.

Gregorio Cortez then sought to escape, fleeing to Martin and Refugia Robledo's home on property owned by Henry Schnabel, a county constable, outside Belmont. His family was taken into custody. Cortez was soon found by county Sheriff Robert M. Glover and his posse, and both Sheriff Glover and Schnabel were killed in the resulting gunfire. Cortez once again went on the run as he headed for Laredo. Cortez was finally apprehended on June 22, 1901, when an acquaintance turned him in. He faced several trials and spent time in numerous jails, receiving a life sentence before being pardoned in 1913. He returned to Mexico and fought in the Mexican Revolution before dying of pneumonia on February 28, 1916. Cortez ultimately became a legend among both Mexicans and Anglos for his ability to elude capture by the famous Texas Rangers in the largest manhunt in the state's history at that time. Many Mexican Americans viewed him as a hero who was unjustly targeted for his race, while many Americans felt he was a dangerous criminal who fit their stereotype of Mexicans and deserved punishment. At one point a lynch mob of 300 people unsuccessfully attempted to break him out of jail and hang him. His legend was retold in the ballad titled *El Corrido de Gregorio Cortez* (The Ballad of Gregorio Cortez). His story was also told in the 1958 book *With His Pistol In His Hand* by Américo Paredes, and the 1982 Hollywood movie *The Ballad of Gregorio Cortez*, starring Edward James Olmos.

to serve in the American armed forces, both at home and with the American Expeditionary Force that fought with the Allied Powers in Europe. A lack of records of the Hispanic Americans who served makes an exact accounting of the numbers difficult. Due to America's late entry into the war, new recruits and draftees had to be trained quickly, a problem for those who spoke little or no English. The military developed what became known as the Camp Gordon Plan, in which soldiers would be divided into units based on their native languages, and led by officers who spoke that language to facilitate the training process. Camp Gordon was located in Georgia.

The U.S. military was still segregated during World War I, preventing most minority soldiers from serving in combat duty along the front lines in Europe. Minority soldiers were usually stationed in non-combat zones and assigned to menial labor. Some Hispanic Americans refused to register for the draft in protest of their discriminatory treatment. Puerto Rico provided one of the

Private David Barkley

David Bennes Barkley was born on March 31, 1899 in the border town of Laredo, Texas. His father, Josef Barkley, was stationed there with the U.S. Army when he met and married his mother, Antonia Cantu, a Mexican American born and raised in Texas. Barkley was forced to drop out of school at the age of 13 when his father left the family, and worked at various jobs to help support his mother and sister. He was 17 when he decided to enlist in the army and fight in World War I. He became a private, eventually joining Company A of the 356th Infantry, 89th Division in France. He hid the fact that he was Hispanic American because the military was still segregated, and he did not want his minority status to prevent him from serving on the front lines in Europe.

David Barkley, a Medal of Honor recipient in World War I whose Hispanic heritage was not known until 1989.

In France, he and a fellow soldier answered a call for volunteers to swim the Meuse River in order to gather information on German positions behind enemy lines. Barkley completed the mission, mapping the enemy's locations, but drowned in his attempt to swim back across the river on November 9, 1918. His partner on the mission was able to carry the intelligence the rest of the way, leading to a successful attack. Barkley was posthumously awarded the Congressional Medal of Honor, which was presented to his mother in San Antonio in 1919, as well as the French Croix de Guerre and the Italian Croce Merito de Guerra. When his body was returned to San Antonio in 1921, it lay in state at the Alamo. He was laid to rest in the San Antonio National Cemetery.

Barkley's Hispanic heritage remained unknown until 1989, at which time the army recognized him as the only Hispanic Medal of Honor recipient of World War I. A San Antonio elementary school and a U.S. Army camp were named in his honor. In 2002 Laredo, Texas, built a memorial honoring the 41 Hispanic soldiers who had received the Congressional Medal of Honor in David B. Barkley Plaza, and a statue of Barkley also stands there.

largest groups of Hispanic-American soldiers, most of whom served in segregated units based on the island or in the newly acquired Panama Canal Zone. A few Hispanic Americans saw combat duty in Europe by hiding their cultural heritage, including Private David Barkley of the 89th Infantry Division's 356th Infantry Regiment, the only Hispanic American to win the Medal of Honor during World War I. Other Hispanic Americans receiving recognition for heroism in combat included Nicholas Lucero, who was awarded the French Croix de Guerre; and Marcelino Serna, who was awarded the Distinguished Service Cross, the French Croix de Guerre, a Victory Medal, and two Purple Hearts.

DISCRIMINATION AND POLITICAL ORGANIZATION

Hispanic Americans faced discrimination on the home front as well as in the armed forces. World War I presented many Hispanic Americans with their first experiences in mainstream American society. Many hoped that this opportunity to display their patriotism, willingness to defend their country, and ability to perform difficult work would help counter the rampant discrimination they faced on a daily basis, as well as lead to postwar social and economic opportunities. America's involvement in the war helped secure the passage of the 1917 Jones Act, which granted citizenship to residents of Puerto Rico, in part to help ease wartime labor shortages and the need for

This lector read aloud from books and newspapers of the workers' choice while they rolled cigars in a factory in Tampa, Florida, in January 1909.

soldiers. The Jones Act increased the flow of Puerto Ricans to the mainland, especially New York City, as word of job opportunities spread. The need for workers opened positions in new occupations such as munitions, as well as the more established manufacturing and service industries.

Early political organization among Hispanic Americans came in the field of workers' rights. For example, in 1901, the Puerto Rican *Federacion Libre de los Trabajadores* became affiliated with the American Federation of Labor (AFL), representing the AFL's first acceptance of nonwhite members. In 1903 Mexican beet workers joined with Japanese-American workers to lead a strike in Oxnard, California and form a farm workers union. Cuban and Puerto Rican *tabaqueros* (cigar workers) were often in the vanguard of the fight for workers' rights, as well as other political and social causes. Tabaqueros frequently employed lectors out of their own wages to read daily news and political and literary tracts while they rolled cigars. Bernardo Vega, a tabaquero and labor organizer who moved to New York in 1916, documented the daily life of workers in his memoirs. In 1929 the League of United Latin American Citizens (LULAC), an organization that has long combated discrimination against Hispanics and promoted education and voting rights, would be formed in Corpus Christi, Texas.

CONCLUSION

The reforms undertaken by the Progressive Movement and the need for the participation of many Americans in World War I as soldiers and workers sped the assimilation of the many new Hispanic immigrants who arrived in the United States in the early 20th century. These new immigrants, who were Mexican, Spanish, Cuban, and Puerto Rican, arrived to find well-established Hispanic communities and a mainstream American society that continued to misunderstand and discriminate against them, while still seeking to use their labor. Although there was little large-scale political organization among Hispanic Americans during the early 20th century, their experiences during this time set the stage for later struggles for equal rights.

MARCELLA BUSH TREVINO
BARRY UNIVERSITY

Further Reading

Acuña, Rodolfo. *Occupied America: A History of Chicanos*. Third edition. New York: Harper Collins, 1988.

Baker, Lindsay T. *More Ghost Towns of Texas*. Norman, OK: University of Oklahoma Press, 2005.

Carrasquillo, Angela L. *Hispanic Children and Youth in the United States: A Resource Guide*. New York: Garland Publishing, 1991.

Chambers, John Whiteclay. *The Tyranny of Change: America in the Progressive Era, 1890–1920*. New Brunswick, NJ: Rutgers University Press, 2000.

Christian, Carole E. "Joining the American Mainstream: Texas's Mexican Americans During World War I." *Southwestern Historical Quarterly*. Vol. 92, No. 4, 1989.

Daniels, Roger. *Coming to America: A History of Immigration and Ethnicity in American Life*. New York: Perennial, 2002.

Davis, Mike. *Magical Urbanism: Latinos Reinvent the U.S. City*. New York: Verso, 2000.

Dolan, Jay P. and Gilberto Miguel Hinojosa. *Mexican Americans and the Catholic Church*. Notre Dame, IN: University of Notre Dame Press, 1994.

Eisenhower, John S.D. and Joanne Thompson Eisenhower. *Yanks: The Epic Story of the American Army in World War I*. New York: Free Press, 2001.

Fernández, Virgil. *Hispanic Military Heroes*. Austin, TX: VFJ Publishing, 2006.

Fernández-Shaw, Carlos M. *The Hispanic Presence in North America from 1492 to Today*. New York: Facts on File, 1991.

Gabaccia, Donna R. *Immigration and American Diversity: A Social and Cultural History*. Oxford: Blackwell, 2002.

Gann, Lewis H. and Peter Duignan. *The Hispanics in the United States: A History*. Boulder, CO: Westview Press and Stanford, CA: Hoover Institution on War, Revolution, and Peace, 1986.

García, John A. *Latino Politics in America: Community, Culture, and Interests*. Lanham, MD: Rowman and Littlefield, 2003.

González, Gilbert G. *Guest Workers or Colonized Labor: Mexican Labor Migration to the United States*. Boulder, CO: Paradigm, 2005.

González, Juan. *Harvest of Empire: A History of Latinos in America*. New York: Viking, 2000.

Kanellos, Nicolas and Claudio Esteva Fabregat. *Handbook of Hispanic Cultures in the United States*. Houston, TX: Arte Publico Press, 1994.

King, John, ed. *Cambridge Companion to Modern Latin American Culture*. New York: Cambridge University Press, 2004.

McGerr, Michael E. *A Fierce Discontent: The Rise and Fall of the Progressive Movement in America, 1870–1920*. New York: Oxford University Press, 2005.

McWilliams, Carey. *North from Mexico: The Spanish-Speaking People of the United States*. New York: Greenwood Press, 1968.

Milkis, Sidney M. *Progressivism and the New Democracy*. Amherst, MA: University of Massachusetts Press, 1999.

Portes, Alejandro and Robert L. Bach. *Latin Journey: Cuban and Mexican Immigrants in the United States*. Berkeley, CA: University of California Press, 1985.

Sánchez, George J. *Becoming Mexican American: Ethnicity, Culture, and Identity in Chicano Los Angeles, 1900–1945*. New York: Oxford University Press, 1993.

Shorris, Earle. *Latinos: A Biography of a People*. New York: Avon Books, 1992.

Stavans, Ilan. *Spanglish: The Making of a New American Language*. New York: Rayo, 2003.

Takaki, Ronald. *A Different Mirror: A History of Multicultural America*. Boston, MA: Little, Brown, 1993.

Vega, Bernardo. *Memoirs of Bernardo Vega: A Contribution to the History of the Puerto Rican Community in New York*. Edited by Cesar A. Iglesias. Translated by Juan Flores. New York: Monthly Review Press, 1984.

Votaw, John F. *The American Expeditionary Forces in World War I*. Duncan Anderson, ed. Oxford: Osprey, 2005.

Weisman, Alan and Jay Dusard. *La Frontera: The United States Border with Mexico*. New York: Harcourt Brace Jovanovich, 1986.

CHAPTER 6

The Roaring Twenties and the Great Depression: 1920 to 1939

THE TWENTIES NOT only produced the first man to fly solo across the Atlantic, the first woman to swim the English Channel, and arguably one of the most phenomenal baseball players ever known, but the decade also helped shape a generation of ideas and attitudes. The 1920s ushered in the modern era with rapid changes in cultural, economic, and political ways of life. The "buy now, pay later" consumer credit mindset prompted the notion that everyone could have not only amenities such as automobiles and washing machines, but a piece of prosperity. Much of the change largely evolved from developments in the previous century, when industrialization and immigration turned America into an increasingly innovative and urbanized society.

From agricultural workers migrating to major metropolitan areas to recent immigrants, newly minted city dwellers fashioned an even more complex definition of what it was to be an American. Characterized as the New Era by contemporaries because of modernization efforts, the decade experienced a backlash in redefined gender roles, sexual mores, and the reinterpretation of a true-blue citizen. In many ways American institutions, and by extension the larger society, defined a citizen as white, socially integrated, culturally linked to European roots, and racially devoid of Mexican, Native-American, African-American, Asian-American, and Hispanic-Caribbean heritage. Thus many Americans remained outside the reach of the new, affluent, consumer revolution culture, and were relegated to second-class citizenship mired in the producer economy of the 19th century.

THE CHANGING U.S. WORKFORCE

A growing proportion of the unskilled workforce consisted not only of women, African Americans, and Asian-American subgroups, but also of Hispanics. Mexican immigrants, and Mexican Americans with long-standing roots in the southwest. Mexican Americans formed the majority of Hispanic Americans in the early 20th century, and also comprised the majority of manual labor. They worked for low pay, primarily on railroads and construction sites and in mines, fields, and factories. Working on railroads was particularly challenging, because most of the terrain was desert, semi-desert, or mountainous. By the late 1920s, ethnic Mexican workers constituted two-thirds of the railroad labor force. In Texas, Hispanics supplanted African Americans in a number of unskilled and semi-skilled occupations. By 1928, for example, 75 percent of construction workers in Texas were ethnic Mexican. The population of south Texas alone jumped from 160,000 in 1920 to almost 325,000 a decade later. By 1930 four out of 10 Mexican-born U.S. residents lived in Texas.

Similarly, Hispanics comprised much of the workforce in Pennsylvania and Ohio steel mills. They also were prevalent in copper and coal mines. In fact, approximately 45 percent of copper mine workers in the southwest were ethnic Mexican by 1927. Three years later, ethnic Mexican laborers supplanted Japanese workers in the citrus industry. By 1930, 40 percent of all ethnic Mexicans worked in farming. Agricultural work often included gathering cotton, beets, lettuce, and citrus fruit. Responsibilities in factories called for processing fresh fruit, dried fruit, and fruit cocktail. Canning and packing goods such as nuts, vegetables, beans, tomatoes, and pumpkin was commonplace. Additional low-paying positions disproportionately held by ethnic Mexicans included that of painter, store clerk, bookkeeper, food service worker, barber, craftsman, ditch-digger, janitor, machinist, laundry worker, and sewage services worker. A growing number of Hispanic women also found work in textile mills and domestic service as maids and housekeepers.

Nearly half a million Mexicans entered the United States in the 1920s, making up 12 percent of all U.S. immigration—more than any other national group. Coupled with an already sizable Mexican-American community, there was no shortage of Hispanic labor. With the United States experiencing a record expansion in manufacturing, Hispanic labor was in demand. Most Mexican immigrants were poor and uneducated farmers, craftsmen, and day workers. Because of this reality, many Americans assumed that all Mexican Americans were poor and uneducated, which in turn reinforced stereotypes about Hispanics. There were, however, a small number of businesspeople, intellectuals, journalists, and former elected officials who also found new homes in the

This Mexican woman accompanied by several children may have been part of the increased participation of Hispanic women in the U.S. workforce in the 1920s and 1930s. The group was returning home
by truck to the Rio Grande Valley after a stint as migrant cotton pickers in Mississippi in 1939.

United States. These educated immigrants were often responsible for spear-
heading community support organizations and Spanish-language newspapers
targeting middle-class Hispanics. Ignacio E. Lozano, for instance, founded *La
Opinión* in Los Angeles in 1926 after immigrating to San Antonio in 1908.

NEW IMMIGRATION PATTERNS

Hispanic immigrants in the 1920s settled not only in traditional southwest
regions like Texas, California, and Arizona, but also Midwestern and western
states. In fact, the Midwest Mexican-American population skyrocketed by
more than 600 percent during the decade. To cite one example, Chicago's
Mexican-American population increased from 4,000 to more than 20,000
between 1920 and 1930, making it the largest Hispanic urban community
beyond the southwest. Hispanics in Midwest urban settings shared a number
of common adjustment experiences akin to Polish, Irish, and Italian immigrants. Mexican Americans in Chicago developed their social acclimatization
strategies in part because of day-to-day encounters with prejudice. In contrast
to long-standing Mexican-American communities in the American southwest, Hispanics in Chicago were initially unaccustomed to inequitable and
antagonistic relations with other ethnic groups, notably Anglos. Coming to
terms with this ethno-racial dynamic compelled a generation of newly minted

This Mexican agricultural worker was working in the sugar beet fields of Minnesota in October 1937. In 1927, up to 95 percent of the beet workers in the Midwestern states of Michigan, Indiana, Minnesota, Colorado, Ohio, South Dakota, and North Dakota were Hispanic.

Chicagoans to reevaluate their worth in a society that only accepted upward mobility through "whiteness." Yet Chicago Hispanics worked to retain and develop a strong cultural identity, especially through participating in communal celebratory activities.

Hispanic culture also spread in Michigan, Indiana, Minnesota, Colorado, Ohio, and in South and North Dakota. By 1927 Hispanics made up as much as 95 percent of sugar beet workers in those states. States such as Wyoming, Oregon, and Washington also gained an appreciable number of Hispanics during the late 1920s. Even Alaskan fisheries called for ethnic Mexican labor, extending the Hispanic diaspora even farther. Like ethnic Cubans 30 or so years later, many Mexican immigrants intended to return home after finding work. Yet many inevitably forged new communities in the United States.

Other Hispanic subgroups, such as ethnic Cubans and Puerto Ricans, continued to journey to different pockets of America. A modest number of Cubans immigrated to Miami and Tampa during the 1920s as political refugees and hurricane survivors. Many joined the ranks of a small, but important group of tobacco workers. By the 1930s about 34,000 people of Cuban heritage relocated to the United States. With the passage of the Jones Act in 1917, which granted U.S. citizenship to all citizens of Puerto Rico,

The Paradox of the "Perfect Worker"

Characterized as cheap labor that needed little money for survival, Mexican Americans were often considered beasts of burden who personified the perfect worker because they were thought of as docile, dim, and separate from Anglos. Further, many believed that Mexican Americans belonged to a race that was both culturally and physiologically suited to perform the arduous manual labor required in the underbelly of American's workforce. Notwithstanding, some powerful forces in the agricultural world argued that Hispanics were lazy and incapable of doing as much work as others. W.H. Knox of the Arizona Cotton Growers' Association dismissed anti-Mexican worker worries by declaring to the U.S. House of Representatives in 1926:

Have you ever heard, in the history of the United States, or in the history of the human race, of the white race being overrun by a class of people of the mentality of the Mexicans? I never have. We took this country from Mexico. Mexico did not take it from us. To assume that there is any danger of any likelihood of the Mexican coming in here and colonizing this country and taking it away from us, to my mind, is absurd.

Within months of this declaration, countless agricultural leaders, including the Arizona Cotton Growers' Association, began lobbying for changes in immigration legislation so growers could have access to more ethnic Mexican laborers. This was especially important after the 1921 and 1924 U.S. immigration acts, because such legislation greatly reduced immigration from eastern and southern Europe, as well as Asia. Between 1926 and 1930, Mexican immigration was investigated by House and Senate committees, thereby leading to congressional hearings. A number of high-ranking officials representing the interests of railroads, mining, cattle, agricultural, and various manufacturing labor markets testified about the importance of ethnic Mexican labor to their overall prosperity. Many, however, questioned the logic of racial ordering with continued immigration of Mexicans and not southern and eastern Europeans.

the Puerto Rican population grew from a few thousand to roughly 55,000 by 1930. Ten years later the population increased by nearly 20,000 more. Many of these new citizens settled in cities such as Philadelphia, Chicago, Boston, Miami, New Orleans, and New York. The population of Puerto Ricans in New York City grew to nearly 7,500 by 1920 alone. East Harlem, also known as "Spanish Harlem," quickly became an effervescent cultural center for Puerto Rican history and life.

Not all Puerto Ricans migrated directly to urban regions in the United States. By the 1930s, U.S. agricultural businesses turned to Puerto Ricans for farm labor. Comparable to Cuban immigration, a number of Puerto Ricans came to the mainland because of natural disasters, such as a series of earthquakes in the fall of 1918, as well as a major hurricane 14 years later that encouraged migration to New York City. Although the Jones Act made Puerto Ricans instant citizens, it did not free them from the stigma of the "foreigner" label, mainly because much of American society did not differentiate one Hispanic subgroup from another. Another important source of Hispanic immigrants came from Spain. In the early 1920s a small number of Spaniards immigrated for economic reasons. By the late 1930s, many more immigrated to U.S. shores in order to avoid the turbulence of the Spanish Civil War (1936–39).

IMAGE, IDENTITY, AND IDEAS OF INCLUSION

Adding to the U.S. population, Hispanic immigrants were not welcomed by some, despite meaningful contributions in various labor markets. A rise in nativism, a philosophy that favored native inhabitants as opposed to immigrants, fueled the idea that foreigners were the main cause of the economic conditions facing Americans. This sentiment gave rise to proposed restrictive legislation in 1926 and 1930, which was intended to limit Mexican immigration. During this period anti-foreign ideas and practices began to exert greater force throughout America. People were defined ever more sharply on the basis of their nationality, language, religion, and ethnicity. Certain cultural groups were increasingly limited in their legal status, voting privileges, and the jobs they could obtain.

Degrading images of Hispanic subgroups such as Mexican Americans, Cubans, Puerto Ricans, and a smattering of Central and South Americans became part of popular culture in song, commerce, and illustrations in books, magazines, and media. Among the most common types of these images in the 1920s and 1930s were depictions of Uncle Sam as the national personification of the United States undermining Hispanics or the nations they represent, as well as a wide swath of other ethnic groups. These and other caricatures often characterized Hispanics in a negative way, such as the lazy Mexican at siesta, the corrupt dictator, the bandito, and the sexualized señorita. In one particular example, Uncle Sam showed up on the cover of the *Saturday Evening Post* during U.S. friction with Mexico, dealing with a diminutive, sombreroed bandito.

Scientists worsened the situation by filling scholarly journals and books with alleged evidence of the superiority of the "Caucasoid race." Citing the size and weight of bones of various groups while comparing Hispanics with each other and with indigenous Latin Americans, scientists unwittingly subverted Hispanic heritage. Founded on poor science, this scholarship indulged the researchers' fascination with factors irrelevant to intelligence, such as the skull and jaw projection. Popular attitudes and culture, combined with these one-dimensional images, indirectly allowed many Anglo men to preserve the most stable, well-paying, and appealing jobs for themselves. While circulating ideas suggesting the inferiority of Hispanics and other cultures, some Anglos felt not only justified in calling Hispanics derogatory names like "greaser" or "wetback," but also to ban them from the rights of citizenship, landownership, and elected government. Like African Americans, Hispanics could not testify in court against Anglos or marry outside their heritage without severe repercussions, and had to show unwavering deference to Anglos.

LABOR CONDITIONS AND GROWING ACTIVISM

U.S. employers exercised substantial control over Hispanic workers, "breaking them in" to become pliant, obedient, and committed to helping the overall enterprise. Through company stores, Hispanic laborers could be kept in a system of debt peonage, dependent on the owners for life's necessities. By keeping wages low and prices high, ownership and management kept Hispanic laborers in a perpetual state of debt, with no hope of raises or promotions. Instead of being free-wage laborers like many others, Hispanics worked under a system of labor repression characterized by a dual-wage system, limited job mobility, occupational segregation, and reserve labor status. Hispanics were also called upon to log more hours in dangerous conditions.

Withheld or low wages resulted in children working to help their parents financially. In doing so, children often missed school as child labor laws were ignored. As Hispanic families moved regularly, children often bounced from district to district. On average, migrant children who did attend school seldom advanced beyond the third or fourth grade. One of the

A caravan of Mexican-American workers protesting wage cuts and eviction from labor camps during the 1933 San Joaquin Valley Cotton Strike in Corcoran, California.

most important Hispanic leaders in U.S. history, César Chávez, was deeply influenced by his own childhood experiences in the 1930s. At the age of 10 in 1937, Chávez lived in overcrowded facilities with no running water or electricity, surviving by picking cotton, grapes, and carrots. Working alongside his family in the fields, and helping with chores such as sowing crops, chopping wood, and feeding animals, Chávez never went beyond the seventh grade. Because of his family's migrations, he attended some 50 schools across California.

Hispanics were often forced to retire early due to long-term exhaustion and permanent injury. Some engaged in heavy labor in 115-degree heat, while others died premature deaths due to unhealthy working conditions that included a lack of ventilation in mining shafts, and exposure to high levels of radioactive dust particles. Machinery also exposed them to toxic particulate matter, which led to black lung disease and other respiratory ailments. Even in open fields, Hispanics were subject to pesticide misuse. A generation later, however, the agricultural establishment was compelled to address issues of pesticide irresponsibility as well as reasonable wages, humane work, and living conditions.

Anglo workers resented Mexican-American workers in large part because of concerns that they would take their jobs, and so prohibited them from gaining membership in Anglo unions. However, new labor organizations arose to safeguard Hispanic rights. The Confederation of Mexican Labor Unions (CFLU) was created in 1927 to champion equal pay and end all discriminatory practices. At its apex, the CFLU encompassed 20 chapters and more than 3,000 members. Luisa Moreno, a Guatemala native, was especially active in fighting for the rights of Hispanic workers by organizing labor unions and strikes across the nation. Moreno's pan-ethnic approach was truly groundbreaking, as she successfully orchestrated the first Congress of Spanish-Speaking People in 1939.

ORGANIZED HATE GROUPS

Throughout the 1920s, Hispanics were not just occupationally challenged, but also troubled by organized intolerance groups, namely the Ku Klux Klan (KKK). Formed in 1866 and reestablished in 1915, it took less than a decade for the Klan, under the national direction of Dallas dentist Hiram Evans, to resurface. Spreading chapters throughout the southwest, the Klan established especially strong roots in Texas and Arizona. At its highest point, as many as 40,000 members belonged to the Texas Klan. Phoenix was the first home of the KKK in Arizona. In the spring of 1921, the first Klan recruiter arrived, and on June 7, the Klan publicly announced its reemergence in the *Arizona Republican*. According to Evans, the intention of a Klan chapter in Arizona was to band "together for the purpose of preserving, protecting, and promulgating the principles of genuine Americanism." Between 1921 and 1925 Klan activity spread from the cities of Phoenix, Tucson, and Flagstaff to smaller towns, including rural and mining areas of Arizona, such as Globe-Miami, Glendale, Tempe, and Prescott.

During this time Arizona, along with the rest of the country, was adjusting to many trends from the previous decades such as urbanization, industrialization, and mechanization. In addition, societal changes such as women's suffrage, the immigration of a large number of Catholics and Jews, prohibition, the ensuing increase of bootlegging and gambling, and a variety of political developments gave many citizens the desire to reverse the changes that had come to America. Unfortunately, this longing led some to become vulnerable to the ideology of the Ku Klux Klan. Some joined the Klan because they believed they were upholding decency and traditional values, while others joined because it was economically and politically expedient. Others joined because it presented opportunities to commit crimes against African Americans, Hispanics, Catholics, and Jews.

By 1925 there were five million Klan members, and their presence was felt almost everywhere. The Arizona Klan wanted more law enforcement, and to contain the growth of the Mexican American population, whose Catholicism was threatening to Klan leadership. Klan membership reached all segments of Arizona society—from the secretary of state to newspaper editors and town mayors. By 1922 more than one-third of Phoenix's residents were Klan members, which included several elected officials and superior court judges. With this widespread power, many Mexican Americans were harassed at their jobs and homes. Since many Klan members were working in management at the mines, they used their positions to discriminate against Hispanic miners.

Often this prejudice violated private space, such as when the Klan burned crosses outside of homes. Mexican Americans were also the first racial group lynched in a number of southwestern states, hanged by the hundreds in every part of the southwest as late as the 1930s. Hispanic men, women, and children were vulnerable to the fury of lynch mobs on the most flimsy pretext. As with African Americans, victims were sometimes singled out for being too assertive, or for refusing to show deference to Anglos.

The KKK in Arizona and throughout the American southwest had a short, yet active life. The Klan spread hate and racial rhetoric among not only ordinary residents, but also among the political hierarchy and other organizations. With the slogan, "Native, White, Protestant Supremacy," the Klan attracted aid from several groups. The Masons, for example, were staunch advocates for Klan initiatives, spreading Klan rhetoric through their publication, the *Independent*. However, by 1930, the national Klan organization was in disarray as a series of internal power struggles and sordid scandals eroded support for Klan leadership.

HISPANICS IN THE GREAT DEPRESSION

All the boom-time hope, promise, and illusions of the 1920s imploded in the stock market crash of October 1929 and subsequent depression, which adversely impacted all Americans. Hispanics endured even greater discrimination throughout the depression-plagued 1930s, and the flow of immigration from Mexico slowed. Historians and economists agree that the causes of the Great Depression were various—overproduction of goods and food, high prices, low wages, overexpansion of credit, excessive profits and unequal distribution of wealth, and a grossly inflated stock market.

The Great Depression tested Americans' faith in the federal government to a degree unmatched in U.S. history. It shaped culture, political life, and new public policies, and brought about a sense of shared hardship during a time of national crisis. In 1929 there were 1.6 million Americans out of work, representing 3.2 percent of the workforce. Three years later that figure jumped to 12.1 million, or 24 percent. Wages dropped from 35 cents an hour to roughly 14 cents, and in some cases, down to 10 cents. In 1932 the *New York Times* projected that out of 2.5 million ethnic Mexicans in the United States, two million were unemployed.

The majority of families maintained at least some source of income during the Depression, but it was often severely reduced, causing the average

A Mexican-American boy playing guitar in a makeshift home made from a converted animal corral in Robstown, Texas, where living conditions for Mexican-Americans were poor in the late 1930s.

Depression Life

American labor and civil rights leader Humberto Noé "Bert" Corona recalls life during the Depression in 1934 in El Paso, Texas:

I remember the 1929 crash … I didn't understand what radio and newspaper accounts of the crisis meant for the daily life of people. But I recall that as 1930 came on, the layoffs began in El Paso … People's wages were cut … Jobs became harder and harder to find; there were many unemployed. By the end of 1930 and the beginning of 1931, we saw all the manifestations of a severe economic crisis in El Paso … The election of FDR, however, changed the political climate … The New Deal opened up programs such as the CWA [Civil Works Administration] in El Paso. These work programs provided single men with dormitories and camps where they were housed and fed. The men kept the places clean. They worked if there was work. In the camps, they had recreational activities. They also had discussion groups. Two or three of those camps were opened in El Paso not very far from where I lived, on Anglie and Missouri streets above the second layer of railroad tracks. We lived adjacent to the tracks in a row of houses. This was between 1931 and 1935, the pit of the depression.

Throughout the Depression, federal programs reported countless incidents of racial bias. This reiterated the notion that Hispanics were a threat to labor and social programs, which caused the repatriation of legal citizens (and the expatriation of their American-born children), as well as the banishment of deep-rooted Mexican-American families to south of the Rio Grande. Thousands upon thousands of ethnic Mexicans were sent to Mexico as rights of citizenship were discarded, and families were put on trains that carried them down into an even more economically depressed Mexico. So pervasive were the deportations that they prompted a 1932 U.S. government commission to acknowledge that they were "unconstitutional, tyrannic and oppressive."

The relocation movement of Mexican nationals and Mexican Americans continued throughout the 1930s and 1940s, as those who could not find jobs—or who were no longer needed after seasonal work—were deported to Mexico or pushed across state borders into other unwelcoming states. Relocation is as much a part of the culture and history of Mexican Americans as it is to most Native-American tribes. An estimated 500,000 ethnic Mexicans, many of them legal U.S. residents or American citizens by birth, crossed unwillingly into Mexico. Those who were fortunate to remain in their homes were frequently dropped entirely from public assistance. Perhaps with the exception of the wartime internment of Japanese Americans, the treatment of ethnic Mexicans during the 1930s and 1940s was one of the worst violations of civil liberties by the American government.

citizen to struggle. It took its toll in all areas of the economy; for example, in cattle production, because many Americans could not afford to buy beef. The employment rate in America sunk to an all-time low, and many states fell millions of dollars in debt. Sixty percent of Mexican Americans throughout the southwest were out of work and on public relief, whereas 10 percent of Anglos received such aid. As a result of layoffs, many Hispanics lost their homes. Historian Francisco E. Balderrama wrote, "Many families not only lacked food but also shelter because they were unable to pay rent or mortgages." Homeless and hungry, many Hispanics resorted to gathering wild greens and fruits that were usually fed to cattle. With a stark number of Hispanics dealing with chronic diarrhea and tuberculosis, even sifting through garbage was an option if it soothed hunger.

RESPONSES TO THE DEPRESSION

As the demand for public relief grew, the trend reversed as increasingly more Anglos began to receive public assistance versus Hispanics. In Phoenix, out-of-work minority citizens came up against the Community Welfare League, comprised of 22 Anglo civic agencies, which would not offer them aid. In such cases, Hispanic support organizations such as the League of United Latin American Citizens (LULAC) tried to help. Established in 1929, with its mostly middle-class, educated, American-born membership, LULAC fought for equality for all Mexican-American citizens while providing college scholarships. LULAC successfully campaigned for the U.S. Census Bureau to reclassify Mexican heritage peoples from the racial designation of "Mexican" to "white." This movement was guided largely by the idea that if Hispanics were seen as "white," they would be better protected from racial discrimination. However, this change, which saw the eventual erasure of the separate racial category of "Mexican" in the 1930 census, did little to persuade Americans that ethnic Mexicans were not a racially inferior, nonwhite group.

Other Hispanic subgroups were adversely impacted by the challenging economic times as well. As unemployment increased, so did the rise in crime, especially in New York City. This growing criminal element was aided by seasoned criminals who purchased Puerto Rican birth certificates in order to gain illegal entry into the United States. The cost of these bogus birth certificates was about $500, and close to 2,000 were sold. Legitimate Puerto Rican citizens bore the brunt of this illegal arrangement, as some blamed them for the city's spike in crimes. This resulted in greater disdain for Puerto Rican culture, and growing racial violence throughout the 1930s.

U.S. government programs eventually helped offset some of the problems caused by the Depression. Under President Franklin D. Roosevelt, the government created many jobs for all Americans. Hispanics, especially Mexican Americans, Puerto Ricans, and Cuban Americans, benefited from jobs con-

Spinning wool by a fire in Trampas, New Mexico. The southwest was especially hard hit by the Depression, with 60 percent of Mexican Americans unemployed in the region.

structing roads, buildings, bridges, public schools, housing units, and parks. Roosevelt's New Deal programs also opened up additional jobs for Hispanics, such as planting trees for forests and surveying land. These jobs, however, were open to noncitizens only until 1937, when a change in policy barred them from working on public works projects. The election of the first Hispanic to the U.S. Senate in 1936—Dennis Chávez (Democrat–New Mexico)— gave Hispanics a formative voice that advocated greater job opportunities as well. Because of Roosevelt's efforts and Chávez's stature, a sizable number of Hispanics pledged their allegiance to the Democratic Party, fostering a secure base for decades to come.

SEGREGATION

The majority opinion throughout the 1920s and 1930s was that Hispanics had to be controlled, and that the best way to accomplish this was through

Dorothea Lange photographed this group of Mexican women and a boy who were waiting to enter the United States at the immigration station at El Paso, Texas, in June 1938.

a continued policy of segregation. Whether by de facto or de jure segregation, Hispanics, especially Mexican Americans in the southwest, often found themselves separated in places as wide-ranging as movie theaters, public and government facilities, restaurants, barbershops, swimming pools, churches, dance halls, social and country clubs, hotels, housing, hospitals, drinking fountains, cemeteries, university cafeterias and dormitories, and the public educational system. Wherever ethnic Mexicans lived or worked in large numbers, segregation was the rule rather than the exception. Enforcing this written or unwritten mandate, Hispanics regularly encountered signs and placards posted that warned: "For Whites—Mexicans Keep Out"; "Mexicans and Negroes Stay Out"; "We Serve Whites Only No Spanish or Mexicans"; and "No Mexicans or Dogs."

Swimming pools and places of worship were fixtures in the Hispanic community, so to be refused entry or at best only be permitted to occupy a non-

Mexican Repatriation

Throughout the 1930s, Hispanics comprised roughly 47 percent of all people deported, and yet they constituted only about 1 percent of the total U.S. population. With the help of social welfare agencies, including the Red Cross, nearly 1,800 ethnic Mexicans were deported from the Tucson area alone. Katherine F. Lenroot, reporting on the social and economic repercussions of forcing Mexican-heritage citizens out of the United States in the region of Nogales, Arizona, in 1943, wrote: "Children of repatriated Mexican parents, including many American-born children are causing great concern to the welfare authorities in these areas. It was reported that some 15,000 such children with their parents went through Nogales, Arizona, just across the border from Nogales, Mexico, on their way back to Mexico. Many of these children have drifted back to the United States, particularly older children, and are living from hand to mouth in Arizona."

From 1930 to 1939, one-sixth of all people of Mexican ancestry were repatriated to Mexico. The heaviest years of repatriation unfolded from 1929 to 1932. In November 1931 alone, nearly 21,000 Hispanics were deported. The largest numbers came from Texas, California, Indiana, Illinois, and Michigan. New Mexico was the only southwestern state that did not aggressively pursue the deportation of its Hispanic citizens. This was due to their long-established communities that underscored their "Spanish" ancestry rather than their indigenous heritage, which translated into solid political support. The threat of "deportation roundups" by the U.S. Immigration Service compelled many Hispanics from the southwest and Midwest to voluntarily return to Mexico. In the end, the 1930s marked a decade when more people of Mexican descent returned to Mexico than moved to the United States.

Anglo section of a church was both frustrating and inconvenient. A common practice granted Hispanics guarded permission to swim in public YMCA pools on Saturdays after a week of public swimming, before the YMCA drained and cleaned the pool so it would be fit for the public during the upcoming week. Instead of using public facilities, Hispanics occasionally turned to canals and rivers for swimming. As for churches, Hispanics fought segregation in separate facilities, such as the requirement that Spanish-language mass be held only in the basement of St. Mary's Catholic Church in Phoenix, Arizona, in 1915. "Mexicans *abajo!*" (Mexicans below!)—was a command Hispanics heard throughout the 1920s and 1930s. In Chicago, churches refused to allow Hispanics into their churches at all.

Father Novatus Benzing of Phoenix's St. Mary's Church, whose actions beginning in 1915 infuriated the Hispanic community in the area, asserted that "As all the world knows, Mexicans tenaciously adhere to their own language and customs, and will not amalgamate ... Nor will the American people put up with the untidiness of the majority of Mexican peons that continually come up from Mexico." This outlook with captions that commonly stated, "Mexicans, Go Home," was reiterated by numerous editorials from local periodicals to newspapers with a national reputation. In May 1930 the *New York Times* ran an editorial that read: "It is folly to pretend that Mexicans, who are largely of Indian blood, can be absorbed and incorporated into the American race." It reflected the prejudice that held that mixed-race people were impulsive, unstable, and prone to mental illnesses, and the fear that these characteristics might enter the American gene pool through miscegenation.

SEPARATE SCHOOLING

During the 1930s several seminal studies pertaining to the educational conditions of Hispanic children were published that indicated Hispanics received a second-rate education. Educational neglect of Hispanics was aided through segregation and insensitive practices. Unlike many of its southern neighbors, which carried out stringent segregation laws impacting mostly African Americans, legal education segregation impacting Hispanics in the southwest was not uniform, but varied from state to state and community to community. As a result, school separation in the southwest has been largely neglected in mainstream scholarship, while segregation in the southern and northern United States is well documented. By 1930, 85 percent of Hispanic children in the southwest were in either separate classrooms, or exclusively segregated schools.

Districts that encouraged the separation of Hispanic students established separate schools, universally dubbed "Mexican schools." Mexican schools lacked adequate indoor and outdoor resources, teachers, classroom space, materials, special services, facilities, and up-to-date gymnasiums. Mexican school students frequently lacked textbooks, yet occasionally were given a disproportionate number of outdated and worn textbooks discarded by mainstream schools.

Even without official segregation mandates, other subtle methods were just as effective in denying equal education access. Scholastic strategies such as special education, ability and discipline grouping, curriculum tracking, linguistic lessons, and "Americanization" classes were used to separate Hispanic students from their Anglo classmates. A generation of Hispanics concentrated on civics, hygiene, home economics, and anything else associated with making Hispanics disciplined, domesticated, and docile. The practice of placing Hispanics in slower-learning classes rose significantly in the 1920s, and intensified in later years. These classes, although sometimes housed on Anglo school property, still segregated Mexican Americans by establishing "Mexican" buildings, rooms, sections, and facilities. Teachers, aides, and administrators were routinely insensitive to Hispanic culture, often reprimanding students if they spoke Spanish or brought food or clothing reflecting their culture.

During the years leading up to World War II, Puerto Ricans also endured educational challenges that impeded academic progress. Their concern over public schools inspired the creation of organizations such as the Puerto Rican association Madres y Padres Pro Niños Hispanos (Mothers and Fathers in Support of Hispanic Children). This organization disputed school officials' use of intelligence testing, which channeled Puerto Rican children into classrooms for allegedly "backward" children, rather than appreciating inherent language bias in such testing. As a result of these experiences, Hispanics often dropped out before reaching high school. Such prejudice remained fairly static, which prevented many Hispanics from fully developing their talents during the 1920s and 1930s, and thereafter.

COMMUNITY ORGANIZATIONS

Living in isolated enclaves, Mexican Americans and Puerto Ricans fostered a shared cultural comfort zone, which encouraged unity. As communities expanded, this cohesion was fostered by Hispanic entrepreneurs, who established various stores filled with cultural goods, religious articles, and festive clothing. Restaurants also sprung up, serving a number of traditional foods, while other businesses increasingly accommodated Hispanics. As with other Americans shunned by the public, Hispanics incrementally created their own eateries, barbershops, and civic agencies to address their interests and needs. In an unfriendly cultural world of the 1920s and 1930s, ancestry connections served as a calming force in dealing with episodes of exploitation.

These cultural connections eventually evolved into mutual aid, or self-help organizations. People of all levels of education, occupations, legal status, and central interests were members of *mutualistas*. Some mutual aid societies were created by women for women, while others appealed either to working-class or middle-class people. Hispanic fellowship organizations not only offered financial support and legal advice and services in times of uncertainty, but also offered temporary housing, start-up business loans, medical or life insurance, and resources to confront patterns of segregation and discrimination. In the book *Hispanics and the Nonprofit Sector* (1991), scholar Miguel Tirado underscores the importance of mutualistas during this early period by quoting a 1928 document: "these societies represented the only continuous organized life among Mexicans in which the initiative come wholly from the Mexicans themselves."

Along the way, these grassroots organizations sponsored cultural activities and petitioned government leadership for much-needed social services. Some even organized schools because public schools were unresponsive to

A couple performing a traditional Spanish-American dance in Taos, New Mexico, during a street festival in 1940. Such events reinforced community pride in the face of discrimination.

their students' needs. Although most of these mutual aid societies lacked political clout, thereby limiting their efforts to create substantive change, the creation of such organizations sent a message to broader society that Hispanics were mobilizing in order to defend themselves. By the late 1920s, organizations sometimes called La Liga Protectora Mexicana (The Mexican Protective League) developed across the country. To avoid prejudice, many within the mutual aid organizations abandoned the word *Mexican* and embraced the term *Latin American*. Across the southwest there were a number of Latin American support groups with a mostly Mexican-American membership.

Confronting racial injustices, Puerto Ricans also sought the refuge of a unified, community support system. In New York City, organizations such as La Liga Puertorriqueña e Hispana (The Puerto Rican and Hispanic League) were founded to bridge solidarity among and between Puerto Ricans and other Hispanics. These organizations not only challenged racial intolerance, but also enriched the social and cultural lives of working-class Hispanics. Puerto Ricans in Philadelphia and Hawaii also created flourishing support organizations. The Puerto Rican Civic Club (PRCC) of Hawaii was established in 1931. From social groups to religious associations, Puerto Ricans came together to share and exchange advice, ideas, and resources. As the Philadelphia Hispanic population increased, Puerto Ricans and other Hispanics began to organize their own churches. With Venezuelan and ethnic Cuban and Mexican families moving to Philadelphia from New York, interdenominational places of worship increased.

These gatherings led to a rich tapestry of recreational events like dances, concerts, picnics, graduation celebrations, theater groups, and sports. For example, the Mexican Independence Club, the largest mutual aid society in Santa Barbara, California, had its own amateur baseball team. In communities large and small, sports served as an important coping mechanism and offered an escape from the pressure of striving for acceptance and acculturation. For many Hispanics, finding success and enjoyment on a playing field encouraged them to believe that achievement in the larger aspects of their lives was attainable.

At their peak, almost every community with an appreciable Hispanic presence housed at least one mutual aid society, with some neighborhoods having as many as a dozen or more. However, most mutual aid organizations were financially strapped by the mid-1930s, which limited their ability to help people. Hispanics also drew on the strength of family as a support network against a demanding and indifferent society. Whether they were Puerto Rican, Mexican American, Dominican, ethnic Cuban, or Central or South American, Hispanics used family as a vehicle to preserve customs and culture.

CONCLUSION

By striving for housing opportunities as well as economic and political liberties, Hispanics in early-20th-century America challenged the way that shades of color and levels of income traditionally bestowed different racial privileges. In the 1920s and 1930s, Hispanics forged the way toward asserting their worker and civil rights. It was a step toward creating not only a more pluralistic society, but also toward moving Hispanic citizenship from the margins to the middle. These years were crucial in shaping identity and community coalitions among Hispanics from places as different as Kansas City and New York City.

For many Hispanics, the 1920s represented a decade of immigrant adjustment, whereas the 1930s were a period of assimilation as hyphenated Americans. By the brink of World War II, Hispanic immigrants and their children maintained, in modified character, some of their traditional cultural traits while either directly or indirectly giving way to some of America's cultural characteristics. In turn, Mexican-American, Cuban-American, and Puerto Rican subcultures developed, with attributes from both American and Hispanic cultural norms, but whose arrangement was unique and distinctive from either "Hispanic" or "American" cultures. Toward the end of the Depression era, more and more Hispanics were graduating from high school, and like all Americans were dreaming of better days. Coupled with unprecedented community growth, this raised expectations about the brand of citizenship they experienced. In turn, second-generation Hispanics, especially those from the

Mexican-American generation, set in motion groundbreaking civil rights litigation, legislation, and organizational activities, and participated in an unparalleled level of military service in the next decade.

DARIUS V. ECHEVERRÍA
RUTGERS UNIVERSITY

Further Reading

Acosta-Belén, Edna and Carlos E. Santiago. *Puerto Ricans in the United States: A Contemporary Portrait.* Boulder, CO: Lynne Rienner, 2006.

Alvarez, Robert. "The Lemon Grove Incident: The Nation's First Successful Desegregation Court Case." *Journal of San Diego History,* spring 1986.

Arredondo, Gabriela F. *Mexican Chicago: Race, Identity, and Nation 1916–1939.* Chicago, IL: University of Illinois Press, 2008.

Balderama, Francisco E., and Raymond Rodríguez. *Decade of Betrayal: Mexican Repatriation in the 1930s.* Albuquerque, NM: University of New Mexico Press, 1995.

Cardoso, Lawrence A. *Mexican Emigration to the United States, 1897–1931.* Tucson, AZ: University of Arizona Press, 1980.

Carrigan, William D. "The Lynching of Persons of Mexican Origin or Descent in the United States, 1848 to 1928." *Journal of Social History,* Vol. 37, No. 2, winter 2003.

Carter, Thomas P. *Mexican Americans in Schools: A History of Educational Neglect.* New York: College Entrance Examination, 1970.

Gallagos, Herman, and Michael O'Neill. *Hispanics and the Nonprofit Sector.* New York: Foundation Center, 1991.

García, Juan Ramón. *Mexicans in the Midwest, 1900–1932.* Tucson, AZ: University of Arizona Press, 1996.

———. *Operation Wetback: The Mass Deportation of Mexican Undocumented Workers in 1954.* Westport, CT: Greenwood Press, 1980.

García, Richard A. *Rise of the Mexican American Middle Class: San Antonio, 1929–1941.* College Station, TX: Texas A&M University Press, 1991.

González, Gilbert G. *Chicano Education in the Era of Segregation.* Philadelphia, PA: The Balch Institute Press, 1990.

González, José Amaro. *Mutual Aid for Survival: The Case of the Mexican-American.* Malabar, FL: Robert E. Krieger Publishing Company, 1983.

Guerin-González, Camille. *Mexican Workers and American Dreams, Immigration, Repatriation, and California Farm Labor, 1900–1939.* New Brunswick, NJ: Rutgers University Press, 1994.

Hays, David M. "Drawn from the Same Inkwells: Cartoons, Ethnic Stereotypes, and Uncle Sam" Available online, URL: www2.uah.es/asi /stereo/hays.htm. Accessed March 7, 2009.

Hernández, Jose Amaro. *Mutual Aid for Survival: The Case of the Mexican-American*. Malabar, FL: Robert E. Krieger Publishing Co., 1983.

Hoffman, Abraham. *Unwanted Mexican Americans in the Great Depression: Repatriation Pressures, 1929–1939*. Tucson, AZ: University of Arizona Press, 1974.

Luján, Roy. "Dennis Chavez and the National Agenda: 1933–1946." *New Mexico Historical Review,* Vol. 74, January 1999.

Márquez, Benjamin. *LULAC: The Evolution of a Mexican American Political Organization.* Austin, TX: University of Texas Press, 1993.

Reisler, Mark. *By the Sweat of Their Brow: Mexican Immigrant Labor in the United States, 1900–1940.* New York: Greenwood Press, 1976.

Rosales, F. Arturo. *Pobre Raza: Violence, Justice, and Mobilization Among México Lindo Immigrants, 1900–1936.* Austin, TX: University of Texas Press, 1999.

Sánchez, George J. *Becoming Mexican American: Ethnicity, Culture and Identity in Chicano Los Angeles, 1900–1945.* Oxford: Oxford University Press, 1993.

Vargas, Zaragosa. *Labor Rights are Civil Rights: Mexican American Workers in Twentieth-Century America.* Princeton, NJ: Princeton University Press, 2005.

CHAPTER 7

World War II and the Forties: 1939 to 1949

OUT OF THE decade of the Great Depression, Mexican Americans, the largest population of Hispanics in the United States at the time, emerged from the painful reality of what they symbolized to much of the European-white majority in the country: a foreign, unwanted population. With the forced migration or "voluntary" repatriation of over two million Mexican-American women and men—more than 60 percent of whom had been born in the United States—the 1930s was a period when being Mexican American meant being perceived as someone who was not loyal enough to be a full citizen of the country, much as Japanese Americans would be viewed during America's war with Japan. This perception of Mexican Americans as less legitimate citizens, or less American, intensified during World War II. Repatriated Mexican Americans were ambivalent in Mexico, no longer feeling as though they belonged in the country of their origin.

The U.S. Census Bureau had yet to make up its mind about how to classify and account for peoples of Mexican descent and other Hispanics. In 1930, while acknowledging that many Hispanics were legally "white," the Census Bureau designated "Mexican" as a separate race alongside the other categories of "white," "colored," Indian, Chinese, and Japanese. In 1940, however, the census listed Hispanics under the "white" category. To this day, many polling forms differentiate—or give the respondent the option to differentiate—

between "white" and "white (of Hispanic origin)." In popular speech, both among Hispanics and among Americans of other ethnicities, Hispanics were often the "brown" that existed between "white" and "black."

Despite the challenges Hispanics faced in the 1930s, in the following decade Mexican Americans forged new identities and communities, and fought for their rights. They successfully challenged institutional discrimination in housing, public facilities, and education in federal courts. With the advent of World War II, urban struggles with youth culture and identity, and a national need for a migratory agricultural labor force from Mexico, the 1940s ushered in a new Mexican-American cultural identity. This was to be the decade of the rise of Mexican Americans as a national ethnic group, as well as the advent of the first large wave of Puerto Rican migrants. Although there were also other Hispanics of Central and South American and Caribbean descent, these populations were not numerically significant when compared to Mexicans and Puerto Ricans. Mexican Americans and Puerto Ricans in the 1940s established or strengthened cultural, religious, political, and social institutions of their own, firmly marking their place in the United States.

WORLD WAR II

More than any other event, World War II shaped the lives of hundreds of thousands of Hispanics. The year before the United States entered the war in December 1941, census estimates put the number of "resident Mexican aliens" at around 380,000, and "Mexican Americans," those with at least one parent born in Mexico, at approximately 700,000. Interestingly, according to the same 1940 census, more than 86 percent of the legal resident aliens did not indicate a preference to become naturalized U.S. citizens, demonstrating a relative ambivalence about U.S. citizenship. For Puerto Ricans, 1940 census estimates put their total number in the United States at about 70,000, rising to over 225,000 by 1950. Legal U.S. citizenship was no longer a struggle for them, as Congress had declared them U.S. citizens in 1917.

World War II offered both opportunities and challenges for Hispanics. They were part of the labor force required to send, arm, protect, clothe, feed, and nurse the more than 16 million U.S. citizens and residents who eventually served in the war. However, discriminatory policies did not allow Hispanics to enter the better positions in industry, defense, and warfare. Distrust of foreigners in the country—marked enduringly by the internment of about 120,000 Japanese nationals and Japanese Americans—also targeted many nonwhite Americans, Hispanics included. Racial violence against young women and men of Mexican descent, for example, took place in many of the nation's cities, including Chicago, Detroit, and Los Angeles.

In the popular imagination, memories of World War II have privileged the experiences of white women and men. Video documentaries and museum and library exhibits continue to underrepresent Hispanic contributions. Yet it has been estimated that anywhere from 250,000 to as many as 750,000 Hispanic men and women served in the armed forces during the war (the hazy nature of ethnic identification on official forms accounts for the range of the estimate here). Among their numbers were 13 Hispanic recipients of the Congressional Medal of Honor.

Wartime industries and shipyards also recruited some Central Americans on the West Coast, specifically San Francisco. Mainly Salvadorans and Nicaraguans, these early migrants did not constitute large numbers, but they did begin to settle in neighborhoods that became the foundation for larger communities in later decades. More than 53,000 Puerto Ricans also served in the U.S. military during World War II. Although both women and men served, Puerto Rican women were restricted to administrative positions and nursing. Men served in segregated "Puerto Rican units," unless they resided in the mainland or were fluent in English.

Soldiers of the U.S. Army's 65th Infantry taking a break in Salinas, Puerto Rico, in August 1941, before the United States entered the war. During World War II over 53,000 Puerto Ricans served in the U.S. military, many in segregated "Puerto Rican units."

Reflections of José "Joe" Solís Ramírez

As part of the U.S. Latino & Latina WWII Oral History Project, José "Joe" Solís Ramírez was interviewed in El Paso, Texas, on February 2, 2002, by Andrea Shearer.

I remember I was in a school in Kiowa, Kansas, and I was sitting in this desk that didn't have no desk in front, just a chair. And there was a white girl behind me, beautiful girl. I didn't know what to say. I didn't know how to speak English then . . . She used to pull my hair . . . I wouldn't even look around, just let her pull my hair. 'Til one day she says, "You know, my name is Gail." and I said, "Ok, me José." We never spoke any Spanish once we got going to school. My brothers and friends, we all spoke English. I remember my brother and I, we was home listenin' to radio. My li'l boy Robert, he was a li'l' baby and I had him in a crib. It was cold outside and all of a sudden the radio stopped playin' songs and we heard President Roosevelt announce that we were at war. We felt pretty bad, but we couldn't do anything 'til we got called to go to the service. We were all just like a family. Even the captain would sit down and eat with us. When I came back I bumped 22 guys to get the job that I wanted. And that didn't sit too well with the ones I had to bump! I used to tell the rest of the veterans, the Mexican boys, "Why don't you join the American Legion? It's good for ya's!" And some of 'em said, "Aw, who cares! They're a bunch of gringos!' So I told the commander, "they don't wanna join your legion 'cause y'all are too many gringos here." So he says, "Ok, well, why don't you organize one for your Spanish people?" So I did! I got 15 guys, they paid their dues; we made the application and we got our license! When I returned [to El Paso], I found people different around here. The Latin people are noticing that they can come out and vote, be a candidate, and have businesses, which they never could before. If it keeps goin' like that the Latin people are gonna really be seen in this country.

The immediate postwar period brought many opportunities for Puerto Rican women and men. Contracted workers arrived via windowless cargo planes, in what was likely the first airborne migration of laborers to the United States. While men were contracted to work in canneries, women were hired as domestic workers.

THE BRACEROS PROGRAM

For the nation's Mexican and Mexican-American population, World War II ushered in tremendous growth and change in their communities. As was the case for Puerto Ricans, it was the nation's growing labor demands that served as a magnet for hundreds of thousands of Mexicans. In 1942, the fed-

Mexican farm labor recruits on a train headed for work in sugar beet fields in the Arkansas Valley, Colorado, Nebraska, and Minnesota in May 1943.

eral government announced the Emergency Farm Labor Program, designed to import experienced agricultural workers from Mexico to help harvests, but eventually to also help maintain railroads. Better known as the *Bracero* program, from the Spanish word for arm, *brazo*, which referred to the workers' laboring arms, the program first contracted 500 Mexican workers who arrived in Stockton, California, in September 1942. During that year a total of 4,189 eventually arrived, peaking at 62,091 in 1944. Over 200,000 had worked in the United States by 1947, more than half in corporate farms in California. Despite Mexican-American protests that the program helped keep wages low, the program continued through 1964 with growing, undeniable accusations of labor and human rights abuses. More than 2.5 million people, mostly men, were braceros, working on average between six to 12 months a year.

Labor corruption, worker abuse, and human rights violations were part of the program from the beginning. Texan racism against Mexicans, and Mexican Americans in particular, was so blatant that the Mexican government officially banned the exportation of braceros to Texas from June 1943 until 1947, citing the extreme forms of discrimination Mexican nationals faced in the

Mexican laborers cutting sugar beets near Stockton, California, in May 1943. The first groups of braceros had arrived in Stockton the previous fall.

Liborio Santiago Pérez

In 2002 at age 77, Liborio Santiago Pérez narrated his journey from Oaxaca, Mexico to Northern California, searching for a better livelihood. This oral recollection was documented by the Bracero History Archive.

I was in Oaxaca shopping and there was talk about American agents contracting people to harvest fields [in the United States]. World War II was raging on heavily. I was very young [19], so I struggled to have the Americans contract me. You needed to line up for everything. The contracting center was in Guanajuato. They checked your hands. And I answered them: about what fields were like, how you use a bull yoke. I passed all their tests and they gave me a contract. I went through Ciudad Juarez. Once in the United States ranchers and farmers came to ask for us. They discounted money for all expenses from my checks. It was a dream for us, to wonder where we would work, how everything would be there [in the United States]. They won the war also because of us. What we did counted a lot. Without the harvests, how would they eat, how would they sustain themselves, who would help them? It is not just that they treat us this way. I am thinking about those of us who went in the middle of the war. We helped here [in Mexico] and we helped there [in the United States], on both sides. My first job was in a huge cattle ranch. After San Francisco they took us to Santa Rosa. There were many Filipinos there; then, they spoke Spanish. One felt bad leaving [Mexico]. You leave your family, your friends. Everything was rationed. They used a stamp system. If you wanted shoes, they would tear off some stamps. If you wanted to purchase meat, yet more stamps. Cigarettes or tobacco, more stamps. Same with sugar. The barracks were all made of wood. You would not see cement. The only entertainment would be on Sundays. To go have a hamburger, to have a glass of milk. We would dedicate our time to getting our clothes ready for the work week.

state's schools, restaurants, theaters, pools, and other public facilities. Mexican-American leaders rightly expressed concerns about the new worker import program, recalling how World War I also led to similar projects. Following that war, Mexicans in the United States became "a problem." Wanted for labor, but also discarded at the whim of national needs and perceived threats, Mexicans and Mexican Americans were cautious about what the future held, even with the prospect for a better financial future for themselves and their families through the program. Because many of the braceros never returned to Mexico, but instead married and had families in the United States, their experiences built the foundation for hundreds of thousands of Chicano students in later generations.

Corruption in the program was commonplace; bracero workers complained and revolted against the poor treatment and low wages they received. To make such a life-changing commitment to travel away from their homes and families only for the promise of better opportunities in a foreign country and culture meant that they were serious. They also expected to be justly rewarded for their efforts. Decades after the end of the program, lawsuits finally revealed the extent to which the bracero program constituted one of the greatest global examples of binational labor exploitation. As part of the agreement between Mexico and the United States, the Mexican government was to receive 10 percent of bracero wages to be placed in a savings account, under the assumption that the money would be given to the worker upon his return to Mexico. In 2001 several former braceros who had worked under the program between 1942 and 1946 filed a class-action lawsuit, alleging that the Mexican government never returned the 10 percent of their wages that was forcibly withheld. Once settled, the case guaranteed what amounted to approximately $3,500 for each surviving bracero or their descendants. However, nearly half the braceros affected by the lawsuit had already passed away by the early 2000s.

THE ZOOT SUIT RIOTS AND THE SLEEPY LAGOON CASE

Two events in 1940s Los Angeles exemplified the struggles in Mexican-American communities and their conflicts with mainstream, white institutions. The two incidents brought together wartime reactionary patriotism, violence against Hispanic youth, and police brutality. They also involved the courts and, with the support of powerful allies, some form of justice for Mexican Americans. Both cases brought attention to a distinctly Mexican-American public youth culture taking form in many cities across the United States, the so-called *pachuco* and the female counterpart, the *pachuca*. An urban youth subculture, pachucos first appeared in El Paso, Texas in the late 1920s, the style moving west as Mexican railroad workers spread over the region. Pachucos spoke a mixed Spanish-English slang dialect called *caló*, reflecting a hybridization of cultures that gained more popular currency in the 1940s. Their more characteristic trademark was the clothes they wore—the "zoot suit," a high-waisted, wide-legged, and tight-cuffed trouser ensemble with a long coat, pointy shoes, and long watch chain dangling to the knee or below. Worn by Puerto Rican, Filipino-American, Italian-American, African-American, and Mexican-American youth, the zoot suit represented excess for some, a flashy, immodest, un-American style that did not conform to wartime needs for the rationing of cloth and other resources. The death of a young Mexican-American and related police sweeps and arrests of zoot suit–clad young men thrust national anxieties about young men of color and their urban zoot suit culture into wide news coverage.

In early August 1942, two teenage girls found José Díaz dead near the Sleepy Lagoon reservoir in southeast Los Angeles. Days afterward, Los Angeles Police Department dragnet raids apprehended young women and men, holding the former as witnesses and forcing them to testify in court against the accused men. Only months after the internment of Japanese Americans, racist newspaper hysteria from the *Los Angeles Times* and the *Herald-Express* expressed justification for the indiscriminate arrest of 600 Hispanic youth, based on the assumption that the death was the result of conflicts between Mexican gangs. Twenty-two presumed gang members, 21 of Mexican descent, were eventually indicted and charged with murder and conspiracy. In the trial *People v. Zammora*, which lacked in basic due process, an all-white jury convicted three of the defendants of first-degree murder, nine of second-degree murder, and five of assault, acquitting only five. After the accused began serving sentences starting in January 1943, the Court of Appeal of the State of California reversed all convictions in October 1944. Leftist Mexican-American and African-American community leaders, in addition to renowned historian and attorney-activist Carey McWilliams, led the efforts to this reversal through the Sleepy Lagoon Defense Committee (SLDC).

A young man poses in a zoot suit with typical wide, cuffed trousers and a long jacket in June 1943.

As scholar Catherine Ramírez has documented, Mexican-American women were also targeted by the legal system, beyond their forced role as witnesses against their male neighbors, friends, and boyfriends. Then executive secretary of the SLDC,

Soldiers and sailors armed with clubs converge on a Los Angeles street, seeking Hispanic and nonwhite youth to harass during the Zoot Suit Riots in June 1943.

organizer Alice Greenfield McGrath recalled at least five young women being sentenced to the Ventura School for Girls, a California Youth Authority correctional facility known for its excessive disciplinary measures. Despite their sentencing, none of the women were ever tried or convicted, some remaining wards of the state even after the also falsely accused young men had been released from prison. Well-known Mexican-American advocates and Anglo allies were part of the defense effort, including Anthony Quinn, Rita Hayworth, and Henry Fonda.

Between the 1942 trial of the 22 young men and the reversal of their convictions in 1944 came the even more well known, but erroneously named, Zoot Suit Riots. One of the most noted incidents of white racial violence against Mexican-American youth in Los Angeles, the Zoot Suit Riots were a painful example of national racial turbulence in the World War II period. Between June 3 and 13, 1943, white servicemen roamed the streets and theaters of east Los Angeles, Chinatown, Chavez Ravine, and downtown. Targeting Mexican-American youth decked out in zoot suits, but also Filipino and African-American youth, they stopped and boarded streetcars, and entered private homes and businesses. Vigilante-style, they apprehended youth and beat them, stripped them of their attire, and cut their hair. The violence at the hands of mobs of military and naval personnel, along with civilian accomplices, exacerbated already tense racial relations among Mexicans Americans and Anglos in Los Angeles. As was the case with the Sleepy Lagoon incident, the local press and national publications including *Life* and *Time* magazines justified and celebrated the violence at the hands of the servicemen, referring to the victims as "hoodlums." Based on racist stereotypes and presumed natural propensity toward violence, the beaten youth were arrested by the Los Angeles police department for "disturbing the peace."

MEXICAN SEGREGATION AND *MENDEZ V. WESTMINSTER*

Immediately south of Los Angeles County, Orange County was the setting for a landmark federal court case in 1945 and 1946 that brought attention to the systematic segregation of Mexican-American schoolchildren. Like African-American schools, these Mexican schools typically had shorter school years, larger classes, and less funding, to a degree that could not be ascribed simply to a difference in local income levels. Some retrospective discussion of this disparity has written it off to white indifference, but others suggest more sinister motives, such as the limiting of opportunities for African Americans and Mexican Americans by curtailing their education. As with much institutionalized wrongdoing, the various parties involved likely acted from a combination of motives.

In 1945 the Estrada, Guzman, Méndez, Palomino, and Ramírez families brought suit against the Westminster, Garden Grove, Santa Ana, and El Modena School Districts of Orange County, California, claiming unconstitutional discrimination against their children and the 5,000 other Mexican-American children attending those schools. On February 18, 1946, Senior District Judge Paul McCormick found in favor of the plaintiffs, and when the school districts appealed to the Ninth Federal District Court of Appeals (in San Francisco), it upheld McCormick's decision. The district and appeals courts disagreed over the reason for siding with the plaintiffs; however, the appellate court ruled in favor of the plaintiffs not because segregated schools constituted a case of unequal protection of rights, as the district court had said, but because the California laws that allowed segregation only specified "children of Chinese, Japanese, or Mongolian heritage," not Mexicans—a holdover from California's history of Asian distrust. California law normally considered Hispanics white—a fact important to the other major California racial discrimination case, *Perez v. Sharp* (1948), which challenged California's ban on marriages between blacks and whites when a Mexican-American woman married an African-American man.

The governor of California, who thus repealed Mexican segregation in response to the court's ruling, was Earl Warren—who shortly thereafter became chief justice of the Supreme Court and presided over the *Brown v. Board of Education* segregation case for which *Mendez v. Westminster* had set a precedent. Histories of desegregation often overlook the fact that one of the key pre-Brown court decisions in fact pertained to Mexican schools, not the south's "colored" school districts.

These Mexican-American boys photographed at a Farm Security Administration labor camp in Robston, Texas, in January 1942 were likely working as child laborers alongside their families.

REDLINING

While urban Mexican Americans were stereotyped in popular entertainment as Communist sympathizers, flashy zoot suit wearers, sexual aggressors, and drinkers and carousers, in more rural areas Mexican Americans were considered dirty, shifty, lazy, or untrustworthy.

Similarly, throughout the 1940s, redlining—named for the red outline around neighborhoods considered to be mortgage credit risks, as dictated by the Federal Housing Administration (FHA)—was particularly common throughout the southwest, just as it was in the south and the industrial Midwest, where the practice segregated black and white neighborhoods. The FHA called for the creation of color-coded maps with areas outlined in red, yellow, or blue, depending on the residents' perceived abilities to maintain loan payments. Some of these maps were created by the government; many others were created by private organizations. There was little oversight for the reasoning behind the outlines, much less any questioning of the accuracy or appropriateness of the practice. Neighborhoods with a high concentration of local ethnic minorities were redlined, making it difficult for homeowners to get loans, worsening the terms of loans they could get, and especially making it hard for families to move from a redlined neighborhood to a yellow- or blue-lined one. In many cases race was the only, or the primary criterion for this determination, which resulted in many Mexican Americans being denied loans because of their ethnicity, but without the lender having to directly acknowledge the racial discrimination. This, in turn, reaffirmed the racial characteristics of various neighborhoods, and exacerbated the financial distress of those homeowners. Redlining persisted officially until the Fair Housing Act of 1968.

At the same time, some neighborhood segregation was clearly self-induced—just as newly arrived immigrants traditionally moved into neighborhoods populated by people with similar ethnic ties, some Mexican Americans deliberately chose to live in predominantly Mexican-American neighborhoods. Such ethnic neighborhoods were typically strong in social capital, and provided a support network.

PUERTO RICAN CULTURE AND IDENTITY

The 1940s was an important decade for Puerto Ricans, both on and off the island. In 1947, as the European powers dismantled their empires in order to uphold the precepts of democracy promoted by the United Nations, the United States granted Puerto Rico the right to elect its own governor. Many expected that Puerto Rico would eventually become a state, like Hawaii was in the process of becoming. Luis Muñoz Marín became the first democratically

Young sugar cane workers taking a noontime break from their labor in Rio Piedras, Puerto Rico, in December 1941. In the 1940s many Puerto Ricans left their homes seeking better work opportunities on the mainland.

elected governor of Puerto Rico in 1948. Two years later, a democratic referendum was called to discuss the formulation of a Puerto Rican constitution, which was eventually written and ratified in the 1950s.

Though Puerto Ricans had been granted citizenship in 1917, Puerto Rican migration to the mainland United States reached its peak in the 1940s. Those who settled in New York City began developing a unique ethnic identity, which

"I Have to Learn to Sew"

Migrating from rural Puerto Rico to New York in 1948, a woman named María was attracted to labor opportunities in the city's garment industry. She was also leaving behind poverty and low-wage work on the island. In her recollections, published in *Oral History Review's* "The Stories Our Mothers Tell: Projections-of-Self in the Stories of Puerto Rican Garment Workers," in 1988, she expresses the determination and patience it took to secure employment in the growing garment industry.

Well, I continued working with the intention of looking for something better but every time I went out to find a job all the jobs available were for sewing machine operators and I said to myself, "My God, I have to learn to sew." I told [my husband] that we had to find a school so I could learn to sew. Then I went to a school on 14th Street and Union Square and I signed up for three classes. They charged $25 and the only thing they really taught us was to sew a straight seam. But I took the classes, and I went to look for work as an operator. I didn't really know how to sew. I only knew how to start the machine although I had some knowledge of the machine because my mother had a small manual one in Puerto Rico. I used to watch my grandmother sew on that machine and I thought I could do it. Well, I went to look for work, and oh, my God, wherever I went, whenever I sat down at the machine and touched the pedal the machine seemed to run by itself! I was thrown out of a number of factories, but five minutes here, fifteen minutes there, I kept getting more and more practice. Then, I said to myself, "I'm going to see what kind of machines they have and if I see a Singer machine I'm going to say that I don't know how to sew on that particular machine." I went to a factory at 380 Broome Street and I noticed that they had Merrow machines and no Singer machines. Now, since I had failed so many times I told the man that I knew how to sew but not on the machine they had. I told him I knew how to sew on a Singer. Blanca, because of that lie they showed me how to sew on the Merrow. The man said to me, "If you can sew on a Singer, this one is easier." Then I said to him, "How is that possible with all those spools of thread?" He said, "Well, I'll show you." He sat me down and calmly showed me how to thread the machine, how to tie up the thread when a spool ran low, not to let it run out, and that's where I started working on Chenille robes.

was later called "Nuyorican" culture, blending "Nueva York" and "Puerto Rican." The term sometimes reflected an attitude that developed quickly among other Puerto Ricans—that these Nuyoricans had more in common with New York African-American culture than with other Hispanic groups. In most other parts of the United States, Puerto Ricans assimilated into the rest of the local Hispanic culture; only in New York City did this syncretic identity emerge to such a degree.

Throughout the decade, Nuyorican communities developed quickly in New York City, as the large numbers of migrants formed social and cultural clubs, literary societies, athletic clubs, and veteran welfare associations. Like other ethnic groups, they faced discrimination by whites and by more firmly entrenched groups, and so built up these communities to offer collective support.

CHICANO LITERATURE AND JOSEPHINA NIGGLI

Chicano literature is that written by Mexican-Americans (Chicanos). Technically, it can be dated to the earliest writing of explorers like Alvar Núñez Cabeza de Vaca, but historians of Mexican and Mexican-American culture more typically date the start of Chicano ethnic identity—a Mexican-American ethnic identity distinct from the Mexican ethnic identity—to the aftermath of the Mexican-American War in the middle of the 19th century, when more than half of Mexico was ceded to the United States. For these early Chicanos, they did not arrive in the United States: the United States materialized beneath their feet. Typically, Chicano literature focuses on this theme of identity, especially the works of the genre's golden age.

That golden age began in 1945, with Josephina Niggli's *Mexican Village*, the first Mexican-American novel to achieve mainstream popularity. Born in the Mexican city of Monterrey in 1910, Niggli was the daughter of a businessman and a violinist, both of whom were of mixed Anglo/Mexican heritage. When she was three years old, Niggli moved to San Antonio, so her parents could evade the political turmoil of the country after the assassination of the Mexican president. They spent the next seven years in the American southwest, moving frequently, before returning to Mexico in 1920, where they remained for only five years. When the 1925 Mexican revolution again disrupted the country's peace, Niggli was sent back to San Antonio to complete high school. After high school, she studied philosophy and history at San Antonio's College of the Incarnate Word, where her professors encouraged her to develop her writing. While still a teenage undergraduate, she won a national poetry contest and published a short story in the popular national magazine *Ladies Home Journal*.

More publications followed while she attended graduate school at the University of North Carolina at Chapel Hill, where she earned a Master's degree in drama. Most of her publications through the 1930s were plays and poetry. *Mexican Village,* published in 1945, is a novel of 10 interconnected episodes set in Hidalgo, Mexico, mostly during the 1920s and 1930s. The *New York Herald Tribune* called it "without peer ... a wholly convincing portrayal of Mexican village life as it is," and the book sold widely to white audiences as curious about their Mexican-American neighbors as they were fascinated by stories set outside the United States. After World War I, an increasing amount of American fiction, and foreign stories popular with American audiences, introduced Americans to the rest of the world in the comfortable confines of fiction.

Niggli went on to pursue a career principally in playwriting, teaching, and writing scripts for radio, as well as contributing to the screenplay for *Sombrero*, a movie based on *Mexican Village,* and *The Mark of Zorro.* She published her second novel, *Step Down, Elder Brother,* in 1947.

CONCLUSION

Perhaps more so than in any other decade of the 20th century, the everyday lives of Hispanics in the United States in the 1940s were shaped by struggles to survive economically, to retain their distinct cultural identities despite harassment, and to challenge discrimination and violence at home and abroad.

There was no uniform experience of becoming Mexican American; while many did begin to see themselves as more American than Mexican, an equal number remained ambivalent about what it meant to be of Mexican descent in the United States. Mexican Americans were caught between having to prove how American they were, while at the same time holding on to enough of their Mexican heritage to survive a national climate of disdain for non-Anglos. Although Puerto Ricans were American citizens, they too negotiated their growing visibility in the nation, confronting racism and stereotypes about who they were and what they could offer.

Given the legal, educational, housing, and everyday forms of discrimination that Mexican Americans encountered in the United States, a great number chose to retain their Mexican cultural heritage, the ways of life that rooted them in traditional customs among their families, their foods, and their community organizations.

HORACIO N. ROQUE RAMÍREZ
UNIVERSITY OF CALIFORNIA, SANTA BARBARA

Further Reading

Aguirre, Frederick P. "*Mendez v. Westminster School District*: How It Affected *Brown v. Board of Education.*" *Journal of Hispanic Higher Education*, Vol. 4, No. 4, October 2005.

Alvarez, Luis. *The Power of the Zoot: Youth Culture and Resistance during World War II.* Berkeley, CA: University of California Press, 2008.

Alvarez, Robert R., Jr. "The Lemon Grove Incident: The Nation's First Successful Desegregation Court Case." *The Journal of San Diego History*, Vol. 32, No. 2, spring 1986.

Gamboa, Erasmo. *Mexican Labor and World War II: Braceros in the Pacific Northwest, 1942–1947.* Seattle, WA: University of Washington Press, 2000.

García, Mario T. *Mexican Americans: Leadership, Ideology, and Identity, 1930-1960.* New Haven, CT: Yale University Press, 1989.

González, Gilbert G. *Labor and Community: Mexican Citrus Worker Villages in a Southern California County, 1900–1950.* Urbana, IL: University of Illinois Press, 1994.

Gutiérrez, David G. *Walls and Mirrors: Mexican Americans, Mexican Immigrants, and the Politics of Ethnicity.* Berkeley, CA: University of California Press, 1995.

Montejano, David. *Anglos and Mexicans in the Making of Texas, 1836–1986.* Austin, TX: Texas University Press, 1987.

Mullins, Patrick, Violeta Domínguez López, and Ricardo Valencia. *Bracero Stories.* DVD/VHS, 56 minutes, 2008.

Ramírez, Catherine. *The Woman in the Zoot Suit: Gender, Nationalism, and the Cultural Politics of Memory.* Durham, NC: Duke University Press, 2009.

Rivas-Rodríguez, Maggie. *Mexican Americans and World War II.* Austin, TX: Texas University Press, 2005.

———, Juliana Torres, Melissa Dipiero-D'Sa, and Lindsay Fitzpatrick. *A Legacy Greater than Words.* Austin, TX: Texas University Press, 2006.

Robbie, Sandra Membrila. *Mendez vs. Westminster: For All the Children/ Para Todos los Niños.* Video, 30 minutes, 2003.

Sánchez, George, J. *Becoming Mexican American: Ethnicity, Culture, and Identity in Chicano Los Angeles, 1900–1945.* Oxford: Oxford University Press, 2004.

Sánchez Korrol, Virginia E. *From Colonia to Community: The History of Puerto Ricans in New York City.* Berkeley, CA: University of California Press, 1994.

Smithsonian Institution, National Museum of American History, Bracero History Archive. Available online, URL: www.braceroarchive.org. Accessed December 2008.

U.S. Latino & Latina WWII Oral History Project, Nettie Lee Benson Latin American Collection, University of Texas at Austin.

Vázquez Erazo, Blanca. "The Stories Our Mothers Tell: Projections-of-Self in the Stories of Puerto Rican Garment Workers." *Oral History Review,* Vol. 16, No. 2, fall 1988.

Whalen, Carmen Teresa. *From Puerto Rico to Philadelphia: Puerto Rican Workers and Postwar Economies*. Philadelphia, PA: Temple University Press, 2001.

Whalen, Carmen Teresa and Víctor Vázquez-Hernández, eds. *The Puerto Rican Diaspora: Historical Perspectives*. Philadelphia, PA: Temple University Press, 2005.

CHAPTER 8

The Civil Rights Era: 1950 to 1969

THE 1950s WAS a decade of anxiety, social change, and perceived conformity. Americans were reaping the benefits of a prosperous postwar economy, yet McCarthyism and the threat of nuclear war persisted. Immigration was also an issue of concern during this time of uncertainty. The Immigration and Nationality Act of 1952, also called the McCarran-Walter Act, placed quotas on immigration by limiting entry to mostly northern and western Europeans. Although immigrants from the Western Hemisphere, including Hispanics, were exempt from the quotas, they had to surmount a variety of barriers to clear themselves of being homosexuals or Communists. Then, during the 1960s, in response to more tolerant immigration laws, the United States experienced a third wave of labor migration as workers from Mexico and Puerto Rico poured into the United States. Also, between 1960 and 1980, hundreds of thousands of Cuban Americans were granted entry into the United States, resulting in a significant and largely new community of Hispanic Americans.

Life in the United States underwent massive transformations in the 1960s as the Civil Rights movement, under the leadership of Dr. Martin Luther King, Jr., paved the way for growing demands for equal treatment from minority groups and women. Hispanic-American movements included the Chicano Movement, Brown Power, and union activity. In the grape fields of Califor-

Increased immigration in the 1960s led to the growth of Hispanic neighborhoods around the country. This early 1960s photo shows a busy fruit market in New York City's Spanish Harlem, where 70 percent of Puerto Rican immigrants settled between 1940 and 1960.

nia, labor organizer César Chávez lit a spark that rippled throughout the Hispanic-American community. On college campuses around the country, young Hispanic Americans from various groups joined the fight for a more inclusive curriculum, and more equitable representation among faculty and staff. Hispanics became much more visible during this era, influencing American culture further through music, the arts, language, and popular entertainment, and gaining power in the political arena. During these decades of apprehension, instability, and sweeping social movements, Hispanic Americans, like other formerly marginalized groups, fought to establish a more secure place for themselves in American society.

MEXICAN AMERICANS

Mexican Americans were the largest group of Hispanics in the United States during the 1950s. Americans of Mexican descent had roots in the United States long before there was even the concept of a United States, yet they were faced with continuous racism and discrimination, especially in the southwest. Like African Americans in the south, Mexican Americans were met with hostility and violence, as well as discrimination in employment and facilities.

Mexican Americans were excluded from schools, restrooms, and even restaurants that catered only to whites. However, this unequal living situation began to change. To help abolish segregation, Hispanic Americans formed organizations such as the League of Latin American Citizens (LULAC) and Alianza Hispano Americana. With the ruling of *Hernandez v. Texas* in 1954, Mexicans were seen as a distinct class that needed representation in juries. Even in the state of Texas, where Mexican Americans accounted for a large proportion of the population, Hispanics were rarely represented in juries. *Hernandez v. Texas* gave Mexican Americans equal protection under the Fourteenth Amendment. On the heels of *Brown v. Board of Education of Topeka*, Mexican Americans also gained a victory in the desegregation of schools in Texas with *Hernandez et al. v. Driscoll Consolidated ISD* in 1957. These victories legally gave Mexican Americans more equal rights, but de facto discrimination was very much alive, and laws were difficult to enforce.

The Bracero Program, which had begun as a way of dealing with agricultural labor shortages during World War II, continued through 1964. In the 1950s alone, the program brought over three million laborers from Mexico to work on American farms for low wages. At the same time, illegal Mexican workers began to be seen as a problem for the United States, especially after the war ended and jobs were needed for returning soldiers. The solution was to launch the Immigration and Naturalization Service (INS)–sponsored program "Operation Wetback" in 1954, which deported approximately 3.8 million illegal Mexican immigrants in a five-year period. This program, among others, contributed to the hostile environment for Mexican-American workers. Despite these setbacks, and their exclusion from white American labor unions, many persevered and created their own organizations. Organizations such as the Mexican American Political Association (MAPA) would flourish as part of the greater Chicano movement in the 1960s.

THE CHICANO MOVEMENT

The Chicano movement surfaced on college campuses where there were large numbers of Mexican-American students. The movement was based in part on an atavistic identification with the Aztec Indians, who had become legendary. Followers of the Chicano movement endorsed the concepts of brotherhood and *carnalismo*, invoking courage, loyalty, and love for other human beings. As a result of their efforts, the term *Chicano* came to signify a pride in being Hispanic, and highlighted the need to promote greater political awareness and participation within the Hispanic-American community. Based on their distinct physical characteristics and backgrounds, particular groups of Hispanic Americans announced that they preferred to be identified as Chicana, Boricua, or Afro-Cuban.

The success of the Chicano movement was illustrated by the new prominence of leaders chosen to protect Hispanic-American interests in all levels of government. For the first time, students from kindergarten to colleges and universities saw Hispanic teachers and administrators representing their presence in the total population. Classes on Hispanic history and culture were added to college curricula, and textbooks at all levels began including information about Hispanic Americans. In 1968 the Mexican American Legal Defense and Educational Fund (MALDEF) was founded in San Antonio, Texas. MALDEF became the leading organization for promoting philanthropy and education among Hispanic Americans.

In California, agricultural workers began to take a more active stance as well, demanding better working conditions and more humane treatment. Under the auspices of the United Farm Workers Organizing Committee, the dedicated and passionate César Chávez led migrant workers in a successful strike, and launched nationwide boycotts against offending industries. The tradition of Protest Theater surfaced in the 1960s in conjunction with Chávez's work. Luis Valdez founded El Teatro Campesino in Delano, California, in 1967 to entertain and educate farm workers about their rights. Performance venues varied from protest sites to agricultural fields. Due to the success of Chávez and other activists, legislation passed to provide limited protection for migrant workers.

The new awareness that Hispanic Americans were denied basic rights sometimes spilled out in mass protests. By 1968 frustration and anger had become a major force for change as Hispanic Americans, particularly those of Mexican descent, joined what had become known as the Brown Power movement. A massive 1968 walkout of the Los Angeles high schools, which became known as the "East L.A. Blowouts," protested longstanding discrimination in the educational system. In addition to the protests taking place in high schools and on college campuses, barrio groups such as the Brown Berets focused on serving Hispanic-American interests in their own communities and across the country. In Texas, Hispanic Americans established La Raza Unida party to represent Chicanos in communities where they were the majority.

PUERTO RICANS
The complicated Puerto Rican–American relationship has changed over the past century. Puerto Rico began as a colony of the United States in 1898 when the Treaty of Paris ended the Spanish-American War. In 1952 Puerto Rico became a commonwealth of the United States, but not without resistance—both peaceful and violent. In 1950 Puerto Rican nationalists attempted to assassinate President Harry Truman due to the United States' perceived unfair relations with the island. Then in 1954 Puerto Rican nationalists opened fire in the House of Representatives, injuring five congressmen. Periodically, Puerto Ricans are asked to vote on whether or not they would like to become an American state. Since 1967 Puerto Rican voters have opted to remain a commonwealth.

César Chávez

Born on March 31, 1927, in Yuma, Arizona, César Estrada Chávez grew up among Hispanic migrant farmers in the American west. After a stint in the U.S. Navy during World War II, Chávez returned home and continued to work in agriculture. He also began working with the Community Services Organization in California and became general director in 1958. In 1962 Chávez founded National Farm Workers of America (NFWA), which was devoted to winning a living wage, improving the deplorable conditions under which migrant farmers lived, and gaining access to medical care. Chávez used the organization to launch a five-year strike of California Delano grape pickers, and spearheaded a nationwide boycott of California grapes. Building on these successes, Chávez also led subsequent strikes against lettuce and table grape growers.

In 1966 Chávez's organization merged with the American Federation of Labor-Congress of Industrial Organizations (AFL-CIO), becoming the United Farm Workers Organizing Committee, which later became the United Farm Workers of America. Chávez managed to keep the Teamsters out of the area in 1972, winning sole authority to organize field and farmworkers. In recognition of the need for legislation to provide legal protections for migrant workers, the state legislature passed the California Agricultural Labor Relations Act in 1975, which recognized the right of farm workers to unionize.

Although he had only an eighth-grade education, César Chávez educated himself, anxious to learn everything he could about the subjects that mattered most to him. He was honored within the Hispanic-American community and by the people of the United States as a tireless worker in the struggle for civil rights, environmental protection, and consumer rights. He provided moral, religious, and political leadership by adhering to the theory of nonviolence adapted by Mahatma Gandhi and Dr. Martin Luther King, Jr. In 1990 Chávez encouraged his own supporters to "learn his [King's] lessons and put his views into practice, so that we may truly be free at last." Chávez quoted from an encouraging letter Dr. King wrote him in 1968 during the first of several fasts: "Our separate struggles are really one: A struggle for freedom, for dignity, and for humanity."

When Chávez died in his sleep on April 23, 1993, he was survived by his wife Helen and their eight children. The following year Helen Chávez accepted the Presidential Medal of Freedom from President Bill Clinton on her husband's behalf in recognition of his contributions to the cause of freedom. Chávez's family and supporters carried on his work by creating the César E. Chávez Foundation. In 2000 California declared March 31 César Chávez Day, making it a holiday for state workers. Texas and Arizona also honored Chávez's contributions.

**Free the Five
Puerto Rican Nationalists**

Demonstrate: Nov. 13 - United Nations, N.Y.C.
San Francisco, Calif.
Oct. 30 - Springfield, Mo.

A call for demonstrations in support of the Puerto Rican activists jailed for the attack on Congress in 1954, and the attempted assassination of President Harry Truman in 1950.

Although they were excluded in many ways from American society, Puerto Ricans still maintained their obligations to the United States. This is illustrated by the 61,000 Puerto Ricans who volunteered to serve in the army during the 1950–53 Korean War.

In the post–World War II era, Puerto Rico's economy was transforming from a plantation system to an industrial society. Operation Bootstrap (1948–65) enticed foreign and American companies to invest in the process by offering them cheap labor and tax incentives. Although this program improved the overall economy and lives of Puerto Ricans, it decreased the amount of jobs available to the population. This caused many to move to the mainland during the 1950s.

During the 1950s airfare from Puerto Rico to the mainland was inexpensive and readily available. Many took advantage of this opportunity, especially those who faced unemployment as a result of Operation Bootstrap. From 1946–64, one-third of the Puerto Rican population moved to northern cities such as New York and Chicago, a shift referred to as the Great Migration. Between 1940 and 1960, 545,000 Puerto Ricans came to the United States, with 70 percent settling in East Harlem in New York City.

Although they were legally American citizens, Puerto Ricans were often discriminated against in employment, housing, and education. Puerto Ricans ended up taking jobs that mainland Americans did not want, such as service and factory work. Puerto Rican women were especially prominent in the garment industry. Due to competition in employment, housing, and even street space with other working-class groups, ethnic tensions arose. The very real ethnic rivalries between Puerto Ricans, Irish, and Italians in New York City inspired the plotline in the 1957 musical *West Side Story*, which was turned into a film in 1961.

Puerto Ricans were pushed to assimilate into American society. Puerto Rican children in public schools were pressed to take more Anglo-sounding names and to disregard their culture. Since Puerto Ricans did not fit into the established racial dichotomy of 1950s America, they were compelled to choose between adjusting to life as a black American or white American. Despite this, Puerto Ricans maintained their cultural traditions, and as their numbers grew, were able to celebrate them.

Puerto Rican life centered on religion, and Roman Catholicism was intertwined in cultural traditions. The Caballeros de San Juan (Knights of St. John) in Chicago, Illinois was founded in 1954 by Puerto Ricans to help newly arrived Puerto Ricans in the community with not only social support, but also legal and medical support. By the late 1950s, as a result of the Great Migration, Puerto Ricans were more free to celebrate their culture publicly not only in Chicago, but also in New York City with the Puerto Rican Day Parade in 1958. Puerto Rican culture became a part of the cultural landscape.

In the 1960s, businesses initiated a flight to the suburbs where operating costs were cheaper. This placed a heavy burden on Hispanic-American workers, who had to add transportation costs to living expenses. At the same time, opportunities for doing piece work at home declined drastically. In many states, Hispanics were shut out of jobs by unions. In response to these changes, the number of Puerto Ricans in the United States began to decline as some returned to their homeland seeking a more hospitable and lucrative environment. Even as overall numbers declined, political and community leaders worked to improve the situation in the United States.

These Puerto Rican demonstrators at New York City Hall in lower Manhattan in 1967 protested educational discrimination in the public school system.

One such influential Puerto Rican leader was Antonia Pantoja, one of the founders of the organization Aspira, which helped Puerto Rican youths achieve higher levels of educational and occupational success. Aspire/Aspira was founded in 1961 as a means of raising funds for the education and leadership development of Puerto Ricans and Latino youths. Its name comes from the Spanish word *aspirar*, which means "to aspire." Headquartered in Washington, D.C., Aspira opened offices in states with large Hispanic communities, such as Connecticut, Delaware, Florida, Illinois, New Jersey, New York, and Pennsylvania. The Aspira network was made up of local organizations, school districts, policymakers, and corporate representatives

In 1960, 20 volunteer social workers joined together to meet the needs of the growing Puerto Rican community. Three years later they founded the Puerto Rican Family Institute under the leadership of Augustín González. Its focus was to mitigate the effects of poverty facing Puerto Rican migrant families in New York City. Their work had a ripple effect, as targeted families were invited to join the effort to provide counseling and services for new Puerto Rican migrants. New avenues for funding opened up after the passage of the Economic Opportunity Act in 1964, and the program was able to expand.

CUBAN AMERICANS

Cubans started immigrating to the United States in large numbers at the close of the 19th century. Between 1868 and 1895, Cubans were fighting for their independence from Spain. This prompted about 10,000 people to leave their homeland and resettle in the United States. Many of these people settled in nearby Key West as well as Tampa, Florida. Cubans in Tampa created their own community, called Ybor City, based on cigar manufacturing. This would attract even more Cubans to settle there because of the prior ties to the area. From 1900 to 1950, few Cubans migrated to the United States; those who did came primarily for political reasons.

Some 79,000 Cubans came to the United States from 1951 to 1960. New York was the most important Cuban center in the United States in the 1940s and 1950s. Before 1959, about 40,000 Cubans lived in Miami, Florida. The Cuban Revolution in 1959, in which Fidel Castro overthrew the

This handmade metal boat, which is eight feet long and jury-rigged with the engine from a lawn mower, ferried a Cuban couple to Florida in the mid 1960s.

The U.S. Coast Guard rescued these Cuban exiles from their small craft off Florida during what became known as the Camarioca boat lift of 1965.

U.S.-sanctioned leader Fulgencio Batista, pushed a massive exodus of political refugees north to the United States. Most of these refugees settled in Florida, but others made their way to New York City and New Jersey. Unlike other Hispanic-American immigrants, Cuban immigrants were predominately middle and upper class.

In November 1960 Democrat John F. Kennedy was elected president. Once in office, he became directly involved with events in Latin America. On April 17, 1961, American-trained Cuban exiles launched an ill-fated attack on the Bay of Pigs along Cuba's southern coast with the intention of overthrowing Fidel Castro's communist regime. The Bay of Pigs fiasco tested President Kennedy's leadership abilities to their fullest extent. Many Cuban Americans felt betrayed by Kennedy's failure to check Fidel Castro's rise to power. The president later redeemed himself by standing up to Soviet Premier Nikita Khrushchev and forcing him to remove nuclear warheads from Cuba in October 1962. Kennedy placed an embargo on Cuba in 1963, which remained in place.

Between 1959 and 1962, 215,000 Cubans immigrated to the United States. Even though commercial air flights to Cuba were put on hold in 1962, it did not stem the flow of immigration; Cubans fled the country in whatever vessels they could find. On September 28, 1965, Fidel Castro announced that he would allow Cubans who had relatives living in the United States to emigrate, but only if they were picked up by family members already living in Florida.

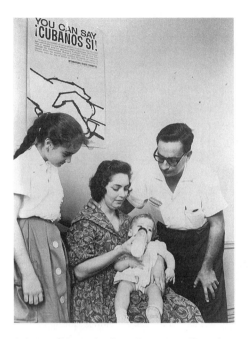

A Cuban refugee family waits at the office of the International Rescue Committee in New York in August 1961.

This action resulted in a barrage of watercraft traversing the waters between the United States and Cuba. As might be expected, a number of tragedies occurred.

To prevent further loss of life, the American government worked with Castro to develop an airlift to remove Cubans and transport them to Miami. These flights, which were called Freedom Flights, Aerial Bridge, or Family Unification Flights, continued until April 6, 1973. By that time an additional 250,000 Cubans had been airlifted out of Cuba, relieving the island of a tenth of its population. According to immigration law, Cuban immigrants were not political refugees, so both Lyndon Johnson and Richard Nixon used the parole system to allow Cuban Americans into the country. It was not until 1980 that the definition of political refugee became more inclusive, encompassing anyone who fled a communist country or anyone with a well-founded fear of political, racial, ethnic, or religious persecution.

OTHER HISPANICS

There were about 57,000 people of South and Central American descent living in the United States in 1950. Central Americans outnumbered Mexicans in the 1950s in the Mission District of San Francisco, creating an environment that was hospitable and familiar by opening stores and businesses that met their cultural, economic, and political needs. Educated Colombians escaping political violence came to New York following World War II.

From the Caribbean, about 1,000 Dominicans per year immigrated to the United States during the 1950s. Dominican dictator Rafael Leónidas Trujillo restricted travel from the country to primarily wealthy people, until his assassination in 1961. The following year, large numbers of Dominicans poured into the United States. Most left for political reasons and settled in New York City. Dominicans had strong economic and political dependency on the United States. Because President Lyndon Johnson was determined to prevent the Dominican Republic from yielding to communism, he began taking an active role in the country's politics.

THE CIVIL RIGHTS ACT OF 1964 AND THE VOTING RIGHTS ACT

Congress passed the Civil Rights Act of 1964 as a memorial to President Kennedy, who had been assassinated in Dallas, Texas, the previous year. The first major civil rights legislation since Reconstruction, the act banned discrimination in employment, education, and public places on the basis of race, sex, national origin, religion, and ethnicity. Title VII, in which Congress set out "to achieve equality of employment opportunity and remove barriers that have operated in the past," prohibited discrimination in advertising, recruitment, hiring, job classification, promotion, discharge, wages, salaries, and other terms of employment. The Civil Rights Act of 1964 had immediate impact since President Lyndon Johnson threw the weight of the federal government into eradicating legal discrimination. The act also created the Equal Employment Opportunity Commission to monitor discrimination, and established Job Corps, the Community Action Program (CAP), and Volunteers in Service to America (VISTA) to provide greater opportunities for minorities. With new legal protections and programs in place, Johnson's War on Poverty generated greater aspirations for Hispanic Americans.

In 1965 Congress solidified the federal fight against voter discrimination with the passage of the Voting Rights Act, which stipulated that "no voting qualification be imposed or applied by any State or political subdivision to deny or abridge the right of any citizen of the United States to vote on account

The 1965 Voting Rights Act improved access to the vote for Hispanic Americans and African Americans. This Puerto Rican woman was registering to vote in New York City in 1960.

Immigration Act of 1965

The first caps on immigration within the Western Hemisphere were instituted when Congress passed the Immigration Act of 1965 (P.L. 89-236) and abolished the national quota system. Cosponsored by Emanuel Celler (D-NY) and Philip Hart (D-MI), the act, which amended the Immigration and Naturalization Act of 1952, represented an about-face in American immigration policy. Immigration within the Western Hemisphere was limited to 120,000 visas per year. Only 20,000 visas per year were allotted for immigrants from the Eastern Hemisphere, but that restriction was an improvement, because earlier laws had almost totally prohibited Asian immigration into the United States.

The policy change in 1965 mirrored the shifting position on immigration within the United States. Instead of emphasizing workers, the new law focused on reuniting immigrants with family members already living in the country. Supporters of the bill insisted that the new act would not increase total immigration into the country, but they were proven wrong. The waiting list for American visas grew steadily, and the immigration caps proved to be particularly troubling as events unfolded in Cuba.

President Lyndon B. Johnson signed the Immigration Bill at Liberty Hill in New York City on October 3, 1965. Johnson downplayed the importance of the bill even while declaring that it would "repair a very deep and painful flaw in the fabric of American justice" and correct a "cruel and enduring wrong in the conduct of the American nation." Invoking the name of John F. Kennedy, the president insisted that the intent of the bill was to ensure that "from this day forth those wishing to immigrate to America shall be admitted on the basis of their skills and their close relationship to those already here." Johnson particularly welcomed Cuban refugees to the United States, ensuring them that American "traditions as an asylum for the oppressed" would continue to be upheld.

of race or color." The ratification of the Twenty-fourth Amendment in 1964, in conjunction with a series of court cases, abolished poll taxes on all elections, making it easier for poor Hispanic Americans to vote. Although the Voting Act was specifically aimed at ensuring the rights of suffrage to African Americans, Hispanic Americans were able to use the act to gain a greater voice in American politics throughout the next decade.

HISPANIC-AMERICAN EDUCATION AND LANGUAGE

Under pressure from Hispanic-American activists and their supporters, in 1968 Congress passed the Bilingual Education Act as Title VII of the Elementary and Secondary School Act. For the first time in the history of the United States, schools were required to develop programs designed to improve education for non-English speaking children and youth, and to promote multiculturalism in mainstream education. Federal funds were set aside to provide bilingual fellowships and teacher-training grants. Because the majority of non-English speaking students in public school spoke Spanish, the new programs had greater impact on Hispanic Americans than on those of other ethnicities.

The new programs varied in content, length, and overall goals. English as a Second Language (ESL) generally offered limited, specialized assistance to non-English speaking students, but all other classes were carried out in English. ESL's focus was to provide students with the skills they needed to survive in the educational mainstream. Bilingual classes were conducted in both English and the student's native language for varying lengths of time. Bilingual classes could be either transitional or monoliterate. In the first case, schools sought to provide students with the basics of English language and communication before moving them into the regular classroom. In the second, students were taught written and oral skills in both English and their native language, but were required to complete all writing assignments in English. Some schools chose to provide bilingual education through either partial or full programs. Partial programs allowed students to be taught in their own language in some classes, while others were taught strictly in English. In full bilingual programs, all education was offered in English and the student's own language.

Six years after the passage of the Bilingual Education Act, the Supreme Court held in *Lau v. Nichols* (414 U.S. 563, 1974) that all children had a right to an equal education regardless of language barriers, assigning school districts the responsibility for carrying out this task. Subsequent studies revealed that teaching children and youths in their own languages and providing them with tools for English communication led to improved opportunities for employment, job advancement, and higher wages as adults. Not all Americans were delighted with the changes, and decades of controversy followed the tacit acceptance of Spanish as a "second American language."

HISPANIC-AMERICAN PROFESSIONALS

With better education and language skills, more Hispanic Americans entered professional fields than ever before, and Hispanic-American teachers, administrators, grant writers, physicians, and lawyers were able to serve not only their own interests, but also those of the Hispanic-American community as a whole. States with large Hispanic-American populations opened up offices dealing entirely with Hispanic-American affairs. A number of notable Hispanics also entered the public arena, such as Representative Henry B. González, a Democrat from Texas who entered Congress in 1961 as the first Hispanic to represent that state in the national legislature.

The End of the Braceros Program

More than four million Mexican workers came to the United States through the Braceros ("the strong-armed ones") Program between 1942 and 1965 to work in the agricultural fields. They labored at whatever jobs were available, including cutting sugar beets, picking cucumbers and tomatoes, and weeding and picking cotton. El Paso, Texas, became a gathering and recruitment area for the Braceros, with some 80,000 Mexican workers passing through each year. Because the contracts negotiated by independent farmers were written entirely in English, Mexicans signed them without always understanding their content. The contracts generally stipulated that permission to remain in the United States was contingent on employment. Workers could return home only in cases of emergency, and only with written permission of their employers. While in the United States, the workers were often harassed by white workers who resented their presence in the country, and relations with local authorities tended to be volatile. By 1960 a fourth of all agricultural workers in the United States were braceros.

Lee G. Williams, the officer employed by the Department of Labor to oversee the Braceros Program, was highly critical of its activities. He maintained that program had become a form of "legalized slavery." By the time it ended, three million braceros had entered the United States. The *El Paso Times* reported on May 30, 1964, that more than 500 workers had crossed the Santa Fe Bridge in the last group allowed in before the Braceros Program ended. After the braceros were forced to return to Mexico, many reentered the United States as illegal immigrants to become chili pickers, joining what Farmworkers.org calls "one of the most exploited labor groups in the U.S." Other Mexicans were employed in assembly plants known as *maquiladoras* that sprang up along the American/Mexican border with the express purpose of ensuring a steady supply of cheap labor for American factories.

With the help of the earlier G.I. Bill, which had allowed many Mexican-American veterans to receive a college education, and the support of Hispanic-American organizations, between 1950 and 1970 the percentage of Hispanic Americans working in white-collar jobs more than doubled in the United States. For the first time in the history of the United States, a class of Mexican-American professionals began to play a role in American politics and society. Nevertheless 60 percent of Hispanic Americans continued to labor in menial jobs.

HISPANICS IN 1950s ENTERTAINMENT

The climate of the 1950s not only created the stirrings of the Chicano movement politically, but also musically. In California, as in many parts of the nation, teenagers influenced by the new phenomenon called rock and roll started creating their own musical groups. Mexican-American teenagers were not excluded from this trend. In fact, they constituted the majority of these groups on the West Coast. One local band from Pacoima, California was called the Silhouettes. Although they never became truly successful as a band, its lead singer and guitarist, Ritchie Valens (Richard Valenzuela), made quite an impression on the musical environment. "Little Richard of the San Fernando Valley," as he was called by admirers, was not only the first Latino rock musician with hits like *Come on Let's Go* and *Donna*, but he brought his heritage into the radios of white America with his updated version of the Mexican folk song, *La Bamba*.

Cuban influence was also evident in American popular culture. Mambo mania took hold of Americans in the 1950s. Afro-Cuban in origin, Mambo infiltrated not only music, but also dance halls and novelty items. Popularized by the musical arrangements of Dámaso Pérez Prado, mambo was soon recorded by Latin and Jazz musicians, as well as popular music artists such as Nat "King" Cole, Bill Haley, Perry Como, and Rosemary Clooney. This also inspired country western and holiday mambo versions such as *Hillbilly Mambo, Banjo Mambo, Jingle Bell,* and *Rudolph the Red-Nosed Mambo.* To reach people all over the nation, in 1954 Tico Records launched a mambo tour entitled *Mambo U.S.A.* that visited 56 cities.

One of the first Hispanic Americans to earn a national reputation in television was Cuban bandleader Desi Arnaz, whose family had fled to Miami during the Batista Revolution of the 1930s. Arnaz met actress Lucille Ball in 1940 while making the film *Too Many Girls*, and the couple married. When Ball and Arnaz's production company Desilu initially pitched the idea for *I Love Lucy* to the networks, executives vetoed the idea of Arnaz playing Ball's husband because they believed the American public would not accept a "mixed marriage." Ball insisted, and *I Love Lucy* (1953–61) proved to be a hit, consistently ranking in the top 10 television shows, and raking in huge profits for CBS. Desi Arnaz and the rest of the cast of *I Love Lucy* made their weekly appearances in American living rooms. This exposed audiences to Cuban culture in a different way—in a family environment. Desi Arnaz played the straight man to his wife's ridiculous antics. Instead of portraying an offensive stereotype, his character, Ricky Ricardo, was a middle-class breadwinner husband who was also unapologetically Cuban. As an overall positive portrayal of Cuban culture, Arnaz seemed to find a balance between resistance and conformity, and was able to fit into the cautious climate of the era.

HISPANICS IN 1960s ENTERTAINMENT

Most Hispanic-American actors on television in the 1960s were depicted in stereotypical or buffoonish roles, or were relegated to playing background characters. Tony Martínez, for instance, played Pepino García on *The Real*

McCoys (1957–63), a show about a poor white farm family. In *The Flying Nun* (1967–70), which was set at the San Tanco convent in Puerto Rico, Carlos Ramírez, a Latino playboy with a heart of gold played by Argentine actor Alejandro Rey, was often the butt of jokes. One of the most visible Hispanic Americans of the period was José Jiménez, a bumbling doorman/elevator operator on *The Danny Thomas Show* (1953–65). The role was filled by Bill Dana, a white comedian of Hungarian-Jewish descent. Even *The High Chaparral* (1967–71), a program about the daughter of a wealthy white rancher who married the son of a wealthy Mexican cattle baron, depicted white actors playing Hispanic roles. Hispanic Americans were cast in background roles, and often had no lines. Television viewers of the 1960s could also see Hispanics in reruns from the previous decade, including Pancho, the sidekick of *The Cisco Kid* (1951–56) played by Leo Carrillo, and the nitwitted Sergeant García on *Zorro* (1957–59), played by Henry Calvin.

PBS tended to portray Hispanic Americans in a more positive light than other networks of the 1960s, generally offering more realistic role models to Spanish-speaking people. This was particularly true of *Sesame Street*, produced by Jim Henson's Children's Television Network. Shortly after the show's 1969 premier, Sonia Manzano joined the cast as María Figueroa. Over time, Maria and the character of Luis Rodríquez, played by Emilio Delgado, fell in

Folksinger Joan Báez, shown here performing with Bob Dylan at the August 1963 March on Washington for Jobs and Freedom, has Mexican and Scottish roots.

love and married on the show. Actor Raúl Julia was also briefly in the cast before he left to pursue a successful career in film.

In the movies, Hispanic-American males had traditionally been played as banditos, buffoons, caballeros, and gangsters, while females were portrayed as overweight mothers, spitfire sirens, or gang members. When sex and violence became more specific in film in the 1960s, positive portrayals of Hispanic Americans were even more difficult to find. Movies such as Clint Eastwood's *The Good, the Bad, and the Ugly* (1966) were perceived as the epitome of the so-called "good-bad bandito" stereotype that had haunted Hispanic Americans. Jewish actor Eli Wallach costarred with Eastwood, playing Tuco the Terrible. Wallach also played a Mexican in other films of the era.

During the 1960s, a number of other Hispanic-American entertainers attracted fans from all races and ethnicities, including Walt Disney, head of Disney Studios, and actors Rita Moreno, Chita Rivera, Ricardo Montalbán, César Romero, Fernando Lamas, and Raquel Welch, as well as folksinger Joan Báez and country artist Freddy Fender. Hispanic Americans were virtually invisible in advertising in the 1960s, except for the highly controversial cartoon figure Frito Bandito, who stole Frito corn chips. The character was voiced by Mel Blanc, who was also the voice of cartoon character Speedy Gonzalez. Hispanic Americans objected to the highly exaggerated accents Blanc used for both characters. The Frito Bandito ad was discontinued in 1971. As the impact of the civil rights and Chicano movements grew, more Hispanic Americans were employed in decision-making positions, and portrayals of Hispanic Americans in the entertainment industry became more realistic.

LITERATURE

In literary culture, the activism of the 1960s inspired Hispanic-American literature that focused on identity and culture, the tone of which was epitomized by the poem *I Am Joaquín* by Rodolfo "Corky" Gonzáles. In the poem, the narrator cries out: "I am Joaquín, Lost in a world of confusion, Caught up in a whirl of a gringo society, Confused by the rules, Scorned by attitudes, Suppressed by manipulations, And destroyed by modern society." Popular subjects in literature of the 1960s were the *barrios*, Hispanic-American neighborhoods; and the *Pachuco*, a group of Mexican-American rebels of the 1930s and 1940s who wore distinctive clothing and exhibited a devil-may-care attitude. Texas and California became the center of activity for Hispanic-American writers in the 1960s. Two of the most noted writers were the poet Alurista (Alberto Urista Heredia), who had a large following among other writers, and Rosaura Sánchez, a scholar and activist who led a cluster of women writers.

CONCLUSION

The oscillations between positive and negative images of Hispanic Americans in the U.S. entertainment industry, exemplified by the contrast between Desi

Arnaz's positive image in the 1950s and the cruel stereotypes of the 1960s, mirror a larger pattern in American culture. Despite the achievements of His-panic-American activists during the 1960s Civil Rights movement, discrimi-nation continued in the years that followed the pivotal decades of the 1950s and 1960s. A new generation of activists, some quite militant and even vio-lent, would work to further the goals of the movement in the 1970s. Again and again, immigration issues would return to the forefront, sparking backlashes against Hispanics in spite of hard-won social progress and increased visibility and political participation.

VANESSA DE LOS REYES
NORTHERN KENTUCK UNIVERSITY
ELIZABETH R. PURDY
INDEPENDENT SCHOLAR

Further Reading

Abalos, David T. *Latinos in the United States: The Sacred and the Political.* Notre Dame, IN: University of Note Dame Press, 2007.

Arnaz, Desi. *A Book.* New York: Warner Books, 1976.

Cafferty, Pastora San Juan and David W. Engstrom, eds. *Hispanics in the United States: An Agenda for the Twenty-First Century.* New Brunswick, NJ: Transaction, 2000.

Chávez, César. "Lessons of Dr. Martin Luther King, Jr." Available online, URL: www.aztlan.net/cesarMLK.htm. Accessed August 2008.

————. Foundation. "American Hero." Available online, URL: www .cesarechavezfoundation.org. Accessed August 2008.

Deck, Allan Figueroa. *Hispanic Ministry and the Evangelization of Cultures.* New York: Paulist Press, 1989.

Delgado, Celeste Fraser and José Esteban Muñoz, eds. *Everynight Life: Culture and Dance in Latino America.* Durham, NC: Duke University Press, 1997.

Farmworkers.org. "The Bracero Program." Available online, URL: http:// www.farmworkers.org/bracerop.html. Accessed August 2008.

Fernández Roberta. "Voces Americanas/American Voices: Thirty Years of Hispanic Literature in the United States." Available online, URL: www.humanities-interactive.org/vocesamericanas/thirtyyears.htm. Accessed September 2008.

González, Juan. *Harvest of Empire: A History of Latinos in America.* New York: Penguin Books, 2000.

Harris, Warren G. *Lucy & Desi: The Legendary Love Story of Television's Most Famous Couple.* New York: Simon & Schuster, 1991.

Heyck, Daly and Denis Lynn. *Barrios and Borderlands: Cultures of Latinos and Latinas in the United States.* New York: Routledge, 1994.

Hovius, Christopher and José E. Limón. *Latino Migrant Workers: America's Harvesters.* Broomall, PA: Mason Crest, 2005.

Jiménez, Alfredo, ed. *Handbook of Hispanic Cultures in the United States: History.* Houston, TX: Arte Público Press, 1994.

Johnson, Lyndon B. "Remarks at the Signing of the Immigration Bill, Liberty Island, New York, 3 October, 1965." Available online, URL: www.lbjlib.utexas.edu/johnson/archives.hom/speeches.hom/651003.asp. Accessed August 2008.

Keely, Charles B. "Effects of the Immigration Act of 1965 on Selected Population Characteristics of Immigrants to the United States." *Demography*, Vol. 8, No. 2, May 1971.

Laezman, Rick. *100 Hispanic-Americans Who Changed American History.* Milwaukee, WI: World Almanac Library, 2005.

Leymarie, Isabelle. *Cuban Fire: The Story of Salsa and Latin Jazz.* New York: Continuum, 2002.

Library of Congress. "Hispanic Americans in Congress, 1852–1995." Available online, URL: www.loc.gov/rr/hispanic/congress/gonzalez.html. Accessed August 2008.

Mendheim, Beverly. *Ritchie Valens: The First Latino Rocker.* Tempe, AZ: Bilingual Press, 1987.

Pantoja, Antonia. *Memoir of a Visionary: Antonia Pantoja.* Houston, TX: Arte Público Press, 2002.

Pérez, Louis A., Jr. *Cuba: Between Reform and Revolution.* New York: Oxford University Press, 2006.

Reyes, David and Tom Waldman. *Land of a Thousand Dances: Chicano Rock 'n' Roll from Southern California.* Albuquerque, NM: University of New Mexico Press, 1998.

Rodríguez, Clara E. *Heroes, Lovers and Others: The Story of Hispanics in Hollywood.* Washington, D.C.: Smithsonian Institution, 2004.

Romero, Mary, Pierrette Hondagneu-Sotelo and Vilma Ortiz, eds. *Challenging Fronteras: Structuring Latina and Latino Lives in the U.S.* New York: Routledge, 1997.

Wilson, Clint C., II, et al. *Racism, Sexism, and the Media: The Rise of Class Communication in Multicultural America.* Thousand Oaks, CA: SAGE, 2003.

CHAPTER 9

A Changing Community: 1970 to 1989

IN THE 1970s the Hispanic-American population of the United States continued the work of political and social movements begun in the 1960s. Both established communities and newer immigrants contributed to forming new political action, lobbying, and direct action groups to lead these movements into the next decade. The groups they formed often had clear roots in specific ethnic or national communities, but a trend toward finding common ground among different Hispanic groups meant that their membership became increasingly diverse as the groups gained strength. Their long fight against discrimination set the stage for the growing visibility of Hispanic Americans in mainstream culture in the 1980s and beyond, when celebrities in the sports and entertainment worlds raised the profile of Hispanics in popular culture to new levels. These public figures were accompanied by growing numbers of Hispanic politicians in high positions in the U.S. government.

The 1980s were marked by the continued immigration of established groups of Hispanics, such as Mexicans and Puerto Ricans, but also by waves of new migrants. These groups included greater numbers of Cubans, and a new exodus of Central and South Americans driven from their homes by a series of wars in Central America and by political and economic fallout from military dictatorships in South America. These new arrivals entered a United States still charged with the old tensions over race, ethnicity, and immigration. However,

159

they also found their way eased somewhat by the work of past generations of Hispanic Americans, who had created many of their own social service organizations, and launched education and labor movements to advocate for their communities. Nevertheless, the statistics for Hispanic Americans in the 1980s showed that many still worked in lower-paid jobs with relatively little social mobility, although a number managed to establish small businesses or find management positions in large firms. A small, but growing number of Hispanic Americans also found work in white-collar professions. For poor Hispanic Americans, however, their circumstances continued to present a stark contrast to the advantages enjoyed by many Americans of British or other northern European heritage.

MEXICAN AMERICANS AND THE CHICANO MOVEMENT IN THE 1970s

Because of population and geography, the Mexican-American population continued to dominate the Hispanic-American community in the 1970s and 1980s. By 1978, of the 12 million Hispanic Americans in the United States, 7.3 million were from Mexico (or descended from migrants from Mexico), 1.7 million were from Puerto Rico (which had become a part of the United States in December 1898), 800,000 were from Cuba (or descended from Cubans), and 840,000 were from families with roots elsewhere in Central and South America.

The Chicano movement, also known as El Movimiento, emerged during the larger cultural and political activism of the 1960s, and peaked by the early 1970s. It found its largest following among young Mexican Americans and those living in California and southwestern states such as Texas, Arizona, Colorado, and New Mexico. Chicanos sought to create pride in their heritage as an important component of their ethnic identity, and to regain control of the construction of that heritage. Chicanos emphasized a rich cultural heritage that began in the mythic homeland, known as Aztlan, of the Aztec people indigenous to Mexico. This culture then blended with Spanish culture after the Spanish conquest of the Aztecs and settlement in the American southwest in the beginning in the early 1500s. Other popular cultural symbols incorporated by Chicanos included the Virgin of Guadalupe, the iconic beret-wearing image of revolutionary figure Ernesto "Che" Guevara, and the distinctive zoot suit, which featured a long padded jacket and narrow trousers. The result was a mestizo, or mixed, culture that they felt could create a sense of pride, rather than inferiority.

Chicanos rejected earlier Mexican Americans' attempts at assimilation into mainstream American society in favor of maintaining their own distinct culture. The movement also emphasized an understanding of the historical wrongs they had endured. They wished to right the injustices perpetrated in American (Anglo) society beginning when the United States acquired large chunks of Mexican territory under the 1848 Treaty of Guadalupe-Hidalgo that ended the Mexican-American War. Chicanos felt that U.S. citizens had illegally claimed Mexican-owned land in violation of the treaty's terms, had segregated and discriminated against them, viewing them only as cheap labor for exploitation. In the 1920s Americans had used the name Chicano as a negative reference to lower-class Mexican immigrants. The Chicano movement sought to appropriate the term with a positive meaning. Chicanos also used literary and artistic avenues such as novels and paintings to express their culture.

The Chicano movement's adopted manifesto, known as El Plan Espiritual de Aztlán, was created at the 1969 Chicano Youth Liberation Conference in Denver, Colorado. The movement sought to create a broad-based national fight for Mexican American civil rights that overcame differences in social class, economic status, political and religious beliefs, and regional identity. The Chicano movement's broad goals were self-determination, cultural pride, and a more equitable social, economic, and political standing. Social goals included an end to racism and discrimination, more access to health care and education, bilingual education, lower dropout rates, more representation in higher education, the inclusion of Chicanos in the teaching of U.S. history, and better relations with the police. Economic goals included lowered poverty rates, better conditions for migrant agricultural workers, and better job training and employment opportunities. Political goals included greater representation in local, state, and national elective offices, an end to legal issues surrounding official use of the Spanish language, and protests over the perceived over-representation of minorities in the Vietnam War.

The Chicano movement sought to achieve its goals through community activism, labor organization, and the formation of new social and political groups that had their roots in the earlier grassroots movements among Mexican Americans struggling for civil rights. They utilized Civil Rights–era tactics such as labor strikes, demonstrations, marches, and sit-ins. Key Chicano groups and organizations included the Mexican American Youth Organization (MAYO); the Brown Berets, a militant group patterned after the Black Panthers of the African-American Civil Rights movement; the United Farm Workers Union, a labor organization fighting for migrant agricultural worker rights; El Movimiento Estudiantil Chicano de Aztlan, which sought curriculum reform, the addition of Chicano Studies programs, and more effort to recruit and retain Chicano students

A group of Brown Beret leaders in Los Angeles in early 1968.

in higher education; and La Raza Unida, a Texas-based political party that achieved local successes, but was unable to achieve national results.

Chicano movement leaders included César Chávez, Dolores Huerta, José Angel Gutiérrez, Rodolfo "Corky" Gonzáles, and Reies López Tijerina. César Chávez and Dolores Huerta were cofounders of the United Farm Workers Union. Chávez emerged as the voice of the Chicano movement for many Americans, while Huerta brought attention to the fact that many migrant workers were women and that Chicanas would also play an active role in the movement. Jose Angel Gutierrez founded MAYO and, with Mario Compeán, organized La Raza Unida. Rodolfo "Corky" Gonzales, who had success in the Democratic Party until he became frustrated with mainstream politics, founded the Crusade for Justice and organized the 1969 Chicano Youth Liberation Conference in Denver, Colorado, where El Plan Espiritual de Aztlán was created. Reies Lopez Tijerina was active in the New Mexico struggle over land rights issues dating back to the 1848 Treaty of Guadalupe-Hidalgo known as the Tierra Amarilla land grant movement.

Key events of the Chicano movement began in the 1960s and continued into the 1970s. César Chávez had led a strike and grape boycott in Delano, California from 1965 to 1970 that received widespread media attention, bringing national attention to the Movement. On August 29, 1970, the Brown Berets led a Chicano Moratorium in opposition to police oppression and the

Members of the Chicano Moratorium Committee protesting the Vietnam War outside a military recruitment office in Los Angeles in late 1969.

Vietnam War in Los Angeles, California, that resulted in a riot and violent clash between protestors and police forces that killed a Mexican-American reporter. Educational activists also sponsored a series of student walkouts in Los Angeles in the late 1960s and early 1970s to protest low funding, inadequate supplies, and excessive dropout rates in area schools. Despite the successes the Chicano Movement experienced, it began to fade on the national level after the mid 1970s. Regional interests, class divisions, and generational tensions made national cohesiveness difficult to maintain. The Chicano Movement's goals and sense of pride remained alive, however, passed on to a new generation of Mexican Americans.

César Chávez at a United Farm Workers rally in Delano in 1974.

MEXICAN AMERICANS IN THE 1980s

During the 1980s 14 percent of all immigrants in the United States came from Mexico, seven percent from Cuba, and 11 percent from Central or South America. By the 1980s many wealthy Mexicans had strong links with the United States, with their children attending U.S. schools and colleges. However, the United States also remained a magnet for large numbers of poorer migrants. Some sought better-paying, white-collar employment in Texas, California, and elsewhere, while others sought laboring jobs.

Although many Mexicans have pursued work in the United States since the 1840s, their numbers have always increased in times of political and economic upheaval in Mexico. Under the presidency of José López Portillo from 1976 to 1982, the Mexican economy developed with increased oil revenue, which allowed the government to nationalize the banking industry and start a spending program based not just on taxes and oil, but also on borrowing. The finance minister, Miguel de la Madrid Hurtado, championed the country's first Global Development Plan. However, by the time Hurtado became president in 1982, the country was facing a major problem following a significant rise in U.S. interest rates. This led the Mexican government to introduce a massive austerity program that saw large cuts in government spending enforced by the International Monetary Fund and World Bank as Mexico sought to pay, or to reschedule the repayment of, government debt. The price of oil within the country doubled, and as Mexico was engulfed in a major debt crisis as well as a breakdown in law due to drug trafficking, many more Mexicans started seeking work in the United States, where the economy was booming.

Increased U.S. border patrols to combat illegal immigrants resulted in tensions between the two countries, as well as resistance to the increasing numbers of Mexican Americans, the vast majority having arrived in the United States legally. Although many politicians wanted to stem the number of migrants, others recognized the economic benefits of low-paid laborers for factories and farms. The result was the Immigration Reform and Control Act—or the Simpson-Mazzoli Act, after sponsors Senator Alan K. Simpson and Representative Romano L. Mazzoli—that passed through Congress in 1986. It managed to attract the support of the United Farm Workers of America, the AFL-CIO, and also the conservative Senator Jesse Helms. The act granted an amnesty to all undocumented workers who had at least two years of continual residence in the United States, but also introduced harsh penalties for employers who hired any newly arrived illegal immigrants. The move led to problems for many Mexican Americans as well as other Hispanic Americans, who were frightened by the racist nature of the debate. However, they supported the amnesty, and saw that the United States recognized the economic role played by many illegal immigrants.

PUERTO RICANS IN THE 1970s AND 1980s

The largest wave of Puerto Rican migration to the U.S. mainland started at the end of World War II in 1945 and continued through the 1960s. Although the numbers began to level off in the 1970s and 1980s, many Puerto Ricans still came to the U.S. mainland during this period in search of economic opportunity in the form of agricultural and industrial employment. This was especially true during the 1970s economic recession that resulted in massive unemployment on the island. Other reasons for immigration included Puerto Rico's large population and high poverty rates, as well as inexpensive travel options and the fact that Puerto Rican immigrants did not need a passport or visa. The Puerto Rican government encouraged this migration in order to reduce unemployment rates. It sponsored migration offices in New York and other U.S. cities with high numbers of Puerto Rican residents that provided assistance with immigration procedures, housing, employment, and battling discrimination. Puerto Rican immigrants also maintained strong ties to Puerto Rico and frequently visited home.

Most Puerto Rican immigrants settled in urban neighborhoods in eastern and Midwestern states such as New York, New Jersey, Pennsylvania, Massachusetts, Connecticut, Florida, Ohio, Illinois, and California. The cities with the largest Puerto Rican populations included New York, Chicago, Newark, and Philadelphia. New York City had the largest number of Puerto Ricans, most located within the Lower East Side neighborhood known as Loisaida in Manhattan and the East Harlem neighborhood known as El Barrio. The Puerto Rican population in the mainland United States also grew through high birth rates. The term *Nuyorican* came into use in the 1960s to describe Puerto

Ricans born in New York City, and their dual cultural identity as both Puerto Ricans and Americans. Challenges faced by Puerto Ricans living in the mainland included the predominance of low-paying jobs in the manufacturing and service industries, the 1970s recession that resulted in an economic crisis in New York, overcrowding and dilapidated housing, police relations, discrimination, and a lack of educational opportunities.

Puerto Rican activists had begun organizing civil rights groups in the 1960s to improve the social, economic, and political status of Puerto Ricans in the mainland United States. Goals included an end to discrimination, more educational and employment opportunities, and better housing conditions. Aspira, founded in 1961, continued to promote high school and college

A young member of the Puerto Rican community in Lowell, Massachusetts, who was crowned "princess" at a community festival on August 22, 1987.

graduation as well as technical training, cultural pride, and leadership skills for the next generation of community activists. The Puerto Rican Legal Defense and Education Fund was founded in 1972 to provide legal assistance to Puerto Ricans facing housing or employment discrimination, among other issues. The National Puerto Rican Coalition, consisting of representatives from other national associations, was founded in 1977 to coordinate national activities. Other active organizations included the Puerto Rican Merchants Association, the Puerto Rican Forum, the National Congress for Puerto Rican Rights, and the Puerto Rican Association for Community Affairs. Active local organizations included the East Harlem Council for Human Services in New York, and the Emergency Tenants Council in Boston. In the early 1970s, Puerto Ricans in New York successfully sued for bilingual ballots, claiming that English-only ballots discriminated against native-born Americans whose first language was Spanish. Puerto Ricans also sought elective offices on the city, state, and national levels. Herman Badillo of the Bronx in New York became the first Puerto Rican elected to Congress with his 1970 election to the U.S. House of Representatives.

In the 1970s there were several organizations that made up the core of the Puerto Rican movement, including the Young Lords Party and the Puerto Rican

Socialist Party. The majority of activists within these radical groups were young. Their goals included cultural pride, an end to discrimination and poverty, labor unionism, and Puerto Rican independence. The Puerto Rican Young Lords was initially formed in the 1960s by Chicago street gang members, led by Jose "Cha Cha" Jiménez. It was a grassroots militant movement similar to the African-American Black Panthers and the Mexican-American Brown Berets. The main base of operations soon shifted to New York, however, due to its larger Puerto Rican population. Young Lords groups also arose in Philadelphia, Boston, Newark, and Connecticut, as well as in Puerto Rico itself.

The Young Lords' main focus was to end the dependence of Puerto Rico on the United States. Other goals included ethnic pride and improving the social, economic, and political conditions of Puerto Ricans living in the mainland United States. Their activities included health screenings, offerings of food and clothing, workshops on Puerto Rican history, strikes, boycotts, and forcible sit-ins at churches and hospitals. They also lobbied the New York City Board of Education for the inclusion of Latino studies in the public school curriculum. They published a New York community newspaper entitled *Pa'lante*. The group began to dissolve in 1972, but reappeared briefly in 1977 to hang a Puerto Rican flag from the top of the Statue of Liberty.

The Puerto Rican Socialist Party (Partido Socialista Puertorriqueno) was founded in Puerto Rico in 1959 as the Pro-Independence Movement (Mov-

A Puerto Rican restaurant in Paterson, New Jersey. Puerto Ricans predominated among small business owners in the city in the 1970s, but were later replaced by Dominicans and Colombians.

imiento Pro-Independencia). The name would be changed in 1971. Communist in nature, the group was influenced by the 1959 Cuban Revolution that brought Fidel Castro to power. Their primary goals were to win Puerto Rico independence from its status as a U.S. commonwealth, as well as to rid Puerto Rico of the U.S. corporations that established a large presence there. They also became active in the anti–Vietnam War movement. Prominent party leaders on the island included Juan Mari Bras and Carlos Gallisa Bisbal. The party faced threats, bombings, and assassination attempts from anticommunist groups.

The Puerto Rican Socialist Party was associated with the U.S. Progressive Labor Party and established their own U.S. presence in 1973, most notably in New York and Chicago. In that year the U.S. branch's First Congress drafted and approved their political declaration, known as Desde Las Entrañas. Prominent U.S. party leaders included Luis Gutiérrez, who would later be elected to the U.S. Senate in the 1990s. The party's October 27, 1974, rally supporting Puerto Rican independence, held in Madison Square Garden in New York, attracted approximately 20,000 people. The party's political philosophy and activities brought them to the attention of the FBI's COINTELPRO program, which sought to infiltrate activist organizations and undermine them from within. In the 1980s members began debating over the use of militant tactics or electoral politics as the best avenue to achieve their goals, causing divisive-ness. Party membership began to decline in the 1980s, although the party would not formally disband until 1993. The party newspaper, *Claridad*, continued to be published.

DOMINICAN AMERICANS IN THE 1970s

Immigration from the Dominican Republic to the United States had begun to increase in the 1960s for both political and economic reasons. The political and economic stability that had come to that country, beginning with the 1966 rule of Joaquín Balaguer and rises in sugar prices and tourism, faded in the mid 1970s. Sugar and coffee demand dropped along with prices on the world market, oil prices rose, several hurricanes devastated the island, unemployment rose to high levels, and inflation further hurt the economy. A mounting international debt continued to expand in the 1980s, resulting in government-sanctioned austerity measures and deteriorating living conditions that impelled further immigration to the United States and Puerto Rico. Some Dominicans came for political reasons, but most based their decision on economic factors.

Most Dominicans entered the United States through a process known as chain migration, in which relatives who were legal immigrants or naturalized U.S. citizens sponsored newly arriving family members under immigration law provisions for family reunification. Most Dominican Americans chose to retain their status as permanent resident aliens, although the number of naturalized U.S. citizens increased steadily beginning in the 1980s. Most Dominican immigrants came from the middle class due to the expense of immigration.

There was also a small population of illegal, undocumented Dominican immigrants living in the United States. Many Dominican immigrants to the United States did not intend to stay permanently. Rather, they hoped to save money and return home with a higher economic and social standing.

Although Dominican Americans remained a small percentage of U.S. Hispanics and did not received national attention, they were one of the fastest-growing U.S. Hispanic immigrant populations in this period. The increase in Dominican immigration to the United States resulted in the development of Dominican-American neighborhoods in a several U.S. cities. Most Dominican Americans settled in urban areas of the northeast, mainly in New York, New Jersey, and Massachusetts. A sizeable number also settled in Florida. Cities with notable Dominican-American populations include New York City, especially within the Washington Heights neighborhood called Quisqueya by Dominicans, Boston, and Miami. They tended to settle together, usually in close proximity to other urban immigrant and minority communities, which sometimes led to conflict over employment, housing, and other community resources.

The majority of Dominican Americans also retained close ties with their home country, and its close proximity to the United States made visits home easier. Consequently, many periodically returned to the Dominican Republic to visit, especially on holidays. Some also maintained businesses there. These returnees were known as *retornados,* and made valuable contributions to the Dominican economy. Many Dominican Americans also regularly sent money to relatives who still resided in the Dominican Republic. These payments are known as remittances.

Many Dominican immigrants to the United States were of mixed African, Spanish, and indigenous heritage. Although many tended to have higher education levels and employment histories in the Dominican Republic before leaving, most were employed in low-paying jobs in industry or service occupations in the United States. Some Dominican Americans worked more than one job out of economic necessity or to earn extra money to send to relatives back home. Birth rates were lower and families were generally smaller as compared to the large extended families found in the Dominican Republic.

Major League Baseball pitcher Pedro Martínez (left), who was born in the Dominican Republic in 1971, making a return visit in 2009 as part of a charitable project for local teenagers.

Although Dominican-American families tended to be smaller and women frequently worked outside the home and took on greater responsibilities for traditionally male endeavors such as the household budget, the importance of family within the culture remained strong. Family needs were expected to come before individual wants. Family members aided each other within the United States, and sent remittances to aid those members still residing in the Dominican Republic or to help pay for the cost of their immigration to the United States or Puerto Rico. Parents also emphasized the importance of education to their children as a key avenue to improving their future job prospects and economic standing. Neighbors, friends, churches, and community-based social organizations also provided support for both settled immigrants and new arrivals. In the 1970s many new arrivals found help with housing and employment through the more established Puerto Rican community.

Dominican Americans became socially and politically active mostly on the local community level. Community improvement began first through Dominican-American social organizations that began appearing in the 1970s. These organizations provided recreational activities, as well as assistance with job training, employment, and language instruction. They also began fundraising for various community projects. In the 1970s several community organizations united to form the *Concilio de Organizaciones Dominicanas* (Council of Dominican Organizations). These activities brought communities together and raised awareness of the benefits of organization in a more political arena. Initial political concerns had centered on politics within the Dominican Republic. In the 1970s the *Asociación Nacional de Dominicanos Ausentes* (National Association of Absent Dominicans) sought to maintain the right to vote in Dominican elections. The focus gradually shifted to U.S. politics.

DOMINICAN AMERICANS IN THE 1980s

Dominican Americans began running for local elective offices in New York City in the mid 1980s. Their culture's emphasis on the importance of education made this area one of their prime political targets. For example, in the 1980s the Community Association of Progressive Dominicans in New York City confronted the local school board to demand bilingual education for new immigrants and an end to school overcrowding in the Washington Heights area. Dominican students were active in higher education within the City University of New York system. Other political issues targeted by Dominican American activists included the plight of illegal immigrants, the citizenship process, housing, discrimination, and police relations. Dominican-American political activists sought to unite Dominican Americans to raise government awareness of their needs.

Culture provided another source for Dominican Americans to enter the mainstream American consciousness. Traditional Dominican culture and lifestyles underwent changes as Dominican immigrants adapted to life in the United States, but Dominican Americans retained strong ties to their cultural heritage as well. Traditional cultural maintenance was strengthened by the phenomenon of the retornados. Most Dominican Americans remained Roman Catholic, the predominant religion of their homeland. Most also continued to speak Spanish while learning English, often blending the two in a practice commonly known as Spanglish or Dominicanish. They prepared traditional Caribbean dishes with ingredients readily available at neighborhood grocery stores known as *bodegas*. The sport of baseball maintained its cultural significance, and Dominican baseball players in the United States became cultural icons. Dominican newspapers were available in New York City Dominican-American communities. In 1985 Casa Dominica was founded in New York City. It promoted Dominican art and culture until a lack of funding forced its closure five years later. By the 1980s aspects of Dominican culture such as the music and dance of the merengue, which came to symbolize the Dominican identity, had even achieved popularity within mainstream American culture.

CUBAN AMERICANS IN THE 1970s

Cuban exiles and refugees had been arriving in the United States in waves since the 1959 communist revolution that brought Fidel Castro to power. The numbers of Cuban exiles seeking U.S. homes ebbed and flowed according to the changing status of political and economic relations between the countries. In the 1970s and 1980s, Castro periodically allowed emigration from Cuba. Cuban immigration numbers declined in the 1970s after the initial flood of exiles lessened, although the "Freedom Flights" begun in the mid 1960s when Castro opened immigration to those with U.S. relatives persisted until 1973. Cuban refugees continued to be political pawns, as the United States encouraged exiles as a propaganda means of discrediting communism and the Castro regime.

Cuban immigrants entered the United States without restrictions throughout the 1970s. Under the Cuban Adjustment Act of 1966, any Cuban exile entering the United States was free and could received permanent resident alien immigration status after a period of one year. The Cuban Refugee Program and Refugee Emergency Center, as well as a variety of private and religious groups, continued to provide assistance with settlement, education, medical care, and employment training. Florida, which had historically been the primary destination for Cuban immigrants, continued to attract most of the new arrivals. Most entered through the south Florida city of Miami in Dade County and settled there permanently, aiding Miami's emergence as a Latin American center of international banking, trade, and tourism. Others dispersed throughout the United States, with some returning to Miami years later.

The 1980 Mariel Boat Lift

The Mariel boat lift had its origins in an incident that caused a rift between the Cuban government and the Peruvian Embassy in Havana in April 1980. After a bus filled with refugees seeking asylum crashed through the embassy gates, Cuban President Fidel Castro announced that anyone wishing to leave the island should immediately go to the embassy. Thousands of would-be émigrés crowded the embassy grounds within days. Others hid in the swamps on the outskirts of

Emigrants arriving from Cuba at Key West, Florida, in 1980.

the northern port city of Mariel, waiting for official permission to emigrate. Both groups suffered from a lack of food and water as they waited. Despite harassment, the émigrés were allowed to leave. Earlier Cuban exiles living in Miami traveled to Cuba in a flotilla of boats of all sizes organized by car salesman and political activist Napoleon Vilaboa in order to bring the émigrés back across the Florida straits to U.S. shores.

Approximately 125,000 so-called Marielitos entered the United States from May to September of 1980 as a result of the Mariel boat lift, most of them remaining in the south Florida area. The U.S. government required all new arrivals who did not have U.S. family members to sponsor them to remain in processing centers or detention camps until their future status was decided. Immigrants were even processed in tent cities and a Miami football stadium, and the process took months to years to complete. The new Cuban immigrants received less federal aid than their earlier counterparts, instead relying more heavily on voluntary agencies for assistance with housing, food, clothing, and employment. The U.S. government provided $10 million in emergency funds to reimburse these groups.

Other problems faced by the new arrivals stemmed from the fact that they were more racially and economically diverse than their predecessors, including large numbers of Afro-Cubans who would suffer the same discrimination as African Americans. They also faced the stigma that their numbers contained dangerous criminals Castro had sent to the United States in the boat lift. Although the number of criminals was small, their presence drew nationwide publicity. The strain placed on south Florida's resources and employment opportunities resulted in increased tensions between the Cuban immigrants and minority groups such as African Americans. In 1980 a race riot erupted in Miami after the acquittal of a Hispanic police officer who shot an African American. Partly as a result of the problems associated with the Mariel boat lift, the 1980 Refugee Act reduced the number of Cuban refugees that would be admitted to the United States annually.

CUBAN AMERICANS IN THE 1980s

The 1980s saw a resurgence in the number of immigrants, most notably during the Mariel boatlift of 1980, which brought approximately 125,000 Cuban immigrants to the United States. Cuban immigrants arrived through a variety of methods, including organized air and boat lifts, as well as more risky trips across the Florida Straits aboard small boats or homemade rafts. Rafters became known as *balseros*. During this period Cuban Americans grew to one of the largest Hispanic groups within the United States. The 1980 Refugee Act lowered the number of Cuban refugees who would be admitted each year, as the U.S. public began calling for overall immigration restriction to ease competition for jobs and public services. Throughout the 1980s, U.S. presidents Ronald Reagan and George H.W. Bush took a hard line on relations with Cuba, refusing to have any contact with the communist government of Fidel Castro. This was a stance welcomed by the Cuban-American community, which flexed its political muscle in Louisiana (especially New Orleans), as well as in Florida's Dade County, home to about 600,000 out of a total of 800,000 Cuban Americans.

The first wave of Cuban immigrants in the 1960s had been mostly white, upper- and middle-class businessmen and professionals opposed to Castro's policies of property expropriation and the redistribution of wealth. They had achieved economic success and the development of close communities such as the "Little Havana" area of Miami, Florida, after realizing that Castro's regime would not quickly fail and that they would consequently remain in the United States for a lengthy period. These older arrivals provided a ready source of resettlement help to newer arrivals in the 1970s and 1980s. Cuban Americans in the 1970s continued the process of establishing close communities in which they maintained their own language, customs, culture, religion, and food. Overall Cuban Americans were more readily accepted into American society and received more federal aid than other immigrant groups due to their political motivations for immigration. According to the U.S. Census, Cuban Americans had higher education levels, better jobs, and higher incomes than those of the general Hispanic population within the United States.

Newer arrivals in the 1980s, such as the "Marielitos" of the 1980 Mariel boatlift, experienced more difficulty and discrimination due to the higher percentage of Afro-Cubans, those without higher education, money, or job training, and those without family members already residing in the United States. Arrivals in the 1980s also had to face the stigma that Castro had used the Mariel boatlift to unload Cuban criminals onto U.S. shores. In Miami, they also encountered racial tensions with African Americans who increasingly viewed them as competition for jobs and resources. Several riots broke out in the city in the 1980s, including a notable 1980 riot begun after a Hispanic police officer who shot an African American was acquitted in a jury trial. The Cuban-American population left a permanent impact on both U.S.

and Florida demographics. Many historians feel the multicultural growth of Florida's population and culture, such as the development of Miami's large Cuban-American neighborhood, is a forerunner of the growing ethnic diversity in the rest of the country.

Cuban Americans remained one of the most politically active immigrant groups in the United States in the 1970s and 1980s. Those exiles who had fled Cuba in the 1960s after Castro came to power retained their anticommunist political activism, as they became naturalized U.S. citizens and acquired the right to vote. Cuban Americans were interested in both local and national politics. The Miami Cuban-American community emerged as the most powerful political voice due to their high concentration in that city. They lobbied the U.S. government to maintain its tough sanctions against Cuba as long as Castro remained in power. Cuban Americans also emerged as an important voting bloc in presidential elections in the swing state of Florida, where the balance between Republicans and Democrats was close.

CENTRAL AND SOUTH AMERICANS IN THE 1970s AND 1980s

In the late 1970s, most of Central America was reeling from the fall of the regime of Anastasio Somoza, the president of Nicaragua, who fled Managua in July 1979 just before it fell to the left-wing Sandinista revolutionary movement. A number of Somoza's supporters and some of the emerging opponents of the new Sandinista government moved to the United States, where they campaigned successfully for support from the U.S. government under President Reagan. The Reagan government started an active policy of helping the Contra rebel movement in Nicaragua, and providing military aid to the neighboring governments of El Salvador and Guatemala, which were both involved in devastating civil wars. As the civil strife in Nicaragua, El Salvador, and Guatemala increased in ferocity, with tens of thousands of people killed in each country, many were eager to flee the conflict for the United States. Many of the Central-American migrants to the United States were, however, the poor looking for jobs in the United States, and often ending up employed in low-paid farming or factory work.

There were also many problems in Panama, which was in a unique position because the Panama Canal Territory was occupied by the United States, but scheduled to be handed back to full Panamanian sovereignty in 1999. In 1989 the United States invaded Panama to oust General Manuel Noriega, a dictator who was involved in drug trafficking and money laundering. He was seized and jailed in the United States in 1992.

The economic crisis that hit Mexico in the early 1980s was also a major factor in the economic and political problems in South America. High interest rates in the United States caused a major crisis over debt repayments by some countries such as Brazil and Argentina. This in turn put great strain on many of the military dictatorships in the region, causing the collapse of the military government of Leopoldo Galtieri in Argentina; the government of João Baptista da Oliveira Figueiredo in Brazil; the government of Gregorio Conrado Alvarez Armelino in Uruguay; and even the government built by longtime strongman Alfredo Stroessner of Paraguay, who fled his palace in Asunción after holding power in his country for nearly 35 years.

After the rise of many of these dictators (and their predecessors) led to the crackdowns of the 1970s and early 1980s, many left-wing and moderate political activists in the region sought refuge in countries around the world, including the United States. This led to a great number of Latin American intellectuals either living or conducting lectures in the United States. Much interest emerged in literature set in Latin America, with writers—not all of them political—such as Gabriel García Márquez, who won the Nobel Prize for Literature in 1982. They became household names in the United States, and raised the profile of many Hispanic-American intellectuals.

HISPANIC AMERICANS IN SPORTS, ENTERTAINMENT, AND CULTURE

Although the U.S. media often focused its coverage of Hispanics on poor Mexican Americans working in menial work as farm hands, factory workers, or cleaners, there were also many skilled Hispanics who found greater opportunities, and even widespread acclaim in the United States in the 1970s and 1980s. One such success story was that of Fernando Valenzuela, who was born in 1960 in Etchohuaquila, a small village in Mexico. When he was 19, he signed a contract to play as a left-handed pitcher for the Los Angeles Dodgers. There were many Hispanic immigrants in Los Angeles, and they became his strong supporters, helping to make him one of the most famous U.S. baseball players 1980–94. His success in 1980 immediately led to stardom, and in 1981, when President Ronald Reagan met with Mexican President José López Portillo, Valenzuela was invited to the White House reception. There were the inevitable racial slurs against him by some of the press, but what investigative reporters eventually found was a real success story for not only Valenzuela, but also for the idea of merit-based fame for Mexican Americans in the United States. For Hispanics, Valenzuela represented one of the greatest triumphs in the United States for a person of Mexican heritage. The contrast of his poor upbringing and his great wealth in the United States remains an inspiration to many Hispanic Americans.

There were many other important Hispanic-American athletes in the 1980s. Keith Hernández, born in San Francisco of Hispanic parents, played for the St. Louis Cardinals from 1974 to 1983, and for the New York Mets from 1983 to 1989. José Canseco, also from a Mexican background, was a designated hitter in Major League Baseball, and eventually earned the American League Rookie of the Year in 1986. He continued to play until his retirement in 2003. Sammy Sosa, who had been born in the Dominican Republic, made his Major League Baseball debut in June 1989 for the Texas Rangers. Other Hispanic-

Mexican-American baseball player Fernando Valenzuela, who pitched for the Los Angeles Dodgers, visiting schoolchildren at the Sheridan Street School in Los Angeles in 1984 as part of a campaign to improve school attendance rates.

American athletes of the decade included Michael Anthony Muñoz from California, who became famous for his tackling agility with the NFL's Cincinnati Bengals from 1980 to 1992; and Alberto Salazar from Cuba, one of the most famous U.S. marathon runners in the 1980s, who performed well in the New York Marathon, as well as the Stockholm and Oslo marathons of 1982.

In the arts, one of the most famous Puerto Ricans during the 1980s was Jean-Michel Basquiat, the son of Haitian and Puerto Rican migrants who had moved to New York many years earlier. A painter, he was influenced by Andy Warhol, Pablo Picasso, and Henri Matisse. His work reflected his career as a rebel and high school dropout, and his involvement in the hip-hop culture as a neoexpressionist.

Emilio Estévez, born in New York of Hispanic ancestry, was involved in the "Brat Pack" group of actors in the 1980s, appearing in films such as *The Breakfast Club* and *St. Elmo's Fire*, released in 1985; and *Young Guns*, released in 1988. Hispanic-American folk singer and political activist Joan Báez wrote her memoir *And a Voice to Sing With* in 1987, which relayed the story of her life in New York City and then in California.

One success story from Panama crossed the line between music, acting, and politics. Panamanian-American Rubén Blades was a successful salsa musician who took up roles in 1980s films such as *Crossover Dreams* (1985)

Franklin Chang-Díaz stands before the space shuttle Discovery *prior to his 1998 mission to the* Mir *space station.*

and *The Milagro Beanfield War* (1988). Blades later returned to Panama City, and in 1994, he placed a respectable third place in the presidential elections in Panama.

The vast U.S. aid effort in Central America did much to encourage the middle class to send their children to U.S. universities and colleges. There were many success stories, some predating the fighting in the region. One of these was Franklin Ramón Chang-Díaz, who was born in San Jose, the capital of Costa Rica. His father was of Chinese, Japanese, and Amerindian heritage, and his mother was Spanish from Costa Rica. Moving to the United States to complete his school education, Chang-Díaz gained his doctorate in science from the Massachusetts Institute of Technology in plasma physics, and in 1980 was selected as an astronaut candidate by NASA, taking part in space shuttle missions until 1986. His daughter, Sonia, became the first Hispanic-American woman elected to the Massachusetts Senate.

Cuban Americans rose to prominence in a wide range of fields. Gloria María Milagrosa Fajardo García—Gloria Estefan—was born in 1961 in Havana, Cuba's capital. Soon after her birth, her family was forced to flee after the Castro government came to power. Her father, a Cuban exile, had been captured in the abortive Bay of Pigs invasion in 1961. As a famous popular music artist who was given the title Queen of Latin Pop, Estefan's single *Don't Wanna Lose You* in 1989 was certified Platinum for sales in the United States, and reached number one on the Billboard Hot 100. Fashion model (and later actress) Cameron Michelle Díaz, born in San Diego, California, was the daughter of a second-generation Cuban father and an English, German, and Cherokee Native-American mother. Modelling for Calvin Klein and Levi's Jeans as a teenager, she soon became famous in the United States.

Another successful Cuban was Carlos Miguel Gutiérrez, born in Cuba in 1953, the son of a pineapple plantation owner whose property was seized by Castro's communist government. The family settled in Miami, where young Carlos worked as a bellhop at the hotel where his family was staying until they gained U.S. citizenship. Gutiérrez then went into business. He became a sales representative at Kellogg's in 1975, working for the cereal manufacturer through the 1980s and 1990s. In February 2005, he became U.S. secretary of commerce, a post he held until January 2009.

One of the foremost Latin American writers who settled in the United States was Isabel Allende, who fled her native Chile after the assassination of her uncle Salvador Allende in 1973. A vociferous opponent of the military dictatorship of Augusto Pinochet, in 1981 she wrote a letter to her terminally ill grandfather, which became her first book, *The House of the Spirits*. Other books followed, and her style of magic realism, welcomed by many Hispanic Americans and others, propelled her to become the most successful woman novelist from Latin America, as well as one of the most high-profile Hispanic Americans in the country. Sandra Cisneros, a writer born in Chicago in 1954, published her book *The House on Mango Street* in 1984. It drew from her memories of growing up in an unstable, poverty-riddled childhood between Mexico and Chicago, and won the Before Columbus American Book Award. She also wrote poetry, and one volume, *My Wicked Wicked Ways*, was published in 1987.

HISPANIC AMERICANS IN POLITICS

Hispanic Americans have long been involved in U.S. politics, and in the 1980s, there were two long-serving Hispanic members of the U.S. House of Representatives for Texas, both Democrats: Henry B. González, for the 20th District 1961–99; and Kika de la Garza, for the 15th District 1965–97. De la Garza was heavily involved in improving U.S.–Mexican relations, and drew much support from poorer Hispanic Americans. In New York, politician and former member of the U.S. House of Representatives Herman Badillo, from Puerto Rico, was deputy mayor of New York until 1979 and remained active in the New York Democrat Party machine through the 1980s. Most Hispanic Americans tended to identify with the Democratic Party, although some Cuban Americans, because of strident anticommunism and their support for the Reagan and Bush policies on Cuba, were Republicans.

Although most Hispanic Americans did vote Democratic during the 1980s, it was President Reagan who, in September 1988, appointed Lauro Cavazos from Kingsville, Texas, as the 4th U.S. secretary of education in September 1988, a position he held until December 1990. Lauro Cavazos—whose brother, Richard E. Cavazos, had become the first four-star, Hispanic-American general in the U.S. Army—became the first Hispanic American to serve in the U.S. cabinet. When George H.W. Bush became president, Cavazos remained in his post (although he was eventually forced to resign over problems with the use of frequent flyer miles) and was joined in the cabinet by Mexican-born Manuel Luján, Jr., whose father had been mayor of Santa Fe. Following his father into politics, he was a member of the U.S. House of Representatives for New Mexico 1969–89, before being appointed as the 46th U.S. secretary of the interior.

Bill Richardson (center) in 1984, when he was the chair of the Congressional Hispanic Caucus. Other caucus members pictured include (left to right) Representatives Henry B. González, Manuel Luján, Baltasar Corrada, Robert García, Antony Coelho, Rod de Lugo, Matthew Martínez, Ed Roybal, and Esteban Torres. The caucus has since added a number of female members.

Other Hispanic-American politicians of this period included Bill Richardson, who was elected to the U.S. House of Representatives for New Mexico in 1983, holding the seat until 1997 when he was appointed as U.S. Ambassador to the United Nations and later becoming U.S. Secretary of Energy; and Frederico Pena, the son of Hispanic migrants from Texas who, in 1979, was elected as a Democrat to the Colorado House of Representatives and became the minority leader. In 1983, Pena managed to defeat the 14-year incumbent William H. McNichols, Jr., to become the first Hispanic elected as mayor of Denver; he was reelected in 1987. In January 1993 he was appointed the 12th U.S. secretary of transportation, and four years later became the 8th U.S. secretary of energy.

The 1980s were also a period when many other Hispanic Americans began their involvement in politics. Alberto Gonzáles, later U.S. attorney general, gained his doctorate in law from Harvard Law School in 1982, and during the 1980s was in private practice in Houston. Ken Salazar also served as chief legal counsel to Colorado Governor Roy Romer in 1986.

CONCLUSION

In the 1970s and 1980s, Hispanic Americans' fight against discrimination began to show significant progress, even as early activist groups disbanded or

changed focus. This progress came about in part though unexpected means, such as the national celebrity of Mexican-American baseball player Fernando Valenzuela, which opened the door for the increased acceptance and even admiration of Hispanic heros in mainstream American culture. Talented artists from new immigrant groups, such as South American writer Isabel Allende and Cuban musician Gloria Estefan, also helped raise the profile of Hispanic culture in the United States. The fact that the achievements of these celebrities were paralleled by growing numbers of Hispanic politicians in Congress and elsewhere appeared to bode well for Hispanic Americans in the 1990s and 2000s.

CHRISTINA V. JONES
SOUTHEASTERN UNIVERSITY
JUSTIN CORFIELD
GEELONG GRAMMAR SCHOOL, AUSTRALIA

Further Reading

Burchard, S.H. *Sports Star: Fernando Valenzuela*. San Diego, CA: Harcourt Brace Jovanovich, 1982.

Fitzpatrick, Joseph P. and Lourdes Travieso Parker. "Hispanic-Americans in the Eastern United States," *Annals of the American Academy of Political and Social Science,* Vol. 454, March 1981.

Fraga, Luis Ricardo, Kenneth J. Meier, and Robert E. England. "Hispanic Americans and Educational Policy: Limits to Equal Access," *The Journal of Politics,* Vol. 48, No. 4, November 1986.

Massey, Douglas S. and Kathleen M. Schnabel. "Recent Trends in Hispanic Immigration to the United States," *International Migration Review,* Vol. 17, No. 2, summer 1983.

Pérez-Brown, María. *Mama: Latina Daughters Celebrate Their Mothers*. New York: HarperCollins Publishers, 2003.

Portes, Alejandro and Robert L. Bach. *Latin Journey: Cuban and Mexican Immigrants in the United States*. Berkeley, CA: University of California Press, 1985.

Ramírez, Amelie G., Alfred McAlister, Kipling J. Gallion, and Roberto Villareal. "Targeting Hispanic Populations: Future Research and Prevention Strategies," *Environmental Health Perspectives*, Vol. 103, Supplement 8, November 1995.

Richardson, Bill. "Hispanic American Concerns." *Foreign Policy,* No. 60, Autumn 1985.

Unterburger, Amy L. and Jane Delgado. *Who's Who among Hispanic Americans 1991–92*. Detroit, MI: Gale Research Inc., 1991.

CHAPTER 10

Hispanic America Today: 1990 to the Present

HISPANIC AMERICANS ARE now the largest minority group in the United States, and by 2050, they are expected to comprise 25 percent of the total population. In 1991 Hispanic Americans made up nine percent of the total American population. By 2002 there were 37.4 million Hispanics living in the United States. Within six years, the number had grown to 45 million. The influence of Hispanic culture on life in the United States has expanded in response to this population growth. The influence has been particularly strong in music and food. While Hispanic Americans share a common language, a history of Spanish colonialism, and similar religious beliefs, they also belong to distinct cultures.

In rank order, the largest Hispanic groups living in the United States are Mexican Americans, Puerto Ricans, Cuban Americans, and Dominican Americans. Other large groups of Hispanic Americans include those from Ecuador, Colombia, Guatemala, and El Salvador. The term "Hispanic" is used to describe all immigrants and their descendants from Spanish-speaking countries, including Mexico, Spain, the Caribbean Islands, and Central and South America. Puerto Ricans are also considered Hispanic, but they are U.S. citizens at birth because Puerto Rico is a territory of the United States. Immigrants from Brazil and Portugal are not Hispanic because they speak Portuguese, rather than Spanish.

181

Three percent of the U.S. Hispanic population is classified as black, including many Americans from Caribbean countries. This Afro-Caribbean dancer performed at the West Indian–American Day Parade in Brooklyn, New York, on September 1, 2008.

Since the 1960s there have been differences of opinion on how Spanish-speaking Americans prefer to be identified; class and region sometimes play a role. The Mexican-American activists of the 1960s preferred the term "Chicano," but it is rarely used in the 21st century. Some Spanish speakers resent being identified as "Hispanics," contending that the term has connotations of slavery. Others object to "Latino," insisting that it is often mistaken for "Ladino," the language spoken by the Jewish people of Spain. The "Latino/Latina" identification is preferred by many Spanish-speaking groups because they believe it is more representative of their Latin American history, and the gains made by Hispanic Americans during the Civil Rights movement. Those who favor "Latino/Latina" also feel that the term better symbolizes the combining of European and indigenous heritages within the United States. The term "Hispanic" is most commonly used, in part because it was adopted by federal agencies in 1970 and has since come to be recognized as a generic term for individuals who identify with the Spanish language and culture. It was not until the 2000 census that "Latino" was included as an option for Spanish-speaking people.

During the colonial period, Europeans, Africans, and indigenous peoples intermarried to produce generations of Latin Americans with "mixed blood" who identified with more than one culture. Before 1980, Hispanic Americans were required by the U.S. Census Bureau to classify themselves as either black or white. After that time, Americans with a Spanish-speaking heritage could classify themselves as Hispanic. In the 1990 census, respondents were given the option of choosing "other" to define race. Less than one percent of non-Hispanics chose that option, but 40 percent of Hispanics selected this category in recognition of the diverse racial backgrounds of Hispanic peoples. Within the Hispanic community, individuals may be white, black, or brown. They may have black, brown, blonde, or red hair, and their eye color may vary from brown to blue. This diversity in physical appearance has created some tension with those African Americans who object to Hispanic Americans being able to avoid discrimination by "passing as white."

Three percent of the Hispanic population is classified as black. Some black Hispanics insist they are discriminated against because of their skin color, even by other Hispanics who associate dark skin with "bad or inferior blood." A number of studies of discrimination have supported this contention, finding that individuals with lighter skin are given preferential treatment in the business world and in American society as a whole. The tension over dark skin is particularly strong among Dominicans because of their intense hatred of black Haitians, with whom the Dominican Republic shares the island of Hispaniola. Most black Hispanics tend to identify more closely with other Spanish-speaking peoples than with African Americans. The number of Hispanics who identified themselves as "white" rose from nine million in 1980 to 18 million in 2000. The number of Hispanics who identified themselves as Hispanics ethnically, but who chose "other" to describe race, rose from 34 percent in 1980, to 44 percent in 1990, and 47 percent in 2000.

DEMOGRAPHICS AND CONSEQUENCES

Hispanic Americans live in every state in the United States, but nearly six of every 10 live in California, Connecticut, Florida, Illinois, Massachusetts, New Jersey, New York, and Pennsylvania. Puerto Ricans and Cuban Americans are more likely than Mexican Americans to concentrate demographically. Some 83 percent of Puerto Ricans live in New York, Florida, and New

Place of Birth of Agricultural Workers in the U.S.

United States 23%

Central America 2%

Other 1%

Mexico 76%

Note: Due to rounding, figures do not add up to 100%.

© Infobase Publishing

Jersey. Approximately 71 percent of Cuban Americans live in the south, as do 30 percent of other Hispanic Americans. Some 67 percent of Hispanic Americans are of Mexican origin. Between 1990 and 2000, the number of Mexican Americans rose from 13.5 million to 20.6 million. The majority of Mexican Americans live in California, Arizona, New Mexico, Texas, and southern Colorado, but their presence in the south has expanded considerably. Some experts believe that as many as 40 percent of Mexicans living in the United States may be undocumented. However, many of the Mexican Americans now living in the United States became documented through a special provision of the 1986 Immigration Reform and Control Act, which allowed 1.8 million people to obtain legal status through an amnesty provision in the law. Another 1.3 million were allowed to remain as part of a special program for agricultural workers.

While many Hispanic immigrants are poor, Cuban Americans tend to come from the upper and middle classes. They are considered political refugees because they came to the United States to escape a communist regime. Some

Immigration Act of 1990

American immigration laws underwent major revisions with the passage of the Immigration Act of 1990 (P.L. 101-649). The stated purpose of the bill was "to change the level, and preference system for admission, of immigrants to the United States, and to provide for administrative naturalization..." In reality, the bill was intended to mend the problems that had surfaced after the passage of the 1965 Immigration Act. Large numbers of immigrants seeking entry into the United States through amnesty and family reunification provisions were put on hold due to administrative overload. Policymakers were also concerned that the number of European immigrants had virtually dried up since the 1960s, while those from Latin America and Asia continued to swell the American population.

The 1990 act capped the total number of immigrants at 675,000 per year. An exception was made for the first two years after the bill's passage to allow immigration workers to deal with the backlog of applications. Using guidelines suggested by the Select Commission on Immigration and Refugee Policy, 55,000 immigrants were allowed to enter the country between 1992 and 1994 under family reunification provisions. However, categories included in this provision were narrowed. At the same time, the number of employment visas was expanded significantly. The quota for a single country was increased from 20,000 to 28,000. Congress also reserved 55,000 slots for immigrants from countries that were considered "underrepresented."

When President George H.W. Bush signed the revised immigration act on November 29, 1990, he called it "the most comprehensive reform of our immigration laws in 66 years" and noted that the new law "recognizes the fundamental importance and historic contributions of immigrants to our country." Unfortunately, the new act did not solve all of the problems with immigration. Six years later the Visa Office of the State Department reported that there was a list of almost 3.7 million persons waiting for American visas. By 1996 a new act had been implemented placing tighter restrictions on immigration, and applicants were required to show they had the means to support themselves in the United States. Further restrictions on immigration followed the terrorist attacks of September 11, 2001.

left Cuba without financial resources, but they became eligible for federally-funded assistance once they arrived in the United States. In Miami, Florida, where Cuban Americans make up 60 percent of the population, tensions are sometimes high between Hispanics and whites over the issue of language. Between 1973 and 1980, Miami was officially a bilingual city. Today around three-fourths of the population speaks Spanish. Public signs may appear only in Spanish, and it has become the language of the marketplace. Many Miami Hispanics do not know how to communicate in English. Whites often find this frustrating since more than 80 percent of the population of Florida is non-Hispanic.

Like Cubans, immigrants who came to the United States from the Caribbean island of the Dominican Republic sought political refuge, in their case from the repressive Trujillo regime. Today Dominicans tend to enter the country under family reunification provisions. They are likely to be poor, but most continue to send remittances home because their families depend on their help for survival.

Since 1990 there has been a strong push to tighten immigration laws and cut down on the number of illegal immigrants entering from Mexico. With considerable public support, Congress completely overhauled American immigration policy with the Immigration Act of 1990. The backlash against illegal immigrants led to a variety of laws and policy changes at both the state and national level. In 1994 Operation Gatekeeper was initiated in California, and federal border patrol agents were increased along a fence that began at the Pacific Ocean near San Diego and extended for 14 miles. They were provided with four-wheel-drive vehicles, infrared night scopes, and electronic sensors to better equip them for seeking out anyone attempting illegal entry into the United States. Critics of the program complain that Mexican immigrants are dying because of the harsh conditions and roundabout routes they take to avoid border patrol. It is estimated that between 1994 and 2000, 450 immigrants died in this manner.

Proponents of strict immigration control argue that Mexican Americans who enter the United States illegally become

The beginning of the U.S-Mexico border fence on the beach at San Diego, California. Increased patrols with more sophisticated equipment followed the 1994 Operation Gatekeeper program.

A team of armed U.S. Border Patrol Agents equipped with boats search for illegal immigrants along the shore of the Rio Grande in Texas.

freeloaders who drain social service programs without paying taxes. Those who disagree contend that the majority of Mexican Americans do pay taxes. They maintain that few undocumented immigrants benefit from social service programs directly. They do, however, send their children to public schools, and some states have attempted to cut that benefit. On November 8, 1994, California voters passed Proposition 187 with 59 percent of the vote, denying public education and benefits to all undocumented immigrants except in emergency circumstances. The law also made it a felony to manufacture, distribute, sell, or use false citizenship or residence documents and required teachers, doctors, and government officials to report anyone suspected of being an illegal immigrant to the proper authorities. By executive order, Governor Pete Wilson banned government services to undocumented Hispanic Americans who were pregnant or residing in nursing homes.

On November 16, 1994, implementation of the law was blocked by a federal district judge, and a recall was instituted for politicians who had proposed the bill. The following year the Immigration and Naturalization Service announced that the number of immigrants seeking American citizenship had risen by 75 percent. In 1996 Congress passed the Illegal Immigration Reform and Immigrant Responsibility Act, which added stronger penalties for illegal immigrants, and speeded up the deportation process.

HISPANIC FAMILY LIFE

Hispanic Americans tend to be younger than the population as a whole, and nearly a third are under the age of 15. About 70 percent of the Mexican-American population is made up of married couples. Conversely, there are a high number of single-parent families among Puerto Ricans. The birthrate among Hispanic Americans is twice that of the population as a whole. With larger families, Hispanic-American women are more likely than other American women to become stay-at-home mothers. *Machismo*, which is defined as an exaggerated sense of masculinity, is strong in Hispanic-American families that are still influenced by Spanish colonial values. In such families, the women's movement is viewed as destructive to both families and communities. In these traditional families, males retain their role as head of the family. Husbands and fathers exercise almost total control over the lives and decisions of all family members, and women are assigned the role of serving the needs of husband and family.

While substantial changes have been going on within Hispanic-American families, many women remain under the domination of males who take anger and frustrations out on their wives. Reported incidences of domestic violence among Hispanic Americans are growing, and some experts believe the number of actual cases may be three to four times higher than what is reported. A 2005 study of domestic violence in South Carolina revealed that 70 percent of 300 respondents had experienced some form of violence in their homes; 43 percent of those incidences had occurred within the previous year. Reasons cited for violence included unemployment, concern over jobs, financial worries, and substance abuse. Barely a fourth of the women included in the study ever reported the abuse to authorities, because they were embarrassed or lacked the language skills necessary to explain what had happened. They were also afraid of repercussions from family members, worried that their children might be taken away, and were unsure that they could support themselves and their children on their own.

Ninety-five percent of the women in the study were in the United States illegally, and experienced a prevailing fear that they would be deported if authorities became aware of the violence. When asked what could be done to help them, the women asked for help with transportation and legal assistance, and with becoming proficient in English. Despite the continuation of traditional gender roles in many Hispanic families, 65.8 percent of Hispanic women are in the labor force as compared to 73.2 percent of white American women. Even though their salaries may be essential to providing a reasonable standard of living for their families, more than 60 percent of female Hispanic workers are employed in low-paying jobs such as sales and service.

In a 2006 study, Monika Stodolska and Carla Almeida Santos demonstrated that the most important influences on Hispanics who immigrated to the United States were family status, work arrangements, and legal status, and

While women in Hispanic families in the United States may often conform to traditional gender roles, Hispanic women's overall participation in the labor force is high at 65.8 percent.

economic, social, and cultural needs. Most of those interviewed declared that they were in the United States to earn enough money to send regular remittances home to their families. As a whole, Mexican immigrants send as much as $10 billion a year to their home country, making these remittances the second-largest source of foreign revenue for Mexico. Either because of their financial situations or because they see their sojourns in the United States as temporary, many Mexican immigrants leave their spouses and children behind. The guilt they feel over this separation often leads to feelings of loneliness and depression. Some Mexican males have married American women and started new families, even while expressing regret over isolation from families left behind in Mexico.

To people of Spanish descent, religion has always been a major part of their identity. The significance is demonstrated not only in their identification with a particular faith, but also in their daily lives. Hispanic Americans frequently say *"Gracias a Dios"* (Thanks be to God). Another common expression is *"Si Dios quiere"* (God willing). According to one study, three-fourths of Hispanic Americans are Catholic, and 19 percent are Protestant. Only 5 percent identify with other forms of religion. Since the 1960s the number of Hispanics who identify themselves as Roman Catholics has steadily declined, dropping from 90 to 75 percent. Some Hispanic Americans have rejected Catholicism to join evangelical Christian churches, which allow greater congregational participation. Other Hispanic Americans have sought out nontraditional churches to fulfill their spiritual needs. Reasons cited for the shift away from the Catholic Church are alienation from the middle-class mentality of mainstream churches, and a rejection of the priest's role in religious rituals.

The fact that so many Hispanic Americans are Roman Catholic means that many daily traditions are associated with Catholicism. Religious icons representing the Virgin Mother and the various saints may be omnipresent in homes. An entire section of the house may become an altar where religious pictures and candles are displayed, along with statues and flowers. These altars may be covered with elaborately embroidered cloths, and incense and holy water are kept nearby for use in religious rites.

ECONOMICS AND EDUCATION

Many scholars contend that Hispanic-American progress has been diminishing since 1980 in response to the backlash against both legal and undocumented immigrants. In June 2007 a 5:4 Supreme Court decision struck down programs in Seattle and Louisville that used race in some instances to assign students to schools. The court's four-member conservative wing said the use of race in school assignments always violated the Constitution's guarantee of equal protection, while the four-member liberal wing declared it acceptable in the two plans evaluated.

With the weak economy that persisted throughout much of the first decade of the 21st century, many small towns were unable to provide programs for Spanish-speaking students with poor English-language skills, causing them to exhibit poor academic performance.

With the exception of Cuban Americans, who tend to come from middle- and upper-class professional families, Hispanics in the United States are more likely to be poor than other Americans, with unemployment and poverty 15 times greater among Hispanics than the national average. Many are classified as "working poor" because their wages reflect an income below the poverty line. Mexican Americans are more likely to live in poverty than other Hispanic Americans. There was some progress in the last half of the 1990s, and the poverty rate fell from nearly 31 percent in 1994 to around 23 percent in 1999. In 2002 nearly 21 percent of all Hispanic families lived in poverty. The economic situation was even more desolate among female-headed families, with 36.4 percent of this group living below the poverty line. Hispanic wages declined 2.6 percent between 2002 and 2003, when the average median family income for Hispanic-American families was $33,000, 69 percent less than that of European-American families. Using data from the 1990–95 Panel Study of Income Dynamics, Scott J. Smith et al. found in a 2005 study that families of Mexican, Puerto Rican, and Cuban descent were less likely than other Americans to demonstrate economic advancement by moving from high-poverty

This mural on the side of a restaurant on Calle Ocho in Miami's Little Havana depicts Cuban and American heroes.

Little Havana

The Cuban influence is so strong in Miami, Florida, that part of the city has become known as "Little Havana." Hispanics make up more than 60 percent of the population in Miami. There were 362,470 Hispanic Americans living in Miami in 2000, and estimates projected the 2010 population at 390,191. Located in the southeastern part of the state near the Atlantic Ocean and the Florida Everglades, the city prides itself on its diversity. In addition to those Cubans who fled Castro's regime, Miami's Hispanic immigrants come from Nicaragua, Colombia, Venezuela, Puerto Rico, Argentina, Ecuador, Dominica, Haiti, and Mexico.

Throughout the city, Hispanic influence is pervasive in music, food, and architecture. Visitors to Little Havana might have *tastada* and *café con leche*, or drink the perennially popular *mojito* cocktail with fresh mint and rum. Southwest Eighth Street is known locally as Calle Ocho and the "Heart of Little Havana." With its plethora of Cuban restaurants, tobacco shops, and art galleries, Calle Ocho draws visitors from around the world.

Traditionally, Miami has been considered a stronghold for Republicans, and residents have supported the party by a vote of approximately 90 percent in recent national elections. In 2004 President George W. Bush placed new restrictions on travel between Miami and Cuba. Cuban Americans were allowed to visit immediate family members only once every three years. Remittances home were restricted to $300 per quarter. Many Cuban Americans reacted to the move with anger. Some rebelled immediately and registered as Democrats. By 2008 Miami's three Republican seats in Congress were in serious jeopardy as Cuban Americans, like the rest of the country, became concerned about what Inocencia Coto, aged 75, identified to a *Time* magazine reporter as "the cost of living, the war, health insurance" and just "too many things getting out of hand." This dissatisfaction, coupled with changing demographics in Miami, has significantly weakened Republican strength in the city.

neighborhoods into lower-poverty communities. Instead, Hispanic Americans were more likely to demonstrate economic decline by moving from low- to high-poverty neighborhoods.

Because many Mexican Americans come to the United States with little or no job experience and training, they are able to obtain only menial, low-paying jobs with few or no benefits. Mexican Americans are also more likely to be unemployed (7.1 percent) than non-Hispanics (4 percent). In the early 21st century, more Hispanics were employed than ever before. Of 2.5 million jobs created between 2003 and 2005, one million were filled by Hispanic workers, but they were mostly low-paying jobs.

A major reason for the high level of Hispanic poverty is that large numbers of Hispanic youths do not complete high school. There has, however, been a significant improvement since 1980, when only 44 percent of all Latinos completed high school. In 2004, 58.4 percent received a high school diploma. This is still far below comparable rates for European Americans (85.8 percent) and African Americans (80 percent). The rate of college graduation among Hispanic Americans is also lower than among other groups. In 1980 only 7.6 percent of Hispanic Americans completed college. By 2004 that number had risen to 12.1 percent, but the completion rate was less than half that of European Americans. The lack of education among Hispanic Americans, particularly those of Mexican descent, contributes to the fact that they remain underrepresented in all professional groups.

Approximately 62 percent of Hispanic Americans are uninsured, a rate triple that of white Americans. This lack of insurance leads to an estimated 15 million Hispanic Americans lacking access to proper medical care. Hispanic Americans who are most likely to lack a healthcare provider tend to be male, young, have a low level of education, and are usually either foreign-born or poorly assimilated into American society. The National Council of La Raza reports that many Latinos in southern states are so intimidated by the language barrier and obstacles such as lack of medical coverage that they often fail to seek needed medical help. Some Hispanic Americans also mistrust the medical system. A 2008 study revealed that eight in 10 Hispanic Americans reported receiving medical information from alternative sources such as television or family, rather than from a healthcare provider. Fortunately, Hispanic Americans tend to be relatively healthy, except for a tendency toward diabetes, but because they are more likely to be overweight than whites, they are at risk for a number of diseases.

POLITICS

Since the Civil Rights movement of the 1960s, Hispanics have been steadily gaining a greater influence in American politics. The Civil Rights and Chicano movements of that period paved the way for the creation of a plethora of Hispanic-American organizations. Edward R. Roybal founded the National

The Mexican Mafia Gang

In the aftermath of the release from prison of drug lords convicted during the anti-drug wars of the 1980s and the migration of urban youth whose parents were attempting to relocate them to safer environments, street gangs have proliferated in cities throughout the United States. A Department of Justice Fact Sheet issued in April 2009 reported that there were 27,000 gangs with more than 788,000 members operating in the United States. According to the Department of Justice, 49 percent of all gang members are Latin Americans. Foremost among Latin American gangs is the Mexican Mafia, also known as La Eme or the New Family, which is identified as a "militant revolutionary" organization by the Federal Bureau of Investigation.

While the Mexican Mafia, which was established in the 1950s, remains concentrated in Southern California, membership has expanded into other areas of the United States, including Washington, D.C., Texas, and Oklahoma. Because of a direct link to the powerful Gulf Coast Cartel, which is part of what has been called the most dangerous criminal organization in the world, the Mexican Mafia has substantial human and financial resources at its disposal. In Texas, the organization has articulated its goals in a written constitution that calls on members to engage in drug trafficking, assassinations, prostitution, and a host of other legal activities. Membership is based on recommendations by three existing gang members, and all initiates are bound by a code of silence. Members must agree to refrain from homosexual and cowardly acts. The group is anti–African American and, ironically, endorses the Christian religion. Anyone who disobeys the gang's tenets is given a death sentence.

In 2008 incarcerated Mexican Mafia member Rene "Boxer" Enriquez, who admitted to inside knowledge of at least 70 homicides, broke the code of silence to provide inside information on the group's organization and activities. Enriquez informed authorities that Latin American youths were often anxious to be sent to prison in order to become affiliated with Mexican Mafia members who were conducting extensive operations from inside the California prison system. He stated that inmates learned to make homemade knives and hide them inside their rectums in order to carry out assassinations ordered by gang officials. Officials also learned that drug dealers were regularly sending checks and money orders to incarcerated gang members.

During the economic crisis of the early 21st century, local and state governments witnessed a substantial rise in gang activity, particularly in rising homicide rates, as antigang units were eliminated. The federal government responded by using RICO, the Racketeer Influenced and Corrupt Organization Act of 1970, to convict gang members and seize their financial assets. They also began working with state and local governments to create new task forces designed to eliminate gang-related crimes.

Association of Elected and Appointed Officials in 1976. NAEAO reported in 2008 that 6,000 Latinos were in political office at the local, state, or national level. The interests of Hispanics are also represented by the Mexican American Legal Defense and Education Fund, which is devoted to furthering educational opportunities and protecting the civil rights of Americans with a Spanish heritage.

Hispanic Americans suffered a decline in prominence during the Reagan era, but since the 1990s, they have served in a number of important government positions. Partly out of gratitude for their political support, President George H.W. Bush appointed a number of Hispanic Americans to important positions. In 1990 he chose Antonia C. Novello as Surgeon General of the United States, the first Hispanic-American female to hold that position. Norma Cantú, the former director of the Mexican American Legal Defense and Education Fund, was selected as the assistant secretary for civil rights in the Department of Education. Bush also appointed 25 other Hispanic Americans to government positions.

Global and domestic events of the early 1990s also had a significant impact on Hispanic Americans. The North American Free Trade Agreement (NAFTA) promised to open up new avenues of trading with Mexico. According to a

U.S. Surgeon General (1990–93) Antonia C. Novello (center), with colleagues at a December 1990 conference on minority violence. Dr. Novello made the health of women, children, and minorities her priorities while also tackling underage drinking, smoking, and AIDS.

15-year schedule, tariffs between the United States, Mexico, and Canada were eliminated in a score of industries that included energy, automobiles, textiles, agriculture, and telecommunications. In Puerto Rico, the statehood movement gained support, but Puerto Ricans ultimately voted to remain a commonwealth. When racial strife accelerated in 1991 after a jury exonerated Los Angeles police officers accused of beating Rodney King, an African American, Hispanic Americans joined in the rioting.

Yielding to pressure by Cuban Americans, Bush signed the Cuban Democracy Act, which prevented all American subsidiaries in third-party countries from trading with Cuba, and banned any ships that had visited Cuba from docking in American ports. After major redistricting in California, Florida, New Mexico, New

This sign at the May 1, 2006, Day Without an Immigrant protest in Los Angeles reads "today we march, tomorrow we vote." The nationwide boycott protested U.S. immigration policies.

York, Illinois, New Jersey, and Texas, Hispanic Americans were given a substantial political boost in 1998. Eight Hispanic Americans were elected to the House of Representatives. Two nonvoting Hispanic delegates also took their seats on Capitol Hill. Because they are not states, Puerto Rico, Guam, and the Virgin Islands are allotted non-voting delegates to protect their interests in Washington, D.C.

A number of Hispanic Americans have also risen to positions of power in Congress. One example is Bill Richardson, who was elected to the House of Representatives in 1982. As chief deputy majority whip, Richardson became the first Hispanic American to serve in a major leadership position in Congress, where he remained until February 13, 1997, when he resigned to become the American ambassador to the United Nations. Richardson became secretary of energy the following year in the Clinton administration. In 2003 he was elected governor of New Mexico and was reelected by both Hispanic and non-Hispanic voters in 2006, with almost 70 percent of the vote. Richardson launched an unsuccessful bid for the Democratic presidential nomination in 2008. Within Congress, the Congressional Hispanic Caucus has paid close attention to all

The Puerto Rico–born pop musician Ricky Martin waves from his float during the 2007 Puerto Rican Day Parade in New York City.

Contemporary Hispanic Music

In recent years Hispanic music has gone mainstream, partly because many Hispanic singers grew up bilingual in Spanish and English. Thus the Latin influence is often integrated with influences from the pop mainstream. Marcos Hernández, for instance, who released *About Me* in 2006, grew up listening to Barry Manilow, the Temptations, Michael Jackson, and U2. Hernández's music is described as a mix of Latino and soul. A number of Latino record companies have begun marketing albums to both Hispanic and Anglo audiences, and Hispanic artists are releasing albums simultaneously in English and Spanish. In 2005 Sony founded BMG Latin to market Hispanic artists to a mainstream audience.

Hispanic-American artists who are native Spanish speakers have also helped bring Latino music into the mainstream. Gloria Estefan, who was born in Cuba in 1957, has been one of the most successful artists in that group. Known as the Queen of Latin Pop, Estefan is the founder of the Miami Sound Machine, which won Grammy Awards for *Mi Tierra* (1993) and *Abriendo Puertas* (1995). Marc Anthony, who in October 1997 headlined the first salsa show ever held at Madison Square Garden, grew up speaking only Spanish, even though he was born in New York City in 1968 to Puerto Rican parents. Anthony's debut solo album, *Otra Nota,* appeared in 1993 and he was nominated for a Grammy in 1995 for *Todo A Su Tiempo.* Anthony released his first English-language album in 1999, and "I Need to Know" was a Top Five Hit. Anthony married Bronx-born actress and singer Jennifer López, who is also of Puerto Rican descent, in 2004. López was named the most influential Hispanic entertainer in the United States in 2007 and has sold over 35 million albums worldwide.

Ricky Martin has also been successful at integrating Latino and pop music. Martin, born in Puerto Rico in 1971, achieved teen idol status in Latin America after becoming the lead singer for Menudo in 1984 at age 12. He released *Ricky Martin* in 1991, which began a meteoric rise on the Latin charts. In 1998 Martin released his first English pop album, and the following year, "Livin' La Vida Loca" was a hit on both the Latin and pop charts.

issues concerning Hispanics since 1976. Other Hispanic Americans who have made political contributions include Harry B. González (D-TX); E. (Kika) de la Garza (D-TX); Lucille Roybal Allard (D-CA); and Nydia M. Velázquez (D-NY), the first Puerto Rican woman to serve in Congress.

Hispanic Americans also gained recognition in other fields. On October 11, 1995, Mario Molina, a professor of chemistry at Massachusetts Institute of Technology who studies the impact of chlorofluorocarbons on the ozone layer, became the first Mexican American to win the Nobel Prize. In February 2002 Omar Minaya became the first Hispanic-American general manager of a major league baseball team, the Montreal Expos; and Gaddi H. Vásquez became the first Hispanic-American director of the Peace Corps.

ENTERTAINMENT

A number of scholars have maintained that Hispanics are the most underrepresented minority in American television and film. In 1999 Hispanic Americans, under the auspices of the National Council of La Raza, the Tomás Rivera Policy Institute, and the National Hispanic Foundation for the Arts, launched a campaign to increase the Latino presence in the entertainment industry. The National Hispanic Media Coalition worked with Latino civil rights groups to conduct a "brown out" of the fall schedule. Nielsen Media Research, the organization responsible for generating television ratings, agreed to develop new tools for measuring the Hispanic-American audience. Several Hispanic programs were introduced on mainstream television networks: *Resurrection Boulevard* on Showtime, and *The Garcia Brothers, Dora the Explorer, Taina*, and *Go Diego* on Nickelodeon. Hispanic Americans could also watch *The George Lopez Show* on ABC, or they could opt to watch *Cane*, starring Jimmy Smits on CBS. Hispanic-American viewers could also follow the storyline of Hispanic twins with supernatural powers on NBC's *Heroes* in 2007. Since 2000 a number of websites, including America Online and Yahoo, have begun offering Spanish-language versions.

These acknowledgements of Hispanic Americans are partially a response to a study undertaken in 2004 at Harvard University's John F. Kennedy School of Government, which concluded that Hispanics in the 21st century had less media access and representation than in the 1960s. By examining the 2001–02 television schedule, the study demonstrated that only 5.9 percent of actors, 1.7 percent of writers, 0.8 percent of directors, and 1.7 percent of network executives were Hispanic. By the fall of 2003, Latino actors made up 4.1 percent of all primetime characters. At the same time, the Hispanic presence was absent in 84.5 percent of all television shows. Almost a third of Hispanics in regular programming were found in two shows with Hispanic themes.

By the early 21st century, variety shows, soap operas, and talk shows were broadcast in Spanish. Spanish-speaking Americans could hear their own

América Ferrera

One of the most visible Hispanic Americans in the early 21st century was América Ferrera, the star of ABC's *Ugly Betty*. The show, which is produced by Mexican-born actress Salma Hayek, was based on a Columbian telenovela, *Yo Soy Betty La Fea*. In *Ugly Betty*, Betty Suárez is hired to work at *Mode*, a high-fashion magazine, because she is not considered attractive enough to distract the publisher's womanizing son. When *Ugly Betty* debuted in 2006, it was greeted with both public and critical acclaim. Actors, producers, directors, writers, costume designers, and set decorators were all honored with nominations from the Emmy Awards, the Golden Globes, Screen Actors Guild, Alma Awards, AA Directors Guild, BMI TV Music Awards, GLAAD Media Awards, Teen Choice, and even the British National Television Awards. No one received more attention than the show's young star, who was seen as a positive role model for members of the Latino community and for teenage girls who did not fit the "Barbie doll" image of beauty. Ferrera won a plethora of awards, including an Emmy for Outstanding Lead Actress in a Comedy Series in 2007.

América Ferrera was born in Los Angeles on April 18, 1984, in Woodland Hills, California, to parents who had emigrated from Honduras during the previous decade. One of six children, Ferrera was brought up by her mother after her parents divorced. She earned a bachelor's degree in international relations. Ferrera's first break came in 2002, when she won a role in Disney Channel's *Gotta Kick It Up*. Her first critical success came that same year with the film *Real Women Have Curves*, in which she played a young Latina who refused to give up her dreams of becoming a writer. She won a Sundance Jury Award and an Independent Spirit Award for her performance. Following a number of television and film appearances, Ferrara was given the opportunity in 2005 to play Carmen, a young Hispanic woman seeking to repair a broken relationship with her divorced father, in the *Sisterhood of the Traveling Pants*, and reprised the role in the film's 2008 sequel.

language on a number of all-Spanish television channels devoted to a variety of program types that varied from children's shows, to sports and all-news channels. The first Latin Grammy Award Show, held on September 13, 2000, was broadcast to 120 countries. Hispanic Americans are highly respected in all genres of the entertainment industry. Hispanic-American actors of the 1990s and 2000s included Andy García, Raúl Julia, Martin Sheen, Cameron Díaz, Salma Hayek, Lou Diamond Phillips, and Emilio Estévez. In the music industry, Jennifer López, Gloria Estefan, Ricky Martin, and Marc Anthony became household names. Hispanic-American television personalities included Geraldo Rivera, Sally Jessy Raphael, Charlie Sheen, Benjamin Bratt, Jimmy Smits, América Ferrera, George López, and Hector Elizondo.

CONCLUSION

Despite another round of backlash against illegal Hispanic immigration to the United States in the 1990s and 2000s, one out of four Americans is expected to be of Hispanic descent by the middle of the century. While Hispanic culture has been a part of the United States since before it became a nation, Hispanic influence is likely to expand even further in the 21st century. This growing presence and success was exemplified by President Barack Obama's nomination of Sonia Sotomayor, the daughter of Puerto Rican immigrants, to the U.S. Supreme Court. Sotomayor was confirmed as the nation's first Hispanic Supreme Court justice on August 6, 2009, an event that was hailed as a milestone in Hispanic-American history.

Justice Sonia Sotomayor was born in 1954 to Puerto Rican parents in the South Bronx.

In 2010, Arizona passed SB 1070, a strict and controversial immigration law that was targeted toward illegal immigration from bordering Mexico. The law made it a crime to fail to carry alien registration papers or for illegal immigrants to solicit or perform work. It also allowed police officers to perform warrant-less arrests if there is probable cause that a person committed a deportable offense. An additional provision requires police officers to check the immigration status of any person they stop or detain if there is suspicion the person may be an illegal immigrant. The American Civil Liberties Union and other civil rights groups believe these provisions will result in racial profiling and widespread discrimination against Hispanics. The law has been both praised as a long-needed measure to combat illegal immigration and condemned by civil rights groups as codified racism. The U.S. Department of Justice brought a lawsuit against Arizona claiming the state's law would interfere with national immigration policy. During the proceedings, U.S. District Judge Susan Bolton issued a temporary injunction that blocked several key provisions of the law before it was scheduled to take effect. However, many believe that only a decision by the U.S. Supreme Court can resolve the controversy.

ELIZABETH R. PURDY
INDEPENDENT SCHOLAR

Further Reading

Abalos, David T. *Latinos in the United States: The Sacred and the Political*. Notre Dame, IN: University of Note Dame Press, 2007.

Benson, Sonia G., ed. *The Spanish American Almanac: A Reference Work on Hispanics in the United States*. Farmington Hills, MI: Thomson, 2003.

Bush, George. "Statement on Signing the Immigration Act of 1990." Available online, URL: www.presidency.ucsb.edu/ws/index.php?pid =19117. Accessed August 2008.

City of Miami. "About the City of Miami." Available online, URL: www .miamigov.com/press/pressreleases/miami/AbouttheCity.asp. Accessed August 2008.

Cobo, Leila. "Targeting the New Latino: Hispanic Arts and Their Fans Are Moving Quickly into the Mainstream." *Billboard*, March 11, 2006.

Frey, William N. "The New Geography of Population Shifts." In *State of the Union: America in the 1990s,* Reynolds Farley, ed. Vol. 2. Thousand Oaks, CA: SAGE, 1995.

Hunt, Tena. "South Carolina Study: Domestic Violence Prevalent Among Hispanics." *Black Issues in Higher Education*, May 14, 2005.

The Internet Movie Base. "Ugly Betty." Available online, URL: www.imdb .com/title/tt0805669/. Accessed August 2008.

Livingston, Gretchen, et al. "Hispanics and Health Care in the United States: Access, Information, and Knowledge." Available online, URL: http:// pewhispanic.org/files/reports/91.pdf. Accessed September 2008.

López, Antoinette Sedillo. *Latino Communities: Emerging Voices, Political, Social, Cultural, and Legal Issues*. New York: Garland, 2001

López, John Henry. "Race on the 2010 Census: Hispanics and the Shrinking White Majority." *Daedalus*, winter 2003.

Miyares, Ines M. and Christopher A. Airriess, eds. *Contemporary Ethnic Geographies in America*. Lanham, MD: Rowman and Litlefield, 2007.

National Council of La Raza. Available online, URL: http://www.nclr.org/. Accessed August 2008.

Nickles, Greg. *We Came to America: Hispanics*. Darby, PA: Diane Publishing, 2006.

Noriega, Chon A.. "Strategies for Increasing Latinos' Media Access." *Harvard Journal of Hispanic Policy*, Vol. 17, 2004.

Padgett, Tim. "Big Trouble in Little Havana." *Time*, August 25, 2008.

Rivera, Lourdes M., et al. "Role Models and Acculturation on the Career Self-Efficacy of Hispanic Women. *The Career Development Quarterly,* Vol. 56, September 2007.

Rodríguez, Clara E. *Changing Race: Latinos, the Census, and the History of Ethnicity in the United States*. New York: New York University Press, 2000.

alcalde: A person serving mayoral duties for a town, village, or city.

bandido (bandito): A stereotype that promoted the perception that Mexicans were gun-toting outlaws intent on negatively changing American life. The stereotype would become popular in Hollywood films.

bronco: An untrained or wild horse that is prone to bucking. The term originated in northern Mexico and was used there and later in the western United States and Canada.

californio: A person of Spanish of origin who lived in California. The term was mostly used during the Spanish period and in the years directly following the U.S. acquisition of California after the U.S.-Mexican War. It is not in general use today, although one hears it occasionally.

carabinero: A soldier whose primary weaponry was a carbine, a short version of a musket.

charro: A Mexican horseman who traditionally donned fancy, multicolored clothing. Also known as a *vaquero* in Texas.

cholo: A term that has undergone evolutionary changes. Originally, the term referred to people of combined Native American and *mestizo* ancestry. Later, it meant those who were involved in gang activity.

Cinco de Mayo: A Mexican day of celebration commemorating the defeat of French Emperor Napoleon III at the hands of Mexican forces during the Battle of Puebla on May 5, 1862.

colonias: Areas where Puerto Rican, Cuban, and Spanish residents fled to in the United States during Puerto Rico's and Cuba's difficult movements for independence. These areas were largely in the cities of New York, Philadelphia, New Orleans, and Tampa.

coquina: A material commonly used to construct buildings that is composed of shells cemented by limestone.

corral: An enclosed area designed to keep in cattle and other livestock. The term can also refer to a circle of wagons.

Corrido: A Mexican form of music similar to a ballad that often contained lyrics sympathetic to bandits who stymied the progress of Anglo aggressors.

criollo: A person born in the continental United States and other parts of the New World who is of pure Spanish heritage.

Dia de los muertos: The Spanish phrase for "Day of the Dead." The day commemorates the passing of loved ones in Mexico.

doctrina: A mission or religious conversion area built in large Native American villages with the intent of influencing Native American religious beliefs.

doctrinero: A missionary whose purpose was to convert Native Americans living in large villages to a religious belief system that would not conflict with traditional Spanish religious beliefs.

doblón: A doubloon, a Spanish gold coin worth 32 reales.

empresario: The Spanish word for "entrepreneur." *Empresarios* received a land grant under the condition that they recruit new settlers into the specified territory.

encomienda: A labor system used by the Spanish in their American colonies whereby a person was granted trusteeship over natives in a certain area. The person was required to teach the natives Spanish and Catholicism, and in return was authorized to extract from the natives a specified amount of work or payments. The word comes from the Spanish *encomendar,* to entrust.

***familia*:** Spanish word for "family." In traditional Hispanic-American culture, family was to be placed above all other aspects of life.

***floridano*:** In the Spanish caste system in La Florida colony, a *floridano* was a person of Spanish descent born in La Florida and ranking below the person born in Spain.

***fiesta*:** Spanish word meaning "party" or "festival."

***hacienda*:** A relatively self-sufficient estate employing laborers to work on plantations, mines, or factories.

***lazo*:** A lasso, a length of rope with a loop on the end that is used for capturing animals or other targets.

***machismo*:** The cultural ideal of the Latin American man, or in a more critical sense, the predominant stereotype of males. Characteristics of machismo include being the provider of a household and holding an aggressive and protective identity.

***marianismo*:** The cultural ideal of the Latin American woman, or in a more critical sense, the predominant stereotype of females. Characteristics of marianismo include gentleness, self-sacrifice and sexual purity.

***mestizo*:** In the Spanish caste system, a *mestizo* was a person of mixed European and Amerindian (or indigenous) descent. The *mestizo* generally ranked third in the caste hierarchy below those born in Spain and the *crillos* who were born in the Americas of pure Spanish descent.

***México de afuera*:** A term originating when scores of residents fled Mexico during the Mexican Revolution.

***mulatto*:** In the Spanish caste system, a *mulato* was a person of mixed African and European descent. The *mulato* ranked near the bottom of the caste hierarchy.

***música norteña*:** A brand of Mexican folk music that gained popularity among working class people. The primary instruments for it were the *tambora de rancho* (ranch drum) and *bajo sexto* (12-string guitar).

nuyorican: This term is used among those of Puerto Rican heritage to refer to the culture and people of Puerto Rican descent living in and around New York City.

peninsulares: In the Spanish caste system, a *peninsulare* was a person born in Spain. This was the highest classification in the caste system and enjoyed privileges and dominance over the other castes.

peso: A unit of currency originating in Spain that means "weight" in Spanish. In colonial times, the *peso* was equivalent to 8 *reales* and is the origin of the English phrase *pieces of eight.*

pocho: A pejorative term used to refer to a Mexican American whose peers perceive him or her as having lost his or her Mexican cultural heritage.

presidio: A fortress constructed by Spanish settlers during colonial times that was designed to prevent encroachments from hostile invaders.

rancho: An area specifically used for the grazing of livestock and other farm activities.

real: A Spanish unit of currency.

rodeo: Originating in northern Mexico, this is a traditional gathering where *charros* (horsemen) display their skills of horse riding and cattle roping.

santero: Originating in what is today New Mexico, this term refers to an artist who who constructs religious items such as figurines.

situado: A payment system whereby funds from a mother country are given to a colony, especially during times of hardship such as war, disease, and famine.

tabaquero: A worker employed in the task of rolling cigars. Knowledgeable of political happenings, these workers would often hire people to read aloud newspapers and political magazines while they worked.

tejano: A person of Mexican descent who lived in Texas.

texian: A person who lived in Texas who was of Anglo origin.

visita: A smaller outpost established by missions in or near indigenous villages for the purpose of converting the natives to Catholicism.

INDEX

Index note: page references in *italics* indicate figures or graphs; page references in **bold** indicate main discussion.

PHOTO CREDITS. California State Library: 52. Centers for Disease Control and Prevention: 194. Flickr/Cindy Lu: 195. iStock.com: 11, 186, 189. Library of Congress: 2 left, 5, 6, 7, 10, 32, 33, 34, 41, 42, 51, 55, 57, 60, 62, 65, 66, 69, 70, 73, 77, 79, 80, 84, 85, 87, 89, 90, 91, 94, 101, 102, 105, 108, 111, 112, 116, 125, 126, 128, 129, 131, 132, 140, 144, 145, 148, 149, 165, 166. National Aeronautics and Space Administration: 176. National Archives: 154. National Oceanic and Atmospheric Administration: 15, 56. National Park Service: 2 right. Smithsonian: 27. U.S. Agency for International Development: 168. U.S. Army: 93, 123. U.S. Coast Guard: 146, 147, 171. U.S. Customs and Border Patrol: 187. U.S. Supreme Court: 199. University of California Los Angeles Library: 161, 162, 175. University of North Carolina at Chapel Hill Library: 76. Wikipedia: 25, 29, 178. Wikipedia/David Castor: 31. Wikipedia/Fordmadoxfraud: 182. Wikipedia/Infrogmatic: 191. Wikipedia/Joel Levine: 163. Wikipedia/Ernest Mettendorf: 22. Wikipedia/Daniel Schwen: 46. Wikipedia/Toast to Life: 196.

Produced by Golson Media

President and Editor	J. Geoffrey Golson
Layout Editors	Oona Patrick, Mary Jo Scibetta
Consulting Editors	James S. Pula, Silvia G. Dapía
Author Manager	Susan Moskowitz
Copyeditor	Barbara Paris
Proofreader	Mary Le Rouge
Indexer	J S Editorial